Broadcast and Be Damned

Alan Thomas

Broadcast and Be Damned

The ABC's First Two Decades

MELBOURNE UNIVERSITY PRESS
1980

First published 1980

Printed in Australia by
Globe Press Pty Ltd, Fitzroy, Victoria 3065, for
Melbourne University Press, Carlton, Victoria 3053
U.S.A. and Canada:
International Scholarly Book Services, Inc.,
Box 555, Forest Grove, Oregon 97116
Great Britain, Europe, the Middle East,
Africa and the Caribbean:
International Book Distributors Ltd
(Prentice-Hall International),
66 Wood Lane End, Hemel Hempstead,
Hertfordshire HP2 4RG, England

This book is copyright. Apart from any fair dealing for the purposes of private study, research, criticism or review, as permitted under the Copyright Act, no part may be reproduced by any process without written permission. Enquiries should be made to the publisher.

© Alan William Thomas 1980

National Library of Australia Cataloguing in Publication data

Thomas, Alan William, 1954–
   Broadcast and be damned.
   Index
   Bibliography
   ISBN 0 522 84198 8

   1. Australian Broadcasting Commission — History.
   2. Radio broadcasting — Australia — History. I. Title.
384.54′0994

For Sally

Contents

	Acknowledgements	xi
	Abbreviations	xii
	Introduction	1
1	Great Expectations	6
2	Programmes and Personalities, 1932–4	20
3	Cleary and the ABC	45
4	The Politics of Broadcasting	77
5	Wartime Programming	92
6	The Other Side of War	122
7	The Return to Peace	142
	Conclusion	168
	Appendices	
	1 ABC Programme Analysis, 1939–45	174
	2 ABC Organization, 1932 and 1948	175
	3 ABC Stations, 1932–48	176
	Notes	177
	Select Bibliography	214
	Index	226

Plates

		facing
1	W. T. Conder in his early days at 3LO (Conder Papers, National Library)	52
2	Hospital patients listening to community singing broadcasts during the Depression (*Australian Broadcasting Company Year Book, 1930*)	52
3	The ABC's first outside broadcasting van (ABC Archives)	53
4	Some early radio personalities (*Australian Broadcasting Company Year Book, 1930*)	53
5	Cleary the bushwalker (Cleary Papers, National Library)	68
6	Bernard Heinze, Cleary and Moses at work (Cleary Papers, National Library)	68
7	Cleary, Moses, and the British conductor, Dr Malcolm Sargent (Cleary Papers, National Library)	68
8	Adelaide schoolchildren during a 'Music through Movement' broadcast (*Australian Broadcasting Commission Annual, 1939*)	69
9	Jim Davidson (conductor) and Peter Finch (compere) of 'Colour Canvas', October 1937 (ABC Archives)	69
10	The ABC Dance Band entertains the troops, June 1940 (ABC Archives)	132
11	James Pratt helps evacuee children speak with their parents in England (ABC Archives)	132
12	Chester Wilmot records Scottish troops at Tobruk, 1941 (ABC Archives)	133
13	An ABC 'Listening Group' (ABC Archives)	148
14	Wilfrid Thomas and Dick Bentley in 'Out of the Bag', November 1940 (ABC Archives)	148

15	Australian Broadcasting Commission conference, early 1939 (Cleary Papers, National Library)	149
16	Australian Broadcasting Commission conference, 1943 (Cleary Papers, National Library)	149

Acknowledgements

I wish to thank Dr J. A. Merritt of the Australian National University who supervised the PhD thesis on which this book is based. Dr C. N. Connolly also made useful suggestions in the early stages of the project.

Miss Pat Kelly, the senior ABC archivist, displayed an unfailing readiness to answer my many requests for records and information: to her I owe a special debt.

Among the many other people I would like to thank are the staff of the ABC Federal Reference Library; Miss C. Santamaria of the National Library Manuscripts Section; Mr E. Rutlidge of the Australian Archives; Mrs Pauline Watson who kindly granted me access to the papers of her father, William James Cleary, and who agreed to be interviewed on a number of occasions; Mr Talbot Duckmanton, present general manager of the ABC, for his co-operation in releasing the Cleary Papers for my use; Philip Geeves of Amalgamated Wireless Australasia Ltd; Professor W. Macmahon Ball, Mr T. W. Bearup, Ellis Blain, Mrs Sophie Kave (*née* Rockman), Sir Charles Moses, and Mrs Wilga Wind (*née* Armstrong) who agreed to talk to me about their experiences in the ABC; and Carole Lambert who typed the manuscript.

A version of chapter four of this book has appeared in the journal of the Australasian Political Studies Assocation, *Politics*.

For permission to reproduce photographic plates I am indebted to the National Library of Australia, the ABC, and Mrs Pauline Watson.

Finally, I wish to thank my wife, Sally Borthwick, for her encouragement and help.

July 1979   AWT
Canberra

Abbreviations

AA	Australian Archives
AAP	Australian Associated Press
ABC	Australian Broadcasting Commission
ABCA	Australian Broadcasting Commission Archives
APRA	Australasian Performing Rights Association
AWA	Amalgamated Wireless Australasia Ltd
BBC	British Broadcasting Corporation
CP	Consolidated Press
CPD	*Commonwealth Parliamentary Debates*
CPP	*Commonwealth Parliamentary Papers*
DOI	Department of Information
SMH	*Sydney Morning Herald*
UAP	United Australia Party
WP	Watchman Papers, ABC Archives

Note

Imperial measures have been retained throughout. Approximate metric equivalents are as follows.

    1 foot = 30 cm   1 mile = 1.6 km

There were 12 pence (d.) in 1 shilling (s.), and 20 shillings in 1 pound (£). When decimal currency was introduced in 1966, £1 was equal to $2.

Introduction

Even forty-eight years after the Australian Broadcasting Commission's foundation, little of substance has been written of its early history. This book is concerned with ABC policy and practice between 1932 and 1948, a period during which most of the issues that have borne on ABC thinking were either resolved or raised. I do not claim to have written a comprehensive history of the ABC in these years. My purpose is largely to explain ABC policies in terms of the political, social, and cultural forces which sustained or threatened them, and in terms of the ideas and actions of the institution's leading participants.

I have attempted to answer three basic questions. What ideas had the early ABC controllers of the role of broadcasting in society? To what extent were they able to realize their hopes for the ABC between 1932 and 1948? And in what ways did ABC policies reflect, and in what ways (if any) did they help to shape, the society in which they were evolved during the 1930s and 1940s? These in turn lead to further questions: from where did the controllers derive their ideas, did their ideas change over time, and, more importantly, to what extent were their resolutions mere abstract statements of purpose which bore little relation to the realities of ABC programming?

The ABC began in 1932 with six state branches and a Head Office in Sydney. It has not been possible to discuss the development of the branches in detail. Significant gaps in the states' records dictated that the main concentration be on central organization and high policy. A more fundamental reason for this emphasis is that during the period 1932—48, apart from the first two years, the ABC was a highly centralized institution, and almost every important policy decision was taken in Sydney. The only qualification to this was in relation to propaganda broadcasts during the war years when many policy decisions were taken by the Department of Information in Melbourne. Overall, however, a high percentage of programmes in the 1930s and 1940s were relayed from Sydney, so that Head Office programming was often synonymous with ABC programming.

Western Australia and Tasmania are partial exceptions and their special circumstances have been described in the text.

Some areas of policy have been considered in greater depth than others: staffing policies, for example, have been discussed at some length, since they are inseparable from programme policies. News policy, on the other hand, has been touched on only briefly, as the period immediately preceding the establishment of the independent news service in 1947 has been dealt with in great detail by other writers.[1] Although the sources made it difficult to delve into the lower echelons of the ABC organization, I have attempted to present a picture of the internal structure and dynamics of the bureaucracy as they relate to my broader themes. I have especially looked at the way the ideas of the chairman, other commissioners and senior management found practical expression in the methods of recruitment, in the treatment and type of performance required of ABC employees, and in the form of organizational structure evolved.

To study the ABC is to study more than an institution. At a wider level, it is to investigate the acceptance of a new 'technological wonder' in Australia. I have tried to avoid, as Asa Briggs put it in his history of the BBC, the 'temptation to treat the events and policies ... as sufficient in themselves, to paint an intimate portrait rather than to fill in part of a much bigger canvas'.[2] Within the confines of scope and space, I have explored the ABC's changing functions and place in society, how it confronted, avoided, or overcame the many obstacles put before it by governments, interest groups, and the community generally. There are excursions into Australian political and social history as it affected the ABC although I have tended to assume that the reader will be familiar with much of the political and military context within which many key decisions were taken. Most space in this book is necessarily devoted to the ABC itself, its aims, its methods, its achievements, and its problems.

While audience response to ABC initiatives is one of my interests, I have resisted the temptation to establish causal connections between ABC programmes and changes or continuities in the attitudes and behaviour of Australians. Nevertheless, I have pointed to occasions on which an 'impact' on the community appears discernible or at least probable.

I have used the term 'Commission' throughout to refer to the chairman and commissioners acting in isolation from the 'ABC organization' which more narrowly defines the management and bureaucracy. 'The ABC' refers to the combination of Commission and organization. It should be emphasized, however, that the divisions between the various entities which collectively made up 'the

Introduction

ABC' were not clear cut in these formative years.

A considerable amount of biography is unavoidable in writing about any organization. My emphasis on central organization means that lives and interests of the ABC's leading figures have been a major concern. There is William James Cleary, the guiding light for over a decade, his successor as chairman, Richard Boyer, and to a lesser extent other commissioners. On the management side, W. T. Conder and Charles Moses stand out clearly as figures of considerable interest, but there is frequent reference to other executives: Keith Barry, B. H. Molesworth, M. F. Dixon, Frank Clewlow, and so on. There are also the broadcasters, too many in number to list but all vital to the ABC's purpose. However, I have not been concerned to write a broadcaster's account of the ABC, concentrating on the mechanics of programme production, studio equipment and the technical details of performance: these aspects have and should be dealt with by those people more qualified for the task.[3]

Much of this work is based on the ABC's own records, both those held in the ABC's substantial archives and those lodged with the Australian Archives. Where possible, I have checked and supplemented these records with material from newspapers, evidence given to parliamentary committees of inquiry, government department files, and the personal papers of some of the participants. More detailed documentation of the sources used is available in the PhD thesis on which this book is based (Australian Broadcasting Commission Policy and Practice, 1932—48, Australian National University, 1979). Many statistics about programmes and staffing were not available, especially for the 1930s. ABC records before 1936 are chaotic, reflecting in part the state of the administration up to that time. Interviews with a number of former ABC employees filled some gaps in the written records, but the interviews were of more use in helping me develop a sympathetic understanding of the 1930s and 1940s.

Published works on the ABC are few. A biography of Herbert Brookes, the first vice-chairman of the ABC, contains but one chapter on this period in his life.[4] G. C. Bolton's biography of Sir Richard Boyer remains the only substantial analysis of an ABC personality, but it deals in detail only with the period after 1945.[5] There is the standard legislative survey article by Joan Rydon, quoted in almost every piece of writing on the ABC,[6] but there is as yet no published history of the ABC, official or otherwise.

Two former ABC employees have produced reminiscences of their time with the organization. Both works have proved invaluable sources. M. F. Dixon's *Inside the ABC* tells the story of the early

ABC news services from his point of view as the first federal news editor. It also gives insights into the internal politics of the ABC. Ellis Blain's book, *Life with Aunty*, is especially valuable for presenting aspects of ABC history from an announcer's perspective. I have made considerable use of his work in the sections on ABC staff.[7]

G. R. Curnow's MA thesis on the history of wireless telegraphy and broadcasting in Australia to 1942 is now nearly eighteen years old and it was written mainly without access to ABC files. However, it proved a useful introduction to the topic, and it has been cited frequently throughout the text. It was Curnow's suggestion about the ABC's relationship with the 'Establishment' which prompted me to develop this theme further.[8]

The book is divided into seven chapters, roughly in chronological order. The first deals with the passage of the ABC Act and the appointment of the first commissioners. In chapter two, I look at the gaps between policy and practice in the ABC's first two years. Chapters three and four examine William James Cleary's ideas in relation to each area of ABC programming. Chapter three also describes the emergence of tensions between the Commission and its staff, while chapter four analyses relations with government. The fifth and sixth chapters deal with the war, both in respect of programming and its place in the Australian war effort, and in relation to the strains placed on the ABC organization. Chapter seven examines the transition back to peacetime, identifying continuities or the lack of them.

The year 1948 provides a suitable termination date for a number of reasons. First, the passage of the 1948 Broadcasting Act marks the beginning of a new phase in ABC history and distinguishes 1932—48 as a self-contained period for studying policy initiatives within a fairly stable legislative framework. Second, it provides an opportunity to gauge the effects of the war on the ABC, and to observe three years of post-war operation under a new chairman. The third reason is practical: under the thirty-year access rule for government and ABC records, it was not possible to see files created after 1948. Although other types of records were available, it was felt that a better balance of documentation could be preserved by concentrating on these 'open' years. Finally, 1948 falls virtually at the end of two very special decades for Australian radio. Some people might even term them 'golden years' of broadcasting; certainly, some of their sheen did not continue into later decades. Perhaps the introduction of television accounts for the changes, or

Introduction

possibly the emergence of a generation more blasé about technological developments. In any event, this book provides some justification for J. A. La Nauze's description of the 1930s and 1940s as 'that unique era before broadcasting was relegated to "steam radio" '.

1
Great Expectations

Radio broadcasting was one of the few industries to escape the downward trend of the Depression years in Australia. From 1929 to 1932, the number of licensed receiver sets increased by nearly 69 000. As well, there were numerous illegal receivers. Over the same period, private telephone subscriptions fell by 22 000 and car registrations by 54 000. Cinema audiences shrank despite the arrival of 'talkies'. Attendances at race meetings and Melbourne football matches, membership of some sporting clubs, and consumption of tobacco and alcohol also fell.[1] Radio boomed because it was a cheap form of entertainment. Anyone who could not afford a proper receiver, costing from a few pounds to £50 for a deluxe model, had the alternative of a crystal set made from cat's whisker and a galena crystal.[2] Those people who possessed no receiver at all usually had access to one. It was thus in a climate of growing attachment to radio and rising expectations of its potential that the Lyons government established, on 1 July 1932, the Australian Broadcasting Commission.

In the decade preceding the creation of the ABC, Australian governments gave poor leadership to the broadcasting industry. It was left mostly to enthusiastic amateurs to explore the wonders of wireless. By September 1923, there were thirty-seven amateur radio clubs in New South Wales alone. Their members subscribed to a growing number of journals, such as the *Popular Radio Weekly* or the London *Popular Wireless and Wireless Review,* and attended the electrical and radio exhibitions held annually in most large centres of Australia. The Australian public were fed small doses of broadcasting's progress. At one demonstration in Melbourne Town Hall in 1921, the programme pamphlet said that it was 'quite unnecessary for any of the windows to be open as the wireless waves are not hindered by obstacles, however thick'.[3] Radio's novelty value and scientific mystique were sufficient attractions at this stage: the type of programme mattered little. Recalling these years, C. Porter writes:

1 Great Expectations

This was still the era of the cat's whisker crystal set, or the one and two valve with separate loudspeaker. Listening then was a participating, not merely a spectator, sport. With a crystal set, one sat with head-phones clamped against the ears, endeavouring in an agony of anxiety delicately to waggle a piece of wire on to a more sensitive 'spot' on the crystal, and hence improve reception. The remainder of the household sat hushed and wondering whilst the struggle went on. Yes, a listener in those days really had to contribute something to the game.[4]

In the meantime, a very successful commercial firm, Amalgamated Wireless Australasia Ltd (AWA), was contributing to the development of radio technology in Australia. The company was formed in July 1913 under the guidance of Ernest Fisk, and during the war won contracts to install radio communications equipment in many British merchant navy ships. In 1921, it broadcast a series of concerts in Melbourne and early in 1923 submitted plans to the Commonwealth government for a regular radio concert service. Seeing an opportunity to raise revenue through issuing licences, the government called a conference of interested parties in May 1923.

From the conference emerged the 'sealed-set' licence system. Operating licences were to be granted to approved companies, and listeners were to pay a subscription of between 10s. and £4 4s. per annum according to the number of stations they wished to receive. PMG officials would adjust each set to prevent it then receiving more than the number of stations covered by the licence. Four broadcasting companies took out licences under the new regulations: 3AR (Associated Radio) in Melbourne, 6WF (Westralian Farmers) in Perth, and 2SB (Sydney Broadcasters, later changed to 2BL, Broadcasters Ltd) and 2FC (Farmer and Co.) in Sydney. 2SB commenced broadcasting on 13 November 1923, followed by 2FC on 5 December, 3AR on 26 January 1924 and 6WF on 4 June.[5]

Perhaps predictably, the sealed-set system proved a failure. There was no effective means of preventing the skilful amateur from converting his set to an 'open' one the minute he returned home, and only 1400 listeners bothered to take out a licence.[6] Thus in July 1924, the Bruce—Page coalition government introduced a dual system of broadcasting unique to Australia. All stations became either A- or B-Class stations. Both sets of stations were run by private companies under government licence, but A-Class stations were financed by listeners' licence fees whereas B-Class stations were dependent on advertising revenue.

By 1927 there were eight A-Class stations, twelve B-Class stations, and 225 240 licensed listeners, but the number of listeners would have been considerably higher had the government done more to regulate the distribution of broadcasting stations.[7] Many country people still had not heard a radio broadcast. It became obvious that unless the government intervened, broadcasting stations would continue to cater mainly for heavily-populated city and coastal areas where the maximum advertising or listener licence revenue was to be obtained. The government's solution was to set up a royal commission into broadcasting in Australia.

Out of the inquiry came a government recommendation that some of the broadcasting companies amalgamate, but this idea was abandoned after it became clear that a monopoly situation might develop. Instead, the coalition introduced a semi-national scheme in which the Postmaster-General's Department controlled the technical services of A-Class stations, but programmes were to be provided by private companies under government contract. B-Class stations remained unaffected.

The postmaster-general took control of the A-Class stations throughout 1929 and 1930, and a three-year contract for the provision of programmes was awarded to the Australian Broadcasting Company, an organization formed by Greater Union Theatres Ltd, Fullers' Theatres, and J. Albert and Son (Sydney music sellers), with Stuart Doyle as chairman. The Company failed to make an impression on the public, and pressures continued to be applied on the government to introduce a truly national system of broadcasting;[8] but before any action could be taken, J. H. Scullin's Labor Party defeated the coalition at the October 1929 federal elections.

The altered political situation was accompanied by an even more drastically altered economic situation, for within days of Labor's victory the Western world was plunged into severe economic depression. The Wall Street share market all but collapsed and almost overnight Australian prosperity, long believed unending, appeared finished. In these circumstances, broadcasting was accorded low government priority. Scullin did draft a Bill in 1931 to place all A-Class stations under a broadcasting commission, but it lapsed amid political manoeuvrings within the Labor Party over conflicting economic remedies. Jack Beasley led one breakaway group which supported the policies of J. T. Lang, the premier of New South Wales. Another group formed around two of Scullin's ministers, J. A. Lyons and J. E. Fenton. It moved so far to the right that in May 1931 it merged with the opposition Nationalists to form the United Australia Party. Lyons was sworn in as prime minister on 6 January 1932.

One of the first acts of the new government was a Bill to establish the ABC. What lay behind this decision?

1 Great Expectations

The most immediate pressure came from H. P. Brown, head of the Postmaster-General's Department. Ever since the 1905 Wireless Telegraphy Act granted the postmaster-general exclusive rights to issue broadcasting licences, his department had been the single most important voice in Australian broadcasting policy and administration. Brown became head of the department in 1923, after twenty-five years' experience with the British Post Office. He quickly built up a position of power, and was intimately involved in all discussions about broadcasting. Brown was 'very insistent' that a national broadcasting organization be established to enable station managers, hitherto competing for facilities, to co-ordinate their demands nationally. He was equally insistent that the Postmaster-General's Department should continue to control the technical side of broadcasting, an indication that he wished to retain an important say in broadcasting matters.⁹ One newspaper argued that a broadcasting commission had in practice been in existence under Brown's 'chairmanship' since 1929.¹⁰ That was an exaggeration but it did point out the extent of Brown's influence.

Within the community, there were widely divergent expectations about the proper role of a national broadcasting authority. The more educated and perhaps intellectually aware citizens saw a higher purpose for the ABC than mass entertainment. One well-known contemporary publicist, William Macmahon Ball, writing after the ABC was formed, argued that a national broadcasting system should be 'the chief organ for the education . . . of democracy', and further that broadcasting possessed the power 'if used with wisdom and imagination, to bridge the gulfs of ignorance and misunderstanding that now divide the nations'.¹¹ Like-minded people made representations to the postmaster-general, J. E. Fenton, early in 1932, urging that the British system of broadcasting control be adopted. One deputation, on 20 January, included Mrs E. M. R. Couchman (a later member of the Commission) who suggested that any broadcasting body should have at least one woman member.¹² Another deputation from Victorian artistic and educational organizations, which included Frank Tate (a former director of education) and the historian Ernest Scott, argued for a commission modelled on BBC lines comprising people of culture and standing.¹³

These were the desires of a fairly small cultural elite and there is no evidence that the majority of ordinary Australians shared them. One worried country listener wrote to the *Sydney Morning Herald*:

> The wireless is a great asset to the country people, but I doubt if the licences of many would be renewed if a professor of music was directing the broadcast . . . We people do not like what is called classical music, as we are not educated for it. How many are?¹⁴

His was not a lone voice, but many would have argued that his letter clearly demonstrated the need for a national broadcasting authority to provide just this type of education.

Some people's doubts went deeper than the type of programme to be provided by the ABC. They began to wonder about radio's long-term social effects. Was radio an 'enemy of thought'? Would it produce a new superficiality of analysis and a tendency to conform? Could children be expected to complete their homework with the temptation of radio in the next room? If the establishment of the ABC caused an upsurge in radio's popularity, would the problem of noisy radio sets late at night get out of hand?[15]

One member of the Anglican church, the Rev. R. B. S. Hammond, had no such doubts. He thought the development of national broadcasting networks brought divine possibilities: 'Christ may quite likely return within the next twenty years — maybe ten — and when he does he will probably tell the world by radio . . . One of the bodily difficulties that surrounded the return of our Lord has been removed with the discovery of wireless.'[16] At another extreme, one citizen expected the ABC's services to include finding his lost dog!'[17]

The most serious resistance to the spread of broadcasting services came from sections of the entertainment industry and from sporting organizations. Both were struggling to survive the Depression. In the entertainment industry, audience figures were poor, as were sales of sheet music. One contemporary believed that the 'music business had slowed down to a walk'.

> No one bought it, and as for the artists, they starved. In the streets of Melbourne you would come across some of our best musicians playing the fiddle or singing, trying to earn a crust. There were parades of unemployed marching up Bourke Street trying to attract attention to their plight.[18]

The Australasian Performing Rights Association (APRA) blamed radio for this state of affairs.[19] Depression cost artists their livelihood, but the spread of broadcasting facilities, as evidenced by the creation of the ABC, was perceived as a more fundamental, long-term threat to a way of life. At least one major musical firm, Allan's, met the threat of radio by diversifying and going into broadcasting for itself. It was for a time associated with 3LO, and later started 3AW with the theatrical firm J. C. Williamson and the *Age*.[20] The press also bought interests in radio as a means of controlling its influence, and having done so, was prepared to try and influence the provisions of the ABC Act to safeguard its investment.

Sporting organizations feared the effects of live broadcasting on attendances. The racing clubs of New South Wales eventually asked

1 Great Expectations

the postmaster-general to prohibit all racing broadcasts until the end of the day's meeting.[21] Cricket officials were alarmed by reports that the broadcasting of matches had added tens of thousands of radio licences to New South Wales figures.[22] Later in the 1930s, when the ABC was firmly established and there were many more licensed listeners, attendances at the Sydney cricket ground rose.[23] Thus the lower attendances in the period 1929—32 probably were attributable to the Depression, but at the time cricket officials were convinced that radio was to blame.

Notwithstanding these different attitudes towards the establishment of the ABC, the *Argus* believed it had identified a consensus in January 1932 when it said:

> The present system of control is unsatisfactory from many points of view, and licence-holders are unanimous in demanding that complete public control be established over the service. That demand arises primarily from a feeling of dissatisfaction with the standard of the programmes and, in the second place, from the widespread conviction that the time is ripe for the establishment of an independent public authority which would control every phase of broadcasting.[24]

However, members of the Commonwealth Parliament in Canberra were not yet part of this consensus. Each of the major parties had already indicated its support for a publicly controlled body to administer A-Class stations, but there had been little consideration given to the future of the B-Class stations.

The Country Party leader, Dr Earle Page, favoured the idea of a broadcasting commission and promised to support the establishment of the ABC during the 1931 election campaign.[25] Page mainly hoped for a better service for country listeners. Nine years earlier, at the opening of a wireless and electrical exhibition in Sydney, he anticipated his party's support by saying:

> The 'Lonely Bush' has long been a phrase that Australians have not liked. Hence, where we find that by wireless 'the music, song and story' of our city can be spread to the most remote of country homes that word 'lonely' will be eliminated from Australian life, and all who love Australia will welcome the day of the medium wireless.[26]

The Labor Party saw the ABC mainly as a potential counterbalance to the 'partisan' coverage of ALP activities in the commercial media. It was acutely aware of the political dangers and possibilities of radio. J. T. Lang, the New South Wales Labor leader, early acknowledged that 'the future of politics in Australia was going to be bound up with the future of broadcasting'.[27] The New South Wales Labor Council sought and obtained a licence to operate station 2KY in 1925. In Queensland, the Labor government gained the only A-Class licence and started station 4QG. However, the Labour movement's entry into broadcasting was an attempt to prevent monopoly control of radio by business interests, traditionally anti-Labor, and was not an attempt to create Labor propaganda stations; it wanted balance and a fair coverage not slanted to the advantage of any political party. Apparently, there was a similar motive behind Lang's plan to create a network of state-controlled radio stations throughout New South Wales. Although the press claimed the plan was 'intended as a blind for the more important and insidious scheme of making the public pay for a means of propaganda by which the present government may be kept in office',[28] there is no evidence that Lang intended to use radio in an overtly partisan political way.[29]

That federal Labor shared the same concern for an impartial media is indicated by the pressures placed on Scullin by his own party members to stop 2FC and 3LO broadcasting blatant anti-Labor propaganda in 1931. It was these pressures, plus information that the Company did not intend to seek renewal of its contract in 1932, which had prompted Scullin to draft his abortive broadcasting Bill.[30] He even contemplated nationalization of all broadcasting services, a proposal which would undoubtedly have brought strong opposition from the commercial stations. Now, in opposition, Labor still believed that radio as a great public utility should not be 'a means of private profit', but many members were prepared to settle temporarily on a dual system of national and commercial stations.[31]

The Bill which Scullin's Cabinet drafted was obviously acceptable to Lyons, for he resurrected it almost unaltered. He had the support, in principle, of all major political parties, large numbers of ordinary citizens, influential educational organizations, and the Postmaster-General's Department. Moreover, Lyons personally admired the BBC and believed that Australia should possess a similar organization. He identified with the attitudes of the Australian cultural elite who defined themselves in terms of educational and cultural levels. There is no evidence that he acted from conscious political motives. Later in its history, the ABC did become an instrument of repression of certain political and moral views,[32] but there is nothing to indicate that this function was behind its establishment.

Fenton introduced the Australian Broadcasting Commission Bill on 9 March 1932. He opened with a reference to the government's

1   Great Expectations

decision to adopt, in principle, the British system of control. The establishment of the ABC, he said, constituted a great step forward for Australia and the Empire. He predicted that

> under the Empire broadcasting system, it will be possible for naked blacks to listen-in in the jungle to the world's best operas. We may also reach the period when brown-skinned Indians will be able to dance to one of England's best orchestras, and when fur-clad Canadians in distant snow-bound outposts may listen to a description of the running of the English Derby.[33]

Whether the people mentioned would have felt equal exhilaration is questionable. Moreover, this was a strangely imperial conception of civilization for one only recently from the Australian Labor Party.

The press were not enthusiastic, and described the Bill as being in some respects 'colourless and disappointing', in other areas 'positively mischievous and disquieting'.[34] One newspaper advised Fenton to 'RUB IT OUT AND START AGAIN'.[35] The contentious aspects of the Bill were the postmaster-general's right to prohibit certain broadcasts and to control the ABC's technical services, the ABC's right to accept sponsored programmes, and the poor status and pay of the commissioners and chairman.

Many politicians had similar reservations. Dr Page agreed with the spirit of the Bill but likened the awkwardness of some of its clauses to 'a child with club-feet, who requires some orthopaedic treatment to put the feet straight before it can walk and perform any useful function in the community'.[36] Further dissension within the government ranks was evident from the attitude taken by William Morris Hughes, a former prime minister, who attacked the clause making the ABC directly responsible to the postmaster-general and said that he would be satisfied with nothing short of the type of independence enjoyed by the BBC.[37] The *Sydney Morning Herald* supported Hughes, and argued that the Bill would merely maintain Brown as broadcasting head, as ultimate responsibility rested with the postmaster-general and his department.[38] This may well have been what Brown intended, but Lyons moved quickly to quell dissatisfaction within his own party. Within days came an announcement that the clause subjecting the ABC to ministerial control had been included by accident and would now be deleted.[39] An appropriate amendment was introduced on 17 March, but Hughes and his sympathizers were not satisfied as the minister was left with significant power.

Members exchanged strong words on the section of the Bill relating to the salary and unstated qualifications of the proposed five commissioners. Scullin's Bill gave the chairman a salary of £1500 per annum, the vice-chairman £500, and the other three members £300 each. Fenton's Bill provided for payments of £500, £400 and £300 respectively. He believed that these salaries were adequate in the prevailing economic climate, and would prevent appointments to the Commission from becoming 'jobs for the boys'. Hughes was not convinced. This Bill, he said, 'proposes to place broadcasting in the hands of men who, *ex hypothesi,* are mediocrities. Only mediocrities could be obtained for the salaries proposed'.[40] However, a Country Party amendment to raise the chairman's salary to £1000 was rejected by forty-one votes to eighteen.[41] Nothing could budge the government. As for the qualifications of commissioners, Fenton gave only a vague assurance that the commissioners would be 'men of good standing'.[42] His spokesman in the Senate, Alexander McLachlan, said in similar fashion: 'Men with extensive commercial experience and the necessary qualifications will be appointed, and they will, while providing an efficient service, have regard to the interests of economy. This, it is anticipated, will enable a selection to be made from a larger number of suitable applicants.'[43]

Meanwhile, debate continued on the ABC's right to accept sponsored programmes. Did this mean, for example, that the ABC could broadcast advertisements in competition with commercial stations? To clarify this point, the government inserted a new sub-clause, 'The Commission shall not broadcast advertisements', with the proviso that 'Nothing in this section shall be construed as preventing the Commission from broadcasting, if it thinks fit, a programme supplied by any organization, firm or person, provided that the programme is not, in the opinion of the Commission, being used as an advertisement.'[44] The addition pleased some members, but not the Labor Party, which wanted the ABC to carry advertisements.[45]

Was the insertion of this clause an attempt to guarantee programmes uncontaminated by 'popular' taste and the need to attract sponsors? Or was it a means of preventing competition with the commercial stations? The evidence suggests the latter. Immediately after the Bill's introduction, Lyons received protest telegrams from newspaper groups, including one from the Australian Newspapers' Conference claiming that the clause on sponsored programmes meant 'subsidised Government interference with existing advertising channels'.[46] Protests also arrived from newspaper proprietors' associations in Perth, Adelaide and Melbourne, and from the Federation of Commercial Broadcasting Stations.[47] It is significant that Lloyd Dumas, managing editor of the Adelaide *Advertiser*

1 Great Expectations

and with interests in station 5AD (Advertiser Newspapers Ltd), visited Canberra on 16 March, the day before the amendment of the clause on sponsored programmes. Government members denied they had been influenced by Dumas or the press generally, but it seems more than coincidental that the government's amendment conformed almost word for word with one suggested by Australian Associated Press and the Brisbane Newspaper Company Ltd.[48] Opposition members were convinced that the press had forced the amendment on the government in an effort to protect their investments in B-Class stations. The government pointed out that the amendment had been agreed to before Dumas arrived in Canberra, but that does not preclude the possibility that his visit was anticipated by Cabinet. The successful application of pressure by private interest groups seems undeniable.[49]

Newspapers were not the only group to influence the composition of the ABC Act. The Electrical Federation of Victoria, the Victorian Radio Association, the Victorian Employers' Federation and the Victorian Chamber of Manufactures persuaded UAP and Country Party senators to delete the clause which said: 'Subject to this Act the Commission may do such acts and things as it deems incidental or conducive to the proper exploitation of those things which may be beneficial to broadcasting.'[50] The pressures stemmed from fears that the ABC would manufacture radio receivers. The British Broadcasting Company, out of which grew the BBC, had done just that; but it was after all a company formed by radio manufacturers with the intention of expanding the market for radio receivers.[51] The ABC had no such connections with the radio industry, but Australian manufacturers were not willing to risk the entry of a new competitor.[52]

Despite a lengthy passage, the Bill passed with surprisingly few amendments and became law on 17 May 1932. The chairman, vice-chairman, and three ordinary members were appointed for terms of five, four, and three years respectively. The Commission's main responsibility was to provide 'adequate and comprehensive' programmes, where possible giving encouragement to local talent. It could determine 'to what extent and in what manner' political broadcasts should be presented. It could accept sponsored programmes where the programme provided was from an 'organisation, firm or person engaged in artistic, literary, musical or theatrical pursuits' and was not, in the Commission's opinion, being used as an advertisement, and it could recruit and set the conditions of work of its own staff, except that the salaries payable to the general manager 'and the next six most highly paid executive officers' were subject to the approval of the governor-general. Financially, it was to receive a fixed share of the listeners' licence fees (12 shillings out of every 24-shilling fee collected), and it could also issue tax-free debentures up to a maximum value of £50 000.

There the independence of the Commission ended. As minister responsible for the ABC, the postmaster-general could prohibit the broadcasting of any matter he desired. He could veto any ABC project involving expenditure of more than £5000, or any leasing agreement for a period of more than five years, and his department was to control the ABC's technical services.[53]

Press speculation over the appointment of commissioners had begun as early as January. One prediction for chairman was Stuart Doyle, chairman of the Australian Broadcasting Company, an appointment H. P. Brown allegedly recommended.[54] Even W. M. Hughes' name was mentioned.[55] In all, over 150 people expressed interest to the government, including people like the poet A. B. ('Banjo') Paterson.[56] Two days before the official announcement, the press listed as the five most likely candidates Sir George Tallis, Sir John Higgins, Professor W. K. Hancock, R. B. Orchard and Herbert Brookes.[57] Only the last two predictions were correct. On 23 May Fenton published the official list: Charles Lloyd Jones (chairman), Herbert Brookes (vice-chairman), and R. B. Orchard, Professor R. S. Wallace and Mrs E. M. R. Couchman (ordinary members).

Charles Lloyd Jones was chairman of directors of the Sydney-based retail firm, David Jones Ltd, a former treasurer of the Sydney Chamber of Commerce and former president of the Retail Association. His talents were not confined to the business world. He had studied art under Julian Ashton and exhibited with the Society of Artists in 1916. He founded the journal *Art in Australia* in conjunction with S. Ure Smith. As chairman of a citizens' appeal he helped to raise £130 000 for cancer research. He was director of the honorary board which supervised the Australian National Travel Association, and was a keen yachtsman. Indeed, he was very much a person of 'culture' and 'standing', the two qualities so vehemently demanded by the January delegations.[58]

Herbert Brookes had been Cabinet's first choice for chairman, but he had refused the offer for health reasons. He later regretted that decision, for it eliminated his candidacy for the position when it fell vacant again in 1934.[59] One Cabinet member informed Brookes that Jones was chosen for his business acumen and to counterbalance an alleged tendency to overlook Sydney in the past. Brookes was included on the Commission as a representative of the 'classical and

1   Great Expectations

intellectual side of things'.⁶⁰ Like Jones, Brookes was a businessman with broad interests. He was former president of the Associated Chambers of Manufactures, and had been a member of the Board of Trade and the Tariff Board. From 1929 to 1930 he was Australia's commissioner-general in the United States. Both he and his wife, Ivy, were well known for their patronage of Melbourne cultural life, and were prominent figures in the movement to establish a Melbourne symphony orchestra.⁶¹

Professor R. S. Wallace was vice-chancellor of the University of Sydney. He had graduated with first-class honours from the University of Aberdeen in 1904, and held academic posts in classics and English at the universities of Oxford and Melbourne before moving to Sydney. While on the one hand he represented 'highbrow culture', his past membership of the Film Censorship Appeal Board meant he was experienced at assessing more popular standards of taste.⁶²

Mrs Couchman had been active in the Australian Women's National League for twenty years and was now its president. She was a member of seven public welfare bodies, the University Women's Association and various Empire associations, and was senior vice-president of the National Conference of Women. But because she worked closely with the United Australia Party, her ability to act impartially was queried throughout her ten years as a commissioner.⁶³

The final member, R. B. Orchard, was an ex-Nationalist Party (forerunner of the UAP) member of Parliament. In his early years he travelled the countryside in a wagon selling jewellery and performing vaudeville acts in small country halls. Later he opened a jewellery shop in Sydney and in his spare time appeared in *The Mikado* and other productions of John Wren's Opera Company. In 1913, he became member for Hawkesbury and for part of 1918 was minister in charge of recruitment in the Hughes government. His show-business experience qualified him to some extent to assume the role of broadcasting commissioner, but his past political connections sullied his appointment.⁶⁴

It was not enough that the Commission be impartial: it had to be seen to be impartial. Mrs Couchman supported the government, as did Orchard. Herbert Brookes had helped to found the Liberal Party in 1909, and edited *The Liberal* between 1911 and 1914. Jones was a close friend of the former Nationalist prime minister, Stanley Melbourne Bruce. Wallace alone had no obvious political connections, but he was considered a UAP supporter. As private citizens, the commissioners were entitled to some political preference, but it was expected that the government would make no obvious political appointments to the Commission. That all five people chosen were of above-average ability is beyond doubt. That they all had some claim to the title 'cultured person' is probably equally true. But in appointing people known to be active in anti-Labor politics, the government exposed itself to charges of political favouritism.[65]

Jack Beasley, a member of the Lang Labor group, kept the issue of political bias alive for many years. The government always asserted it was mere coincidence that most commissioners held views favourable to the government, and once made the astonishing remark that the type of person required to run the ABC was unlikely to be found among the ranks of Labor supporters.[66]

The truth of Beasley's allegations is impossible to prove or disprove. More certain is the fact that the first commissioners all belonged to a particular stratum in society. Many were businessmen, all were supposedly 'cultured'. They viewed the ABC as a public institution with a moral obligation to 'realise the taste and improve the culture of the community, to spread knowledge, encourage education, and foster the best ideals of our Christian civilisation'.[67] Their expectations were further expounded in the ABC's first annual report:

> Enlightenment must come through entertainment. The Commission therefore aims to develop side by side its two ideals of pleasing and benefiting, and this it hopes to do by continually striving to render its service pleasing and its pleasing serviceable; it will seek to appeal not to each section of the community in turn, but to all sections at all times.[68]

This was a more ambitious aim than John Reith had for the BBC, for Reith believed that radio was for everybody but not necessarily at the same time. Yet like the BBC, the ABC rejected any suggestion that there should be entertainment for entertainment's sake.[69]

The first meeting of the Commission took place on 26 May 1932 in the postmaster-general's Melbourne office. Its official assumption of responsibility on Friday 1 July was heralded by an inaugural broadcast from the chairman and the leaders of the three main political parties. Jones spoke from Sydney, as did Dr Page. Lyons spoke from Canberra, and Scullin from Melbourne. All speakers emphasized that the ABC would be used to create goodwill among the nations of the world.[70]

These reassuring words partly echoed Jones' comments after the first meeting of the Commission:

> I wish the public to understand the magnitude of the task ahead of the commission. While we are not going to delay action we intend

1 Great Expectations

following in the footsteps of the British Broadcasting Corporation, which refrained from any elaborate organisation for the commission at its inception. With the staff of the Australian Broadcasting Company taken over, the commission is confident that broadcasting will continue effectively while the commission is feeling its way. This action is in harmony with the advice given by the Prime Minister (Mr Lyons) to walk in the footsteps of the BBC and fall in behind Britain.[71]

'Fall in behind Britain' was a phrase which would have appealed to an Australian audience in 1932. The early 1930s were uncertain years. Australians saw their society being divided by extremist groups such as the Sane Democracy League, the All for Australia League and the New Guard on the right, and the Communist Party on the left, as well as by secession movements in New England and Western Australia. Many people took comfort in a common allegiance to the motherland. The 1931 Statute of Westminster granting greater autonomy to the dominions was not ratified by the Lyons government.[72] For foreign policy, and for guidance on many domestic developments, Australia still looked to Britain. Lyons' advice to follow Britain reassured many people, and it was a natural course for the type of political leader he personified: 'Hardworking, honest, kindly, unadventurous, and a devoted family man'.[73] In this climate it was natural that the early ABC controllers should seek to emulate the revered BBC.

The founders of the ABC believed that the qualities they admired in the BBC were transferable to an Australian setting. Unforeseen problems over the next two years were to test fully this assumption.

2
Programmes and Personalities, 1932−4

The 1932 ABC Act theoretically gave Australia its own BBC, but in practice it was difficult to graft even the most desirable features of the British organization on to its antipodean counterpart. Jones clearly wanted to create an Australian BBC, yet he did little to achieve such an objective. Between 1932 and 1934, the ABC lacked the organizational unity to undertake a national cultural mission, its programmes more entertaining than uplifting.

The physical transition from Company to Commission was achieved with relative ease, with the new organization renting the premises previously occupied by the Company in each capital city except Adelaide, where the premises of station 5CL were purchased. The Commission signed short-term leases which did not require government approval and which would enable it to vacate an unsuitable building, acoustic qualities counting for more than aesthetics. Because of the paucity of suitable buildings in Australian cities of the 1930s, the ABC chose to erect new buildings rather than to spend recurrent amounts on renovating old ones. The cost of such a building programme—many hundreds of thousands of pounds—required that the Commission budget for a surplus from the outset. Any attempt to float a loan and embark immediately on an ambitious building programme would probably have been blocked by the government: it was after all the height of the Depression, and the ABC had yet to demonstrate that it was a financially viable enterprise.

Having been granted a limited three-year contract to supply programmes on national stations, the Company had not been prepared to invest in better-equipped studios. Facilities were poorest in Perth and Hobart, where land was purchased immediately with a view to building new studios as soon as possible. In Brisbane the ABC fared much better, installing itself in the State Insurance Building whose twin 100-foot steel-latticed rooftop towers advertised station 4QG's presence for miles around. The Victorian branch occupied a building at 120A Russell Street, while in Sydney studios

2 Programmes and Personalities

were leased in J. C. Williamson's building in Market Street and at 264 Pitt Street.[1] The last-mentioned address became known as Broadcast House and served as Head Office, though it was intended that eventually ABC headquarters would shift to Canberra.

There were twelve ABC stations in July 1932: 2FC and 2BL (Sydney), 2NC (Newcastle), 2CO (Corowa), 3LO and 3AR (Melbourne), 4QG (Brisbane), 4RK (Rockhampton), 5CL (Adelaide), 5CK (Crystal Brook), 6WF (Perth) and 7ZL (Hobart). Station 5CK was purely a relay station, and stations 2NC, 2CO and 4RK supplied only small portions of their programmes. There were 4300 miles of land-line cable which connected these stations with the eight main national stations which produced individual programmes. Various technical difficulties hampered the operation of this ABC network. Climatic conditions north of Brisbane sometimes created interference, as did the very different conditions in Tasmania. As well, some of the smaller states lacked adequate relay facilities. Until June 1933 there was no land-line cable capable of carrying music satisfactorily to Perth, a considerable handicap to station 6WF which could depend on relays for only 2.55 per cent of its programme time.[2] On occasions relays were accidentally cut off, one such incident prompting members of the Western Australian secession movement to complain about neglect of the West.[3] Hobart was also at a disadvantage because there were no telephonic communications with Tasmania at this time. For some years station 7ZL had to be content with picking up and later re-broadcasting programmes. As technical services came within the jurisdiction of the Postmaster-General's Department, there was little the ABC could do about transmission problems except make constant representations for improvements.

The distribution of ABC finances also affected the quality of the programmes in each state. New South Wales and Victoria each contributed about 36 per cent of the Commission's revenue. Western Australia and Tasmania contributed nearer 4 per cent and suffered accordingly, despite the supposedly federal charter of the ABC. Melbourne and Sydney did not always receive preferential treatment, but the size of their resources often enabled them to produce programmes of a higher quality than the stations in the smaller states.[4]

Arguments that the Commission was unable to subsidize the smaller states further looked unconvincing when it finished the first two years of operations with a surplus of £73 000. These funds were purposely accumulated for a building programme, but some people believed that all monies received by the ABC should be spent directly on producing broadcasts. The *Daily Telegraph* and *Truth*, among others, cited the surplus as justification for a reduction in the listener's licence fee.[5] In contrast, the *Sydney Morning Herald* backed the ABC when it was accused of extravagance.[6] It was arguable that until all ABC studio accommodation improved, there could be little improvement in the quality of programmes. But in the economic and political climate of the early 1930s the argument attracted little support from the community where funds were short and unemployment was still extremely high, having reached 28 per cent the month the ABC began to broadcast. Fortunately for the Commission, the temptation to reduce the licence fee and win short-term electoral support was for the time being resisted by the government.

Much of the ABC's ability to satisfy community expectations was dependent on the choice of staff. At the Commission's first meeting, the chairman of the Company, Stuart Doyle, agreed to transitional arrangements whereby the ABC would pay half the salaries of the Company executives up to 1 July. Doyle also intimated that most of the Company's executives would be willing to remain in their jobs after that date if the ABC wished to offer them positions.[7] The ABC adopted Doyle's suggestions and took over many of the Company's executives as state branch managers, though for the time being it delayed the appointment of a general manager.

Who were these state branch managers and what were their backgrounds?

The ABC manager for Victoria, T. W. Bearup, had been associated with the Australian broadcasting industry since its very beginnings. In 1916 he had joined the Marine Staff of AWA and spent five years studying technical developments in broadcasting before transferring to the Shore Staff in 1921 to work on the establishment of radio links between Australia, the United Kingdom, and the United States. During the 1920s he held positions on the staffs of 2FC, 3LO, 3AR, 5CL and 7ZL, eventually becoming Victorian manager for the Australian Broadcasting Company in 1929. A passionate admirer of the BBC, Bearup shared the belief that broadcasters had a responsibility to uplift people's cultural standards, or to produce 'edutainment' as he liked to call it.[8]

In New South Wales, the Commission retained H. G. Horner. After an education at King's College, Cambridge, and extensive travel throughout the British Empire, Horner had settled in Canada. He migrated to Australia in 1914. As a qualified accountant and secretary he held positions with various firms, including Sun Newspapers, before accepting an invitation to reorganize station 2BL. He

2 Programmes and Personalities

made 2BL a paying concern. The Australian Broadcasting Company then employed him as company secretary. The Commission were impressed by his administrative talents and his abilities as a musician.⁹

The manager for Queensland, J. W. Robinson, had held one of the first experimental amateur operating licences in Australia. He worked as a journalist with the *Sydney Morning Herald* while studying part-time at the Marconi School of Wireless in Sydney and in 1923 became assistant manager of 2FC. He was later appointed by the Queensland government to set up station 4QG and had remained manager when the Company took over in 1929.[10]

Western Australia's 6WF remained under the managership of Basil Kirke, or 'Uncle Basil' as he was known to many 2BL listeners in 1929. Before entering broadcasting, he had served in the AIF and for a time worked in the planting industry in the Pacific islands. In 1930, the Australian Broadcasting Company appointed him manager for Western Australia. Kirke had a somewhat aggressive personality which perhaps reflected an attempt to compensate for his sheltered upbringing in the small New South Wales country town of Armidale. It is not clear what the commissioners saw in Kirke, unless perhaps they liked his confidence, even his arrogance. Ellis Blain said of him that he 'was convinced broadcasting had not advanced since he invented it many years earlier'.[11]

The manager for Tasmania was E. J. Lewis, a Welshman who had come to Australia for health reasons at the turn of the century. He fought in the AIF at Gallipoli and was invalided back to Australia where he joined the Victorian Public Service. In 1924, he joined 3LO as director of programmes and in 1929 switched to 3DB. He was manager of 7ZL for the Company and retained that position under the ABC, though only with the title acting manager.[12]

Charles Hosking, the manager for South Australia, had originally worked in the legal profession in Victoria and had done some exploring in Australia's north-west. From there he had gone on to write several plays, and became a music and drama critic and freelance journalist before joining 3LO as publicity director in 1925. The Company employed him as manager in several of their stations.[13]

These six men—Bearup, Horner, Robinson, Kirke, Lewis and Hosking—were given the task of directing ABC activities in the states where most ABC staff were located. Head Office in 1932 was very small, comprising the Commission's secretary, A. L. Holman, a couple of administrative support staff, and the general manager (yet to be appointed). A plan to appoint Head Office programme specialists was considered but rejected, and was not revived until late

1935.¹⁴ The job of state branch manager was thus very responsible. Its holders were of two main types, those who had come into broadcasting via their interest in radio technology, and those who had drifted into broadcasting as another experience in a variegated career. Their common feature was to have worked in *national* broadcasting, thus making it a fair assumption that they would be sympathetic to the stated goals of the Commission.

It is much more difficult to identify a guiding principle in the selection of more junior staff, the studio supervisors, script-writers, and other creative staff, and the administrative support staff, many of whom came to have an influence on programming that was quite unintended. The number of people skilled in broadcasting was fairly limited and again the ABC looked to those people already employed by the Company. At the height of the Depression, Company employees were naturally relieved to learn that they could remain in their old jobs, though under new masters.¹⁵ However, many of these employees were to have short-lived careers in the ABC, sometimes through incompetence but more usually because they failed to meet the often unreasonable standards demanded by the general manager.

The Commission had postponed the appointment of a general manager for some months while it negotiated with Mr Marden, general manager of the Company, but when it became clear that he did not really want the position it was advertised. Over 200 applications were received. Unlike the commissioners, who possessed no radio expertise, the general manager had to be an experienced broadcasting man. As chief executive officer, he would be responsible for recommending initiatives to the Commission, for implementing policies, and for general office management and day-to-day administration. The Commission's choice was H. P. Williams, then news editor of station 2FC. Williams had been for a time editor of the Bathurst *National Advocate* and had established the *Land* newspaper. He was widely travelled, having undertaken a number of overseas fact-finding missions for organizations like the Associated Farmers' Federation of Australia and the Australian Meat Council. In 1928, the New South Wales Broadcasting Company had appointed him assistant manager, and in 1929 he became their news editor and editor of publications.¹⁶ His appointment as ABC general manager seemed an obvious progression. Cabinet generally approved of the appointment, though one minister was annoyed that a political 'rat' from the Nationalists was chosen. Others queried the £2500 proposed salary, as a result of which it was reduced to £2000 per annum.¹⁷

Ill-health and public criticism of Williams' political leanings undermined his attempts to leave a mark on the ABC. In Parliament, Jack Beasley constantly attacked his alleged anti-Labor bias, warning that in the event of a change of government he would be well advised to 'pack up his traps and get out rather than be pushed out'.[18] But Williams did not survive long enough to be pushed out. His death early in 1933 was an untimely blow to the infant Commission.

Pending the choice of a successor, ABC operations were divided into two zones: a northern zone comprising New South Wales and Queensland under the control of Horner, and a southern zone (all other states) under the direction of Bearup. The press meanwhile urged haste in filling the vacancy. The *Sunday Sun and Guardian* recommended the appointment of a 'showman' to replace Williams, someone who could make Australia 'a cultural force to be reckoned with'.[19]

It was Herbert Brookes who, prompted by Professor Bernard Heinze of the University of Melbourne Conservatorium, persuaded Mrs Couchman and eventually the whole Commission that Major Walter Tasman Conder was the best man for the job.[20] Born in Tasmania, Conder had received most of his education at Launceston Church Grammar School where he was school captain and commander of the cadets. He distinguished himself at rowing, boxing, sprinting, and horse-riding, and represented Tasmania in football. In 1908, he became a master at the school, studied part-time at the University of Tasmania, and in 1914 he moved to Victoria to accept a position at Melbourne Grammar.

Conder's subsequent career revealed his very great leadership potential. Wounded at Gallipoli in 1915, he returned to Australia as commandant of Langwarrin Military Camp where he radically improved the living conditions of the soldiers invalided there with venereal disease. He saw that the soldiers received their full pay and equal rations. A brass band was formed for their enjoyment. He also managed to keep the camp free from meningitis. After the war, he became governor of Pentridge Gaol and inspector of prisons for Victoria. His ideas of prison reform invoked the displeasure of some people in authority, but he served a useful term as governor. He again formed a brass band from among the inmates and generally raised prisoner morale. In 1923, he left Pentridge when the theatrical firm, J. C. Williamson Ltd, offered him a very high salary.

Conder's initial task at J. C. Williamson's had been to revitalize a flagging administration and particularly to eliminate ticket-sale abuses, but his main job was to develop the company's new interest in radio broadcasting. He very successfully managed the Broadcasting Company of Australia which later merged with Dominion Broadcasting Pty Ltd (controlling 3LO, 3AR, 5CL, and 7ZL). These were pioneering years in Australian radio, and Conder almost single-handedly made the company's broadcasting operations pay, and pay handsomely. He was completely dedicated to his job, working long hours from his office in His Majesty's Theatre or his room at the Athenaeum Club. He presided over a major technical innovation, the reduction of 3LO's wave-length, and through sheer effort helped to establish radio's popularity in Melbourne. It was once said that 3LO's early success was due to Conder's 'genius for organisation, his vision, and enthusiasm for all things affecting the radio field'.[21]

When the Company took over 3LO in 1930, Conder left broadcasting to become organizer of Melbourne's centenary celebrations. He had applied without success to become the first general manager of the ABC, but was now given a second chance with the death of Williams. He was appointed general manager on 19 April 1933.

Conder was an extremely colourful character, hardworking, always cheery, possessing great humanity. His reported slogan was 'everything on the air but hot air'.[22] A great showman, he persuaded Sir Macpherson Robertson to outlay £10 000 to sponsor a London-to-Melbourne air race in 1933. The broadcast of the race was a first in Australia. Given the stated goals of the ABC, a man with Conder's views and personality might seem an odd choice for general manager; for he believed that as a 'democratic institution' radio should arrange its programmes to suit the masses,[23] in contrast to the Commission's aim to cater for people's needs rather than their wants. But it may be that Conder's appointment was predictable and reflected, perhaps more sharply than anything else, the gap which existed between the early ABC's real and stated goals.

Although state managers enjoyed considerable autonomy in programme matters and in office management, intervention by the general manager was not uncommon. Conder's approach to staff relations was a strange combination of military efficiency—and ruthlessness—and private-enterprise freedom of action. His mixed approach brought an equally mixed reaction from staff, some warming to his flamboyant, jovial manner, others suffering under what they believed to be a reign of terror.[24]

It would have been difficult to classify the ABC as a good employer in its first two years. The main reward offered employees was the dubious privilege of being part of the ABC. Unlike employees in the Public Service, ABC staff enjoyed no security of tenure, no superannuation, no overtime payments, no long-service

2 Programmes and Personalities

leave, no assurance of promotion, and no regular hours. Officially, staff worked a six-day, forty-and-a-half-hour week, but in fact many worked between sixty and ninety hours. The only extra benefit enjoyed by ABC staff was three weeks' annual leave to compensate for holiday and Sunday work. There was no regular method of recruitment. The state manager could hire his own staff, and did so mainly through personal connections. Vacancies were rarely advertised. Some years after leaving the ABC, Horner recalled how in the early days vacancies were not advertised even among the existing staff. Even by 1934, only 'responsible' positions were publicly advertised, and then at the discretion of the general manager.[25]

Conder preferred to keep the number of permanent staff small and to treat them like the artists he had employed while at J. C. Williamson's. This meant awarding short (usually sixteen-week) contracts.[26] As a result, the number of permanent ABC staff remained at around 265 for the duration of his term as general manager.[27] The short-term contracts applied mainly to creative staff, but the administrative staff in practice felt little more secure. Many people were dismissed during the first few months of Conder's taking office; and while in some ways this was a predictable weeding-out process in a new, expanding enterprise, there was an abruptness about the dismissals which made many staff fear for their positions. It appears that in a number of cases, a suggested resignation was the first indication of unsatisfactory service.[28]

There can be no doubt that Conder expected very high standards from staff. Ellis Blain has noted one Hobart cleaner's comment that Conder always ran his hand along the top of studio doors to check for dust.[29] Close inspection of staff performance extended to those higher up in the organization. On one occasion, when Charles Moses (then sporting broadcaster and later general manager) was visiting Melbourne to conduct a series of cricket broadcasts, Conder wrote to the ABC manager for Victoria: 'I want you to watch this gentleman very closely while he is in Melbourne to see whether he shows signs of becoming swelled headed. He has shown one or two signs here, and has had to be brought to heel.'[30] The style of operation suggested by this memorandum induced many people to resign, but it must not be thought that Conder's methods merely sorted out the weak; for a number of capable people who were eased out of the ABC during his general managership immediately secured lucrative positions with commercial radio stations. One good man lost in January 1934 was Robinson, the manager for Queensland. He clashed with Conder, 'resigned', and was replaced by Lewis from

Tasmania, who had been Conder's batman during World War I.³¹

Conder's hard line on staff conditions caused a minor revolt early in 1934 when he attempted to reduce salaries in line with a suggestion from the Postmaster-General's Department. Public Service salaries had all been reduced during the Depression. ABC salaries had not, but most ABC staff already received less than their equivalents in the public service and other government agencies. In Tasmania, for example, in September 1933, the most highly paid person next to the manager was the programme controller who earned £8 10s. per week. The lowest paid employees were the messenger boy and switchboard operator who each received £3 per week. In contrast, Public Service juniors could earn £4 per week with provisions for annual increments, and an executive anything up to £20 per week.³² Following strongly worded letters from most branches, and particularly from the South Australian manager, Hosking, the plan to reduce salaries was dropped.³³ From the point of view of industrial relations, Conder handled the matter poorly in the early stages. The clumsy manner in which the decision to reduce salaries had been taken and then rescinded in itself revealed the *ad hoc* nature of ABC staffing policy.

One fairly distinct group of staff was the announcers. The ABC's choice of announcers clearly revealed the kind of image it wished to project. Announcers had to possess a voice appropriate to ABC functions, in practice something approaching the educated accent of BBC announcers.³⁴ An ability to pronounce foreign names or musical titles was equally important. Quite a few announcers, including Heath Burdock ('Peter Possum'), Captain A. C. C. Stevens ('Uncle Steve'), Norman McCance (special descriptive broadcaster), and Charles Moses, had migrated from Britain and had grammar-school backgrounds. During Conder's time as general manager, a useful additional qualification was to have worked for J. C. Williamson Ltd. Among the many announcers who could claim this experience were Conrad Charlton (leading announcer at 2FC), Burdock, Stevens, Frank Hatherley ('Bobby Bluegum') and Maurice de Lacy Dudley ('Billy Bunny').³⁵

Announcing was a relatively new career which demanded special personal qualities in addition to the right image. The announcer's life was lonely, often involving many solitary hours in a studio with no human being in sight other than the technician on the other side of the control booth.³⁶ The salary though not large was adequate: most began at £3—£4 per week, rising ultimately to between £8 and £9 with bonuses for extra services. The announcer had to be a Jack of all trades at this time, for support staff were few. The official

2 Programmes and Personalities

workload could be very heavy. In the early 1930s, Frank Hatherley performed general announcing duties between 4 p.m. and 11.30 p.m., conducted the children's session each day between 5 and 6.30 p.m., and ran the community singing programme.[37]

Yet there were apparently enough attractions in an announcer's life to entice many aspirants, for the ABC had a large number of private inquiries.[38] For the first few years, the ABC generally did not advertise announcing positions but filled most of its few vacancies by personal contact. For the very first year, it relied heavily on the announcers of the old Company.

The choice of announcers also illustrated a central dilemma facing the early ABC: how to project an air of cultural respectability without also projecting an air of smugness or cultural snobbery which caused loss of listeners and threatened the ABC's viability? The fact that announcers wore formal evening dress on all occasions did not help. Basil Kirke spelled out what most of the commissioners were thinking in November 1933 when he wrote to Conder: 'We Australians are not an austere, reserved, phlegmatic type of people and I can never really believe that the stiff formality will ever be acceptable to the average Australian.'[39] Kirke was probably right, for to the present day the ABC has had only limited success in shaking off an image of stuffiness.

The dilemma mentioned above was nowhere more obvious than in the selection and production of programme material. In theory the ABC was committed to broadcasting programmes which entertained and educated, but in practice it was very difficult to evolve working definitions of 'entertainment' and 'education'. How far were the difficulties of providing both these things reflected in the type of programme broadcast by the ABC from 1932 to 1934? To what extent was programming influenced by Jones' belief that 'enlightenment must come through entertainment', and to what extent by Conder's desire to please the masses?

As of 1 July 1932 an additional £400 per week was to be spent on national programmes, but the Commission consciously avoided broadcasting 'wonderful programmes' at first, fearing that a high standard might not be sustainable.[40] Though radio had long since ceased to be regarded as a toy, many early programmes had purely novelty value. There were broadcasts from the bottom of the Yarra, from an aircraft, from the back of an elephant, or from the scene of a famous event. Even the 1932 Christmas broadcast by King George V, which commenced in Edinburgh and was relayed through Belfast, Dublin, the liner *Majestic* in the Atlantic, Montreal, Toronto, Winnipeg, Vancouver, Wellington, and finally through the ABC network, attracted listeners as much for its novelty as for its content.⁴¹ However, there were many more broadcasting hours to be filled each week, all of which could not rely on gimmickry.

The practice of broadcasting continuously from the earliest hours to midnight and beyond is comparatively recent. In the early 1930s, ABC hours of transmission were much shorter and were not continuous. A typical schedule was that of station 2FC:⁴²

7.00 'Big Ben'; Song of Australia
7.03 Weather, News, Cables, Commentary
7.35 Musical Interlude

8.00—9.15 Close

9.15 Musical Miniatures
10.15 Racing Talk
10.30 Salon Music
10.45 Good Housekeeping — 'The Simple Art of Cooking Meat Perfectly'
11.00 AWRA Session
11.10 Organ Interlude
11.15 Religious Devotion

11.30—12 noon Close

12.00 'Big Ben'; Studio Music
12.15 News Commentary
12.30 Musical Items
1.00 News, Cables, Weather
1.15 Racing broadcasts; Music

5.00—5.30 Close

5.30 Children's Hour with Bobby Bluegum
6.30 The Family Physician
6.45 Sporting Results
7.25 News, Cables
7.35 Weather, Stock Exchange Report
7.40 Musical Interlude
8.00 National Programme — 'The Laughter of Fools'
9.15 Military Band Concert
10.30 Weather
10.32 Dance Music
11.30 National Anthem, Close.

It was some years before regular time-slots for particular programmes became common, but even in these earliest days the entire

2 Programmes and Personalities

Saturday afternoon was, then as now, devoted to sporting sessions. Other regular programme items were the Children's Hour, commencing usually at 5.30 or 5.45 p.m., a church service on Sundays at 11 a.m., dinner music at 6 or 6.15 p.m., plays on Sunday, Tuesday and Friday evenings, community singing on Thursdays at 8 p.m., talks on foreign affairs on Mondays at 8.20 p.m., and news nightly at around 7.50 p.m.

For information about programme schedules, listeners relied on the guides published in the newspapers or on specialist radio magazines such as the Sydney *Wireless Weekly*, the *Listener-In* (Melbourne), the *Broadcaster* (Perth), or *Radio Call* (South Australia). The ABC did not publish its own programme magazine until 1939. Most radio magazines were within the price range of the ordinary person: the *Wireless Weekly*, for example, cost threepence in 1932. People who wanted greater detail on programme content, on the people who made them possible, or on the latest technical information, could turn to the *Broadcasting Year Book,* the *Australian Radio News and Film Review* (published by the *Bulletin*), or one of the many short-lived journals such as *On the Air* or the *Radio Monthly*.[43]

Planning of programme content, length, and time-slotting was not co-ordinated nationally until the creation of a federal programme committee in 1936. From 1932 to 1934, these matters were largely the responsibility of the state branch managers, some of whom enjoyed the assistance of a programme controller. At the Head Office level, the general manager would make recommendations about various programmes, but the Commission's role in programme planning was kept purposely general by Jones. Discussion at Commission meetings centred on questions such as the percentage of time and money to be devoted to musical or other types of programme, the percentage of relays, hours of transmission, or the proportion of recorded programmes to live broadcasts.[44] Individual commissioners occasionally took an interest in programmes which they believed fell within their area of competence. Wallace, an academic, used his university connections to approach potential speakers.[45] Brookes and Mrs Couchman drew up lists of records which they considered the ABC should possess.[46] But overall, the Commission was more concerned with making explicit its assumptions about taste, and seeing that in its view the ABC was providing 'adequate and comprehensive' programmes, than it was with programme details.

Strained relations between some of the commissioners limited the Commission's direct role in programme planning. During Brookes' time as vice-chairman, he spent many hours discussing broadcasting matters with Mrs Couchman, and his diaries reveal that many of the guests at his household were people associated with broadcasting.[47] But this close-knit Melbourne group had its differences with the Sydney section of the ABC.

In particular, Brookes believed that Jones lacked sufficient dedication to the job of chairman, and that he too willingly abdicated the primary role in programme policy formulation. His diary impressions record that Jones 'can't play the game properly' and is 'weak and slippery and vain'.[48] To some extent the feeling was mutual, and for the first few months chairman and vice-chairman were continually at loggerheads. In September 1932, Jones wrote Brookes:

> The work of this Commission if it is to run along smoothly, and we are to carry out a successful stewardship, needs a much more generous spirit of co-operation than I have received from you in regard to some matters up to this date. The state of things that has existed in which I, as Chairman, have by suggestion and innuendo been made to suffer indignity, cannot continue if we are to be successful in our undertaking.[49]

Brookes' clashes with Jones cannot be dismissed as the result of a personality failing, for he enjoyed close relations with other people and was popular with ABC staff.[50] His working relationship with Mrs Couchman was solid and lasting. He got on well with the first general manager and for most of the time with Conder. He once said of his friendship with H. P. Brown: 'It has not only increased my knowledge and intensified my Service but it has also enriched my life'.[51] And despite the professional conflicts the personal relationship between Brookes and Jones was reasonably cordial.[52] There was possibly an element of 'sour grapes' in Brookes' attitude (he had only narrowly missed becoming chairman himself), but he possessed too strong a sense of public service to allow a personal disappointment to mar the Commission's operations. The tensions seem more accurately explained as the product of inter-state rivalry.

It was the practice of the Sydney and Melbourne members of the Commission to hold separate meetings and there is plenty of evidence that relations between the two groups were strained. As early as June 1932, before the official assumption of control, Brookes protested against 'Jones and Sydney's' appointment of Horner as manager for New South Wales.[53] Later he attacked Jones' appointment of Arthur Mason as the ABC's London representative, and the Sydney section's failure to agree to the appointment of

2 Programmes and Personalities

Bernard Heinze as musical adviser.[54] Jones answered Brookes' complaints as follows:

> I have reached the limit of my patience in regard to your suggestions and innuendoes that I am either directly or indirectly influencing the policy of this Commission on the grounds of personal friendships. This must cease, and in making this claim I am confident that I hold the fullest support of the majority of the members of the Commission.[55]

But Jones' support came only from the Sydney members, Orchard and Wallace.

The biggest trial of strength between the Sydney and Melbourne 'clubs' came when the Commission was forced to decide on Conder's future as general manager. Hitherto used to the extravagant, glamorous life-style of a commercial entrepreneur-manager, Conder found it a difficult transition to the general managership of a public institution. Jones gave Conder a free hand in decision making, too free according to Brookes who recorded in his diary on 15 February 1933: 'Extravagant service. A weak chairman has given loose rein and let executive run away with us'.[56] At times, Conder's lavish outlays on furnishings and carpets and the entertainment of artists was brought into question.[57] But the matter which most divided the Commission concerned a personal radio-telephone call costing £23 that Conder allegedly charged to the ABC. Jones suspended Conder and had all but persuaded the Commission to ask for his resignation when Brookes intervened and swayed opinion in favour of granting Conder another few months' trial.[58] The Melbourne members' support and sympathy for Conder related to the fact that they had pushed for his appointment in the first place, but there was also a determination to prevent Jones from replacing their man with one from Sydney—or 'Sydney "Australia" ' as Brookes usually referred to it in his diary.[59] It is perhaps to Jones' credit that he was prepared to compromise rather than to force a split in the Commission, but the incident possibly hastened his eventual severance from the ABC.[60]

Lack of a strong policy lead from the commissioners may have contributed to the predominance of musical programmes in the early days. Music accounted for nearly 53 per cent of all broadcasts during the 1932/3 year.[61] Radio seemed to lend itself naturally to music; in addition, music was safe: it was unlikely that any public fuss would be caused by a musical programme, save perhaps some expressions of opinion about taste. Musical programmes were relatively easy to produce, usually requiring merely the playing of a record, or the positioning of an artist in front of a microphone.

The greater number of live performances was the main difference between musical broadcasts of the early 1930s and those of the present day. In its first year, the ABC gave opportunities to 17 067 musicians and singers.[62] Artists who wished to appear on ABC radio appeared before either the state audition committee or a travelling federal committee. If rejected, artists had right of appeal to the general manager, but very few ever exercised that right.[63] Many of the people who appeared before ABC microphones were unemployed entertainers who were feeling the pinch of the Depression.[64] The ABC's presence in J. C. Williamson's building in Sydney and Conder's past connections with the firm were used to full advantage in securing artists; but the two organizations would have enjoyed greater co-operation had not the days of rivalry with the Australian Broadcasting Company left a bitter taste in J. C. Williamson's mouth.[65]

Listeners received a variety of musical items in their homes. Dance-band music took up 5.68 per cent of total programme time in 1932/3, and community singing broadcasts, though occupying only 0.87 per cent of programme time, were always very popular.[66] They were first introduced to provide people with an opportunity to sing away their Depression blues.[67] The concerts were held in different town halls each week and were broadcast live. Proceeds from the concerts went to various charities or were used to purchase radio sets for hospitals. A typical community singing programme was that broadcast on 2BL on Thursday 17 August 1933 at 8 p.m. In addition to the usual selection of sing-a-long numbers, which included well-known favourites such as 'Home Sweet Home', 'Old Folks at Home', 'Ching Chong', and the 'Blue Danube Waltz', the programme featured Mark Erickson (an entertainer) and the North Sydney Tramway Mouth-Organ Band.[68]

Community singing or dance-band music was fairly easily identifiable as entertainment. As a body committed to uplifting taste, the ABC broadcast large amounts of serious classical music as well. This meant broadcasts of something more than Beethoven's Fifth Symphony or Tchaikovsky's 1812 Overture. A large number of grand operas were broadcast, among them *Il Trovatore, La Traviata, Un Ballo in Maschera, Carmen*, and *La Boheme*, together with a selection of light operas such as *The Mikado, The Pirates of Penzance*, and *The Yeomen of the Guard*.[69]

Large-scale musical productions required orchestras. Their establishment and maintenance was to be one of the most significant innovatory roles played by the ABC. By 1936, the Commission was

2 Programmes and Personalities

financing permanent symphony orchestras in each state, but for the first few years it relied extensively on established bodies such as the Melbourne Symphony Orchestra and the orchestra of the Sydney Conservatorium of Music. These orchestras were supplemented or combined as required to meet the needs of visiting conductors and artists of international repute brought to Australia by the ABC to give listeners first-hand experience of world standards. Sir Hamilton Harty, the British conductor, was the first international figure to conduct a series of ABC 'Celebrity Concerts' in Sydney and Melbourne. He did a grand tour of the two cities in 1934, conducting nine concerts. Most of these were broadcast. Although some newspapers questioned the cost, the Harty visit received a good press and a favourable response from the public who attended the performances or who listened-in on their radios.[70]

The ABC played another highly innovatory role in its sponsorship of composers' competitions. Dr Keith Barry, music critic, chairman of the committee of management of Music Week 1933, and a later ABC federal controller of programmes, said of the first such competition that it would 'do for Australian composers what the Archibald Prize has done for our artists'.[71] The first competition was announced officially on 24 February 1933 and offered prizes totalling £450, with individual awards of between £5 and £50. The challenge was readily taken up, the ABC receiving over 800 entries.[72]

In launching the composers' competition, the Commission said that it hoped to 'lay the foundation of an essentially national musical literature, which will reflect worthily the spirit and the aspirations of our people'.[73] But what was this 'national musical literature' to be? The Commissioners did not expect or wish that a peculiarly Australian musical form or style would emerge from among the entries received. What they hoped for was an Australian Beethoven or Bach. The highest category of award was for symphonies, the musical form nearest the commissioners' hearts.

The commissioners' veneration of the classical symphony revealed their cultural conservatism. This conservatism was also reflected in the ABC's first annual report, which gave most prominence to the visits of distinguished conductors, the building up of orchestras and the broadcast of classical symphonies and operas. Jazz did not rate a mention, nor did dance-band music. The influence of Bernard Heinze, professor of music at the University of Melbourne Conservatorium, and conductor of the Melbourne Symphony Orchestra and of the Philharmonic Society, was paramount in leading the Commission in this direction. For these first few years at least, ABC musical policy, while directed from Sydney, certainly owed much of its impetus to the efforts of those in Melbourne. Heinze was not appointed musical adviser to the Commission until April 1934, but his close relationship with Brookes placed him in a position to wield influence from the outset.[74] Together these men had evolved a model of high culture which was to have a profound effect on ABC thinking in many areas other than music in the years ahead.

Notwithstanding the preference for live artists, a substantial amount of ABC air time was occupied by recordings. In the first few months, recordings accounted for anything up to 61 per cent of programme time.[75] This figure had fallen to 37.5 per cent by 1934,[76] a figure still significant enough to sustain the fears of record manufacturers who believed broadcasting was responsible for their falling profits. In November 1931, the record manufacturers had banned all broadcasting stations from using their records, but on 9 September 1932 the ABC received permission to play them, provided the title and brand of the record were advertised and the frequency of use strictly limited. For the time being, the manufacturers refused to enter into a similar agreement with the commercial stations who broadcast for longer hours and who played a greater percentage of recordings.[77]

The problem of the manufacturers settled, the ABC had still to face the demands of the Australasian Performing Rights Association (APRA) over the payment of copyright fees to composers whose recorded works were broadcast. The APRA insisted that sales of sheet music were decreasing because of overexposure of compositions by radio stations. One of Williams' first acts as general manager had been to negotiate a copyright payment of 5 per cent of ABC revenue, but he continued to complain that these payments were exorbitant.[78] The government intervened in 1933 by setting up a royal commission into performing rights. At the hearings it became clear that the APRA was demanding a very high price. The BBC paid £63 500 per annum to the Performing Right Society in Britain, whereas under the rates proposed by the APRA the ABC would pay nearly £170 000 per annum.[79] Mr Justice Owen recommended in his report that the ABC pay 6 per cent of its revenue to the APRA, but a deadlock ensued over the definition of revenue: the APRA claimed it meant the total monies collected through licence fees; the ABC insisted it meant only the ABC's share of the fees. The issue remained unresolved for many years.[80]

The APRA and the record manufacturers were resisting the spread of a new medium which threatened to take over their role in the provision of entertainment. The same phenomenon, of competition between established interests and the intruder, was evident in

2 Programmes and Personalities

the ABC's relations with other bodies such as sporting organizations and the press.

Sport, an entertainment session, occupied over 9 per cent of broadcasting time in the ABC's first year.[81] Ellis Blain has said that sport was 'something of a cinderella'[82] in ABC programming in the 1930s; but while that is an accurate description of the situation in the late 1930s—when sport failed to attain the status of a separate programme department with a federal controller—from 1932 to 1934 sporting sessions rated well in terms of ABC resources. The reason, of course, was that sporting broadcasts were known to be very popular, and the ABC was as keen as any broadcasting body to attract listeners.

Some sporting bodies, fearing a drop in attendances, drove a hard bargain on broadcasting rights.[83] The proportion of running descriptions of sporting events appears to have been higher in Australia than in Britain where live coverages were usually reserved for events of special significance like the Derby or the Davis Cup. In Australia, as the *Wireless Weekly* pointed out, listeners were fortunate in that

> running commentaries of almost every major sport, and many minor sports, are on the air almost every day in the week. This does not merely indicate that we are a sport-loving nation . . . but more importantly, that our broadcasters take the job of serving the demands of listeners seriously and carry it out efficiently.[84]

The editorial especially praised ABC sporting broadcasts.

Sporting organizations were not the only group to express opposition to ABC running descriptions. For moral reasons, racing broadcasts drew the odium of the police, the churches, and other community groups. The New South Wales police commissioner asked the ABC to discontinue race broadcasts which he believed encouraged the growth of illegal SP betting. Church leaders warned of the 'unholy alliance between the radio and the man loving a convivial glass, so that he can bet'.[8] The *Daily Telegraph* cited the ABC's stated goals and queried the 'cultural value' of racing broadcasts.[86] The ABC responded to the public outcry by altering the time and format of the broadcasts, but it refused to eliminate them altogether. Racing broadcasts, like other sporting programmes such as cricket, attracted large numbers of listeners whose usual preference lay with the commercial stations.

The provision of news services proved to be one of the ABC's most pressing and continuous programme problems. At a time when the BBC was building up an enviable news service, the ABC was just embarking on what would be fifteen years of negotiations with the

Australian press for the right to broadcast news. The Australian press, despite its recognized power and influence in the 1930s, feared ABC competition might cause a decline in newspaper circulation figures. The press also wished to preserve the prerogative of being first with the news. The ABC argued that news bulletins would help to stimulate sales of newspapers, but without success.[87]

The need to bargain with newspapers for broadcasting rights was unique to Australia, for in both Britain and the United States broadcasters had dealt with news agencies which agreed to supply broadcasting stations with a special news service. The problem was complicated for the ABC by the fact that as a national broadcasting authority it believed it had an obligation to provide impartial news services, but since it possessed limited resources it was compelled by force of convenience to secure its news from sources that were far from impartial.[88]

The ABC thus had little choice but to sign agreements with the Australian Associated Press and the Australian Newspapers Conference, which limited the timing, nature and duration of news broadcasts. As the Newspapers Conference was not a corporate body, the agreements were technically only 'gentlemen's agreements', but were regarded as legally binding by both parties. For a nominal sum of £200 per annum, the ABC could broadcast two morning bulletins, between 10 and 11 a.m., and one evening bulletin of five minutes' duration, but not before 7.50 p.m. A further agreement for overseas news with AAP (which in turn had rights to Reuters and Associated Press) limited the amount of news received to 200 cabled words per day.[89]

Many listeners blamed the ABC for failing in its early news broadcasts, ignorant of the restrictions under which they were produced. In addition to timing restrictions, the agreements forbade the ABC from collecting its own news, from supplementing the items it selected from the metropolitan dailies, and from checking the accuracy of stories. Thus most early ABC news bulletins degenerated into an announcer reading articles from a newspaper. There was no policy on what constituted news, the selection being merely the personal preferences of the announcer on duty.[90]

Despite the general conditions laid down in the agreements, the precise details varied considerably from state to state, depending largely on the attitudes of the local newspaper proprietors. In Brisbane, the ABC was able to broadcast five seven-minute sessions daily, mainly because the source of news, the *Evening Standard,* was not a member of the Australian Newspapers Conference. In contrast, the power of the newspapers in Sydney was such that they could force 2FC and 2BL to reduce their five-minute sessions each to three minutes' duration.[91]

Thus in a programme area that was later to achieve a high status within the ABC organization, the Commission's role as the arbiter of programme time-slotting and content was usurped by private interests. The ABC was attempting to move into a field where entrenched interests were determined to maintain their effective monopoly. Jones could have taken a much tougher stance against the newspapers but tried co-operating;[92] this was ultimately to the ABC's disadvantage, for the Commission's future bargaining position was weakened. It is not clear why Jones did not adopt a more independent solution to the problem of news services from the outset. The 1932 Act authorized the Commission to 'collect in such manner as it thinks fit news and information relating to current events in any part of the world', which suggests there was no direct legislative bar. It is likely that Jones was reluctant to involve the ABC so soon in arrangements which would be subject to government veto (since any attempt to establish an independent news service would certainly have cost more than £5000), especially in an area where Cabinet's vulnerability to outside pressure was high. There is also the possibility that Jones, Williams, and Conder simply did not attach the degree of importance to this aspect of the ABC's functions which some of their successors did.

One far less contentious area of programming which made reasonable beginnings during the first two years was school broadcasts. The first school broadcasts in Australia had taken place as early as October 1924, when thirteen schools listened to a series of broadcasts by 2FC. Victoria was the first state to begin broadcasts on a sizeable scale in March 1932, when Dr G. L. Wood delivered the first of a series of lectures on the geography of Australia. But it was only after the establishment of the ABC that school broadcasts began to take off on a national scale. In 1933, the Commission formed committees of leading educational authorities to help evolve a system of school broadcasts. The broadcasts were officially inaugurated in Victoria and New South Wales in May 1933 and later that year in Queensland and South Australia. An attempt to extend the scheme to Western Australia fell through because of lack of interest. But the Commission could still take credit for having launched what was to become an important educational service to Australian schoolchildren, particularly those in isolated areas.[93]

The ABC's programmes for young Australians were not confined to educational broadcasts. The 'Children's Hour', a concept borrowed directly from the BBC, from the outset was firmly entrenched in its early evening time-slot. However, until the introduction of a national children's session in 1939, the content of the 'Children's Hour' differed in each state.

During the late 1920s, a succession of performers entertained thousands of young listeners as their radio 'Uncles' and 'Aunts', or as the more colourfully named 'Little Miss Kookaburra', 'Bobby Bluegum' or 'Billy Bunny'. The children's sessions of 1932—4 contained mainly stories, singing, plays, jokes, and birthday calls. The sessions were rarely mentioned at early Commission meetings, and on the whole the initiative was left entirely to individuals in the states: Bryson Taylor and Heath Burdock in Sydney, Judy Lucke in Hobart, Nina Murdoch in Melbourne, and so on.[94]

Nina Murdoch was perhaps the only one to attempt to develop new types of children's programmes. She was keen to diverge from the traditional Uncle and Aunt sessions, and as an employee of the Australian Broadcasting Company had experimented with an Argonauts Club in which children joined Jason in boats that were part of a fleet in search of the Golden Fleece. Children were encouraged to send in poems, songs, stories, or plays, for which they received merit points, each time moving closer to target of the fleece.[95] The programme should have appealed to the Commission with its interest in educating as well as entertaining, but Conder quashed the idea before it ever reached that far, insisting that the whole concept was 'too high-falutin' for children.'[96]

Conder had a quick eye to audience response and was fully conscious of the fact that the ABC's children's sessions were competing for popularity with the very successful programmes on the commercial stations, such as 3AW's 'Chatterbox Corner' with Nicky and Tuppy. His belief that Nina Murdoch's attempts at different types of children's sessions were misguided was shared by many parents. One listener complained: 'Billy Bunny is scarcely heard, the kookaburra laughs no more, we can't understand this piffle. We get all the education we want at school, we only want amusement at the children's session.'[97] Apart from intervening to block Murdoch's experiments, Head Office displayed no interest in children's programmes until 1936, when it began to look seriously at their content and to formulate policy recommendations about them more in line with ABC philosophies.

Talk programmes were in a fairly elementary stage of development. During the ABC's first week, Miss Kathleen De Lauret delivered a talk on 'Travelling Etiquette and how not to act superior to the Natives', and a Mr F. C. Jones spoke on 'The Lure of the Antique'. Dullness was the main identifying feature of early talk

2 Programmes and Personalities

sessions, and sprang from the fact that many talks—or lectures as they were then called—were delivered by university professors, few of whom were accomplished broadcasters. There were exceptions: Western Australia's Professor Walter Murdoch delivered many a well-received literary talk;[98] Professor W. J. Dakin fascinated many listeners with his insights into science; and Professor Charteris became well known for his talks on foreign affairs. In addition, listeners heard the voices of the famous, among them Pope Pius XI and Adolf Hitler.[99]

Only a tiny percentage of broadcasting time was devoted to talks, partly because they were dubious audience pleasers, but also because the ABC wished to eschew broadcast items which might attract government attention. With institutional survival far from guaranteed, it was much easier to play music. This policy of caution was carried to extremes. In May 1933, Dorothy Brunton refused to take part in the production of *Dearest Enemy* after the ABC deleted certain 'blasphemous' phrases ('hell' and 'damn' as expletives).[1] Conder publicly justified the censorship on the ground that the ABC did not intend to 'insult decent Christian people, least of all in their own homes'.[2] He also queried the need for talks or debates on contentious issues, fearing that the ABC might be 'putting ideas of change into the heads of those whose present status leads them to regard any change as desirable'.[3] Excessive caution on controversial issues and a sensitivity to Australia's position as 'part of the British Empire and British race',[4] stemmed partly from the uncertainty of the early 1930s when many people believed that the rise of fascism in Germany and Italy and the growing influence of the Soviet Union posed fundamental threats to Western Christian values. The ABC, through its cautious approach, was to uphold these values.

The remainder of broadcasting time was a mixture of weather reports, emergency announcements, stockmarket reports, shipping and train information, items of interest to country listeners—flood reports, rural news and the like—plays, religious broadcasts, and women's sessions. All these broadcasts together comprised less than 20 per cent of total broadcasting time. Documentaries as we know them today were virtually non-existent.[5]

Plays, which were later to prove one of the most popular of broadcast items, accounted for only 2.87 per cent of programme time in 1932/3. The ABC faced a dearth of suitable dramatic material at first, and for some years it had to be content to import BBC recordings or to broadcast the soundtrack of a popular movie. Listeners were treated to a reasonable selection of plays nevertheless: *The Patsy, The Cardboard Lover, When Knights were Bold,* and *The Merchant of Venice* to name but a few.⁶ However, the radio play as an art form in its own right had yet to reach its heyday.

The 5.58 per cent of programme time devoted exclusively to women's 'particular interests' in 1932/3 could hardly be said to have widened the horizons of the Australian housewife. The bulk of the women's sessions contained 'subjects such as housekeeping in all its many forms, preparation for, care of and upbringing of children, knitting, sewing and fancy work, interior decoration and other matters of essentially feminine appeal'.⁷

It was difficult to ascertain how many people were listening to ABC programmes. By June 1933, licensed radio sets were installed in 469 477 Australian homes. Contemporary observers estimated that this represented a potential listening audience of just under two million (approximately four times the number of listeners' licences);⁸ but this audience was not captive. Newspapers surveys, which must be treated with caution because of the hostility between the press and the ABC and the smallness of the sample, offered an ABC audience figure of under 20 per cent,⁹ very close to present-day estimates but equally unreliable as an accurate indicator of audience reaction to specific programmes.

Given the scant information available to the ABC about its audience, how could it make judgements about audience tastes? Indeed, was it really interested? In his first annual report Jones claimed that the Commission had 'endeavoured to hold the balance equitably between all interests and all competitive points of policy. It has learned much concerning the public wishes and the public needs; and it has endeavoured at once to appeal to these wishes and to fulfil those needs.'¹⁰ But had it? There was no formal audience research at the time. The ABC did receive large numbers of letters from the public, averaging 101 letters per state per day in 1932 and totalling 408 500 letters during the first two years.¹¹ But listeners' letters were not very reliable sources of information. Usually little was known about the author, and letters represented only the views of people who felt strongly enough to lodge a protest or note of approval. It would be safe to say that there were more letters of complaint than of praise, one letter from a group of farmers labelling ABC programmes 'utter tripe';¹² but there was no unanimity of demand. At the annual electrical and radio exhibition in the capital cities the ABC made a token attempt to elicit listeners' opinions by circulating a questionnaire. However, the replies received again represented the preferences of only a few Australians.¹³ In mid-1933, Jones announced that the ABC was to devote more attention to 'humanizing' its programmes by including broadcasts with represented 'the

2 Programmes and Personalities

real things of life'.[14] The vagueness of this commitment suggests that the Commission floundered in the dark whenever it attempted to satisfy a popular audience.

In assessing Jones' chairmanship it should be emphasized that the position of chairman was only part-time. Yet it is clear that the ABC suffered in an economically depressed climate that forced Jones to devote most of his energies to the survival of David Jones Ltd. Pressures of business so increased after the death of his brother early in 1934, that Jones resigned from July.[15] News of the resignation featured prominently in the press on 27 June. The *Sydney Morning Herald* printed a eulogizing editorial, the customary thank-you accorded those who vacate public office.[16] Jones was a competent, able operator, but the ABC was not his first interest and his efforts appear half-hearted compared with those of his successor.

What had been achieved under Jones' chairmanship? Staff, equipment, and buildings had been secured. The Commission had become operational, and aspects of policy were established for all time. In particular, the ABC affirmed its role as a pace-setter in musical appreciation in Australia, and recognized through action the important role of national radio in education. But there were few other achievements. ABC organization remained loose and unstructured. There had been no attempt to divide the organization into divisions or departments—such as news, talks, music, features, and drama—which could develop expertise in their respective programmes. Relations between the Commission and the staff were still at a very informal, personalized level, relecting further the fluid state of the ABC bureaucracy. Programme planning remained chaotic, more like an amateurs' game of blind man's buff than the professional operation expected of a public institution. The commissioners, lacking experience and torn by personal and inter-state rivalry, had contributed little. Brookes and Mrs Couchman took their job seriously, but the rest were far from inspiring. Jones failed to espouse specific policies. Orchard's contribution, if any, is undocumented. Wallace helped to launch school broadcasts but did little despite an overseas trip to examine broadcasting developments.[17]

The public were noticeably impatient with the ABC. Because the Commission's product was so intangible, people readily accused it of failing to meet standards dictated by their own biases. Others criticized its use of scarce monetary resources, so sought after during a time of economic depression. All this public over-expectancy and criticism discouraged the ABC staff, a problem exacerbated by the fact that the postmaster-general in the Lyons Cabinet failed to give the ABC an effective voice in government. Ministers with strong influence usually were on good terms with the press and hence were not anxious to strengthen the position of the ABC *vis-a-vis* the commercial stations.[18] This fact became clear when the ABC asked for exclusive rights to broadcast programmes transmitted from overseas, especially from the BBC. The postmaster-general, Archdale Parkhill, did not force the issue and Cabinet agreed that commercial stations could have equal rights.[19] The ABC considered that it should receive preferential treatment and support in its efforts to enhance its standing as a national broadcasting authority, but Parkhill was neither sympathetic nor particularly influential.

The Commission had to face the realities and politics of survival. While the abstract statement of goals remained constant, circumstances made it essential to interpret these as long-term objectives.[20] Early ABC files abound with illustrations of the fact that, in the interim, it was prepared to chase audiences and get licence numbers up to ensure that there was sufficient public approval and financial support for its continued existence. Shortly after the commencement of operations, an instruction to the ABC's acting manager for Western Australia read:

> I want you to see that the policy of the Commission is not highbrow. Keep your programmes popular. You are dealing with the masses, and while we might aim at a general uplift, at the same time your judgment will be relied upon to see that Broadcasting does not lose its popularity.[21]

At least one state branch manager was offered a bonus of one shilling for every new listener's licence gained in his state![22]

The infant ABC was institutionally weak, lacking a champion for its challenge to vested interests. Its attempts to carve out a territory of its own met with resistance from press organizations, sporting bodies, record companies, the theatre, and commercial radio stations. In these circumstances, it was naturally difficult for a defined institutional ethos to develop. It was to these problems that the ABC's new chairman, William James Cleary, addressed himself.

3
Cleary and the ABC

Between 1934 and 1939, the ABC's organizational structure crystallized. A centralized control system for staff and programming ensured that Head Office philosophies penetrated the lower echelons of the bureaucracy. These changes were largely the result of strong, interventionist leadership by William James Cleary, whom G. C. Bolton has called the 'founding father' of the ABC.[1] Cleary was committed to the ABC as a vehicle for raising the cultural standards of Australians, and was willing to expend the energy and resources necessary to achieve what had hitherto been abstract goals.

Cleary's family background was not one to encourage love of the arts or higher education. He was born on 29 December 1885 in Redfern, at the time perhaps Sydney's roughest working-class suburb, as one of a large family. His father was a foreman at Tooth's Brewery. At fourteen, Cleary was forced to relinquish a scholarship he had won to Sydney Boys' High to join his father at the brewery. This enforced break from education profoundly affected Cleary's outlook, leaving him with a determination to succeed on his own. He did not speak to his father for more than a year, and never forgot the frustrations of his adolescence.[2]

In April 1916, after many years of part-time study, Cleary obtained a Diploma in Economics and Commerce from the University of Sydney. Four years previously, he had left home and married Melanie Newton Lewis from South Australia. They began married life in a tent dwelling on Balmoral Beach, but Cleary's achievements at the university and at Tooth's soon enabled him to live in reasonable comfort. In 1918, after more part-time study, he graduated Bachelor of Economics with first-class honours. Altogether, his undergraduate career achieved nine major prizes, including the Chamber of Commerce prize for the best pass in economics. He continued his association with the university as part-time lecturer in business principles and practice until 1929, and from 1935 to 1939 he was a member of the University Senate.

These distinctions were achieved while working at Tooth's where his record was equally impressive. He saved the company thousands by revising dispatch procedures and later revolutionizing the bookkeeping system. In 1920, the company selected him as assistant manager, ahead of six hundred applicants. Within four years, he became general manager. In the process, the boy from Redfern had graduated from his beach dwelling to a large white house at 1 Awaba Street in the very pleasant north-shore suburb of Mosman.[3]

Despite his success, Cleary yearned for a wider human experience than business alone could offer. He broadened his outlook by a vigorous, self-imposed reading programme of novels, essays, poetry, and drama, and was for five years patron of the Sydney Junior Literary Society. Among his favourite poets were the standard writers of the time: Walter de la Mare, John Drinkwater, and W. H. Davies; but he also enjoyed the poetry of Robert Frost when few others in Australia knew of its existence. The fantasies of J. M. Barrie, Christopher Morley, Patrick Chalmers, and Kenneth Grahame greatly appealed to him. He also loved music and could hum effortlessly compositions by Schumann, Brahms, or Schubert. His large library included works in French, German, and Latin. It was once said that

> if there were assembled all the men holding big positions in the Civil Service of the State, and the conversation swung from departmental management to German operatic lieder, back to control of credits and up in the sky to the Miltonic stanza, Cleary would be the one, perhaps the only one, with discernment wide enough to speak knowledgably about them all.[4]

Cleary passed his knowledge on to self-help groups, such as the Workers' Educational Association, which awarded him life membership for his contribution to working-class education.

There was also an adventurous side to Cleary. He bushwalked hundreds of miles on the Bogong High Plains, in the country beyond Warburton, and in the Gippsland region of Victoria. These expeditions were undertaken with two or three associates, of whom John Klunder (Jack) Jensen was perhaps the closest. The two men's backgrounds were remarkably similar: Jack's education had been interrupted prematurely so that he could begin work as a messenger boy in the Postmaster-General's Department, he had furthered his education part-time, and he later came to hold senior positions in the Public Service. Like Cleary, Jensen read widely, loved music, poetry, and drama, and could write excellent prose.[5] Both men were good examples of self-help Australians, and there can be no doubt that during their many weeks in the bush they discussed their views

3 Cleary and the ABC

on broadcasting.⁶ After their excursions, Cleary invariably wrote articles for bushwalking journals. During troubled periods, his mind usually turned to 'the vision of the road, and camp fires and swags'.⁷

Despite his desires for individual self-fulfilment, Cleary believed one's ultimate responsibility as a citizen was public service. He turned down an offer from the Bavin government to become chief civic commissioner for Sydney in 1927, possibly for fear of being involved in intrigue, but eagerly accepted the position of commissioner of railways for New South Wales two years later, even though it meant a drop of salary of £2000. Money was of little import to Cleary. As the Depression deepened, he voluntarily surrendered part of his salary as an example to others.⁸

Nowadays it is not common for businessmen to forgo lucrative incomes to perform public service, nor to regard such service as the capping of a career. Perhaps such a progression was no more typical for men of Cleary's generation. One newspaper said that Cleary was an 'unusual type' who 'in his lectures and business associations has always emphasised the importance of public service'.⁹ His decision to quit the business world was partly a result of disillusionment, or as he put it, 'the great industrial problems with their false lure of success which experience has told me may easily turn to ashes in the mouth';¹⁰ but his commitment to public service was peculiarly strong. Again, his views were influenced, or at least were reinforced, by Jensen, who wrote that the great reward of public service was 'the consciousness, when one's life is ending, that the time has been spent not in mere money-grubbing but in building up something which will remain even though the builder passes into oblivion.'¹¹

Cleary's first experience of public office was neither satisfying nor rewarding. The Lang government which assumed office in October 1930 objected to his proposals for reducing the railways' deficit. Tensions climaxed when he dismissed a senior official, C. T. Goode, for corruption. Lang retaliated by legislating Cleary out of office. After Lang himself was dismissed in 1932, a royal commission upheld Cleary's charges against Goode who subsequently 'resigned'. The clash with Lang, which caused Cleary great financial loss, illustrated his strong moral and mental make-up. He was persuaded to return as chief transport commissioner, but resigned after a few months when the new premier, B. S. B. Stevens, refused to restructure the transport administration.¹²

After his resignation, Mark Foys Ltd offered Cleary a chance to re-enter the business world at a very high salary. He declined, accepting instead the ABC chairmanship at £10 per week.¹³ His term commenced on 3 July 1934.

Impeccable honesty, decisiveness, a reputation as an 'archbishop of commonsense'[14]—these were the qualities which had induced governments to offer Cleary high office and which now sealed his appointment as ABC chairman. Yet his appointment was never a foregone conclusion. As vice-chairman, Herbert Brookes had been an obvious candidate. One member of Cabinet, Sir George Foster Pearce, assured Brookes that 'no Parkhill & C. L. J. [Charles Lloyd Jones] Hanky' would be appointed ahead of him.[15] Thus it was with 'surprise and shock' that Brookes read of Cleary's appointment in the *Argus* on 4 July. Mrs Couchman questioned Cabinet's wisdom in choosing a 'newcomer', but both she and Brookes became Cleary's staunch admirers.[16]

The press welcomed the appointment. There were testimonies to Cleary's 'breadth of culture', 'public spirit', 'business capacity', and 'strength of mind'.[17] The editor of the *Sun* wrote a personal letter of congratulations in which he claimed some credit for having influenced Cabinet's choice.[18] Even *Smith's Weekly*, one of Cleary's life-long tormentors, heralded his arrival as broadcasting chief with the optimistic lines:

> From a past that is partially beery,
> A bout with the permanent way,
> There raises the figure of CLEARY
> And, lo, all the wave-lengths obey!
>
> The nights will no longer be dreary,
> The sky, let us pray, will be fair,
> When the cheery commandments of Cleary
> Take charge of the Commonwealth air.[19]

Dozens of congratulatory messages were received from organizations as disparate as the Sydney Conservatorium of Music, the Associated Chambers of Manufactures, the Catholic Broadcasting Company, and the Chinese Consulate.[20]

Cleary held firm views about the nature of the society he was commissioned to serve. He told the press that he did not accept the 'standards of today', and viewed the 1930s as a 'restless age, very much machine-ridden, not only in factories but in the councils of men'.[21] The prejudice within the Australian community towards intellectuals or purveyors of 'culture' was his first target. He believed that he could meet the challenge of 'the Philistines', despite the countervailing influence of 'canned culture' from America.[22] His background undoubtedly influenced his approach. He emphasized self-improvement through exposure to radio, a paternalistic but not dictatorial approach. As one who had had to work hard for an

3 Cleary and the ABC

education, he did not apologize for 'trying to open up a wider world for every one', and reacted angrily to accusations that by presenting things of intellectual value the ABC would lose listeners.[23] As well, Cleary wanted the ABC to project an image of community-consciousness. Both notions were often present in his annual New Year's Eve broadcasts and in various public addresses he delivered. When opening Adelaide's station 5AN in October 1937, he said:

> The members of the Commission do not sit like the Gods of Olympus, aloof, unseeing, indifferent: we are not strangers to community life and interests: we are grown up, but we have been children in our time! ... We remain serene under the sneer that we attempt to give education over the air ... We know that the people, as a whole, want the best. We know that they want their children to be more enlightened than the present grown up generation, to live in a saner, a happier, a more charitable world.[24]

Cleary had an all-embracing, yet common-sense, conception of words like 'culture' and 'education'. They implied far more than taste and the three R's, and covered the spectrum of intellectual and aesthetic awareness. In his words, the acquisition of 'culture' and 'education' meant

> the development of sensitiveness, the capacity for making the most of our environment in the way of aesthetic appreciation, touching such questions as art, music, painting, &c, and also for learning to weigh facts, winnow chaff from grain, test theories and see through shibboleths, and to form independent opinions.[25]

Equally broad was his conception of 'entertainment'. It was not merely amusement, but included those things which enriched life, such as 'treasures of literature and music' and 'provocative and illuminating talks and discussions'.[26]

Most commissioners had at least vague commitments to cater for something beyond the average taste. Brookes' commitment was perhaps stronger than any other, save that of Cleary himself. But Cleary was the most persistent advocate of the ABC's educative and cultural responsibilities and ultimately had the most influence.[27]

The ABC members were not alone in condemning cultural torpidity. During the 1930s, a number of creative Australians left their homeland for greener pastures overseas. One of them, Norman Lindsay, said in 1931: 'Minor officials were making an organised effort to stamp out culture ... and the Australian mind could not make the effort necessary to fight them, nor could it make the effort to care'.[28] Partly because of the strong anti-nationalist sentiments of the inter-war years, most intellectuals, the traditional sustainers of cultural life, did not try to develop a distinctive national culture. There were a few attempts to do so and of these Rex Ingamells' Jindyworobak Movement is perhaps the best known.[29] But the ABC controllers had little interest in Ingamells and his supporters. While they saw themselves as belonging to a cultural elite, they aimed to increase cultural awareness that was not specifically Australian in emphasis. They encouraged awareness by Australians rather than awareness about Australia.

The role Cleary envisaged for the ABC required a tight organization staffed by people who shared his philosophy. Major Conder's fundamentally different perception of broadcasting's role in society made disagreements almost inevitable. Conder believed that the ABC should not give Australians something better than they thought they wanted. He did not like talk sessions or controversial broadcasts, and he wanted more sporting programmes and more entertainment for its own sake.[30] Cleary could accept neither Conder's outlook nor his 'barrack-room standards'.[31] The differences between the two men became obvious when, just one month after taking office, Cleary called a conference to discuss talks programmes. Conder dismissed the conference as a 'fad of the Commission's'. The day before it commenced, he told Cleary that the public did not want talks, and that the ABC must guard against the influence of academics. This prompted Cleary to observe to his vice-chairman: 'Heaven help us, with this microscopic outlook!'. Radio, an 'instrument of good', was being threatened by 'scoffing managements'.[32]

Doubts about Conder's personal integrity precipitated his eventual removal. To Cleary, any hint of corruption or impropriety was anathema. Thus when irregularities in Conder's expenditure were discovered early in 1935, Cleary demanded a full explanation. Conder was unable to justify the fact that he had hired cars at ABC expense during a recent visit to Tasmania for purposes quite unconnected with his responsibilities as general manager. Nor could he explain why he had hired cars for friends.[33] The Commission met in Melbourne on Sunday 24 March 1935, but decided four to one against direct action. That evening Brookes wrote in his diary: 'They had stood for dismissal—now fail to act for fear of Com of Inquiry. And yet all realize unsuitability and have ample proof of unreliability. The Major's days are numbered. He himself may take action.'[34] Conder, however, did nothing. On 16 June, the Commission agreed that dismissal was therefore the only option, but in a generous gesture granted him compensation payments equal to one half-year's salary.[35]

3 Cleary and the ABC

Cleary read aloud the notice of dismissal at a full Commission meeting on 25 June. It was, in Brookes' words, 'a tense, silent scene'. Conder offered no comment. 'Afraid G.M. doesn't recognise picture. He is so egotistical and warped', noted Brookes, for whom the business was particularly unpleasant.[36] A later diary entry revealed the extent to which he felt let down by Conder: 'Now the cloud has been lifted we are turning up lies all round. Conder was and is a congenital liar'.[37]

News of Conder's 'resignation' came as a complete surprise to the public. The *Labor Daily* complained of the ABC's 'hush-hush policy of impenetrable silence'.[38] *Truth* suggested that disagreement over programming and staffing had caused the resignation.[39] The Commission never did disclose the official reason, and allowed Conder to leave with dignity, untainted (publicly at least) by the humiliations of dismissal from public office. Given the colour and showmanship Conder had brought to Australian broadcasting in its infancy, it is perhaps a pity that his association with national radio was so brief.

When the Commission refused to comment further on Conder's departure, press speculation turned to possible successors. The ABC's manager for Victoria, T. W. Bearup, was suggested, but Cleary denied he was being considered.[40] On 23 August, Cleary surprised the other commissioners by requesting the appointment of one Charles Joseph Alfred Moses. At the time, Moses was thirty-five years old. He had been in broadcasting four years, and was currently in charge of ABC talks and sporting programmes. Brookes suggested that the Commission should seek a 'higher type' and recommended Dr Wood of the University of Melbourne.[41] When the remaining commissioners indicated that they favoured a trial period for Moses, Cleary became more insistent. He had told Brookes in August 1934 that Moses would turn out to be one of the ABC's best men. Cleary had never had qualms about selecting young men of ability for senior executive positions. Just before leaving Tooth's Brewery, he had chosen a young man to succeed him as general manager, a choice which later proved excellent.[42] Eventually, a compromise was reached by which Moses was appointed federal liaison officer. But Cleary had no intention of letting the matter rest. He was soon to request again that Moses be appointed, and on this occasion had complete success.

The delay in appointing a new general manager had led to questions in Parliament, and given rise to press speculation that the Commission was to be restructured to make Cleary both chairman and general manager. Cleary desired no such change and tried hard to kill the rumours.⁴³ Two things then paved the way for Moses' appointment: firstly, he excelled as federal liaison officer and received a good press; secondly, Brookes dropped his opposition after Dr Wood informed him that his prospects at the university were too good to consider other job offers.⁴⁴ At an ABC meeting on 30 October 1935, there was unanimous agreement on Moses' selection. Conder's salary had been £2000 per annum, but Moses was appointed on £1600 as Cleary was to shoulder some of the responsibility while Moses felt his way.⁴⁵

Cleary and Moses worked together marvellously for the first few years. They agreed on broad interpretations of the ABC Act, and both left their stamp on the ABC organization: Cleary in his ten years as chairman, Moses in his thirty years as general manager. In 1935, nobody suspected that one of them would eventually cause the other's departure.

Moses had a broad background. Born at Atherton, Lancashire, in 1900, he attended Oswestry Grammar School and Royal Military College, Sandhurst, afterwards holding commissions in the British Army and Border Regiment in France, Germany, and Ireland. Seeing little future in the army, he sailed for Australia in 1922 to try fruit-growing in Bendigo. This venture cost him his savings. He moved to Melbourne and worked as a car salesman, but enjoyed his free-lance broadcasting engagements more. In 1930, he joined the staff of the Australian Broadcasting Company, transferring to Sydney in January 1933 to supervise broadcasts of sport, news, talks, and market reports for the ABC. Moses had an excellent broadcasting voice and unusual ability as a commentator. Test cricket broadcasts reached new heights when he used sound effects and information from overseas cables to reconstruct the play, giving the impression of a live commentary.⁴⁶ His flair for sporting broadcasts stemmed in part from his own sporting achievements. He could boast a number of championships, among them the Irish command boxing and shot-putting, and the Victorian amateur heavyweight boxing and discus-throwing. From 1926 to 1932, he also represented Victoria in rugby union, and he was a keen axeman.⁴⁷ He had charm, tact, and considerable charisma, but was not without vanity. Immediately after Conder's dismissal, he told Cleary that he was 'younger, more adaptable, more readily receptive of new ideas than most prospective candidates' for the general managership were likely to be.⁴⁸ Senator Collings, a perennial critic of the ABC, denounced Moses' appointment on the grounds that he possessed no qualifications and was not Australian born.⁴⁹ But the general reaction to the appointment was favourable.

1 W. T. Conder (left) in his early days at 3LO

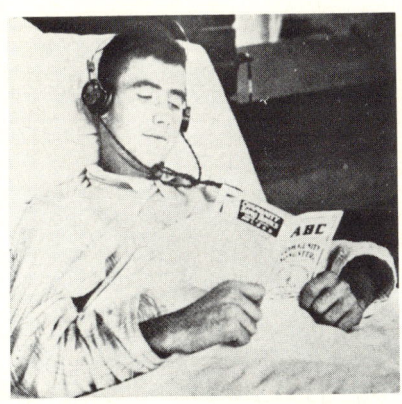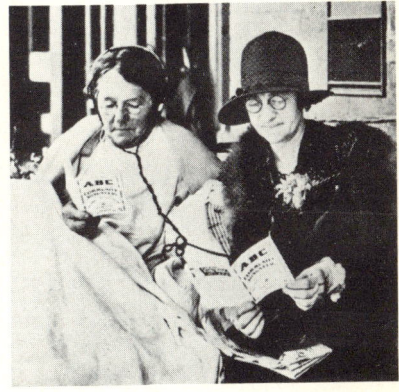

2 Hospital patients listening to community singing broadcasts during the Depression

3 The ABC's first outside broadcasting van

4 Some early radio personalities: 'Brother Bill', Melbourne; 'Bobby Bluegum', Melbourne; 'Plain Peter' and 'Rollicking Rita', Melbourne; 'Billy Bunny', Melbourne; 'Aunty Maxine', Perth; 'Little Miss Kookaburra', Melbourne.

3 Cleary and the ABC

It was while dining at the Cleary household that Moses first learned of his promotion. Neither he nor Cleary's family had any inklings in advance. As the two men arrived at the door, Cleary turned calmly to his daughters and said that he would like them to meet Mr Moses, the new general manager of the ABC. This was typical of the way Cleary liked to handle situations: no fanfare or overstatement, but with an element of drama.[50]

The general managership settled, Cleary could concentrate on wider aspects of the ABC's organization. He set out deliberately to centralize operations in Sydney. In September 1936, Dr Keith Barry, music critic for the *Daily Telegraph* and *Wireless Weekly*, was appointed federal controller of programmes, and over the next twelve months Cleary gathered around him a group of controllers to run specialist federal programme departments. At the end of the decade, the ABC's federal bureaucracy possessed departments of talks, music, drama, news, youth education, concerts, and publications.[51]

All the senior federal appointees shared Cleary's philosophy of broadcasting. B. H. Molesworth, the federal controller of talks, was a first-class-honours graduate of the universities of Queensland and Oxford, and had lectured in economic history at the former until the ABC brought him to Sydney to run the talk sessions. He also had considerable experience in adult education, having been director of the University of Queensland's Extension Service as well as Queensland state director of the Workers' Educational Association. The controller of music, W. G. James, had had a distinguished career as a composer and solo pianist, and had been musical director of the Australian Broadcasting Company. Frank D. Clewlow, the controller of productions, an Englishman, came to Australia after touring extensively with Shakespearean companies in England, India, China, Japan, and the Malay States. He, too, had worked for the Company and stayed on with the ABC. The controller of school broadcasts was Rudolph Bronner. He had lectured in ethics at Adelaide University and had done postgraduate research at Oxford before moving to the University of Melbourne as lecturer in sociology and vice-chairman of the University Extension Board. An interest in the educational possibilities of radio prompted him to accept a job with the ABC in 1935. T. W. Bearup filled the newly created position of federal superintendent, performing duties similar to those of an assistant general manager. As a result of these and associated appointments, the number of Head Office staff rose from 21 in 1935 to 111 in mid-1939.[52]

Centralization was a means of creating and maintaining

organizational unity. There were practical considerations: the opening of new regional stations increased the demand for nationally relayed programmes, which in turn reinforced the need for federal co-ordination. But the desire to encourage and enforce a uniform ABC approach, to create an organizational ethos that rose above state boundaries, was paramount.

Total ABC staff numbers grew from 265 in 1935 to 500 in 1939.[53] Some of the increase was the result of paying greater attention to programme presentation, which required more script-writers, music arrangers, presentation officers, and producers. Extra staff were also needed to produce the many additional programmes broadcast over an expanded ABC network. Eleven transmitters were constructed during these four years, making possible the addition of fourteen medium-wave and two shortwave stations.[54] This expansion was only possible because of a strong financial position. A rise in the number of listeners' licences, from 721 852 in 1935 to 1 131 860 in 1939, increased ABC income from £405 852 to £770 133.[55]

Each of the states developed specialist programme departments corresponding to federal departments. Occasionally, this could lead to confusion, for heads of state departments were responsible on programme matters to the relevant federal controller, but were administratively responsible to the state manager. There was never any doubt, though, that the final say rested with Head Office.[56]

The fact that the first two ABC chairmen were Sydney businessmen undoubtedly influenced the choice of Sydney for Head Office, but it had always been intended that the headquarters be located in Canberra. Successive federal governments, following a post-Depression policy of reduced public spending, were reluctant to finance the construction of new studios and residential accommodation which a move to Canberra would have required. A rumour during Conder's time that ABC headquarters might shift to Melbourne came to nothing.[57] Moses had no desire to shift from Sydney. Unquestionably a great entrepreneur, he considered it imperative to be on the spot where the broadcasting talent lay.[58] A Canberra site had been chosen for Broadcast House, close to where the present Hotel Kurrajong stands, but resistance by Moses and the financial stringencies of the 1930s, and then the war years, enabled Broadcast House, Sydney, to assert its pre-eminence to a point where it was no longer practicable to move to Canberra.

Cleary's decision to regard the chairmanship as a full-time position, together with the relative smallness of ABC staff during his first years, meant that he could exert considerable influence on daily administration. Theoretically, his position differed from that of

3 Cleary and the ABC

John Reith, who both determined policy and oversaw its administrative implementation, in that Cleary was nominally at least in charge of policy matters only. In practice, Cleary acted as both chairman and general manager during the five months between Conder's dismissal and Moses' appointment, establishing a close supervisory working style which he never completely abandoned. Even after Moses assumed full executive responsibility in 1938, Cleary's daily presence at Broadcast House inhibited his freedom of action. Cleary saw nothing wrong in this. In October 1938, he told Lyons that the ABC's 'comparatively inexperienced and untried staff' required close guidance, at least for a few years.[59] As late as 1941, he reiterated this point, saying that there was too much loose talk by 'inexperienced persons' about the Commission having no right to interfere with its staff.[60]

The young and ambitious Moses found Cleary's concern with administrative detail a nuisance. He seized every opportunity to bolster his own position, and was delighted when Basil Kirke organized the presentation of a dress watch-chain, a silver tray, and a scroll bearing messages of loyalty and admiration from the staff in August 1938. Moses especially relished the 'Hymn of Praise' which followed:

> But we've a man with us to-day
> Another Moses — C.J.A. —
> And like his great namesake of old
> He's enterprising, brave and bold.
>
> Ha-ha-ha,
> Hee-hee-hee —
> We are proud as proud can be —
> Ha-ha-ha,
> Hee-hee-hee —
> To have for G.M. such as he![61]

At the time there was a persistent rumour that the ABC Act was to be amended, either to combine the positions of chairman and general manager, or to make the general manager the vice-chairman of the Commission. Kirke was aware that Moses was the likely candidate for the dual post, and his actions were most likely an attempt to court the favour of a possible director-general of the ABC. In any event, Cleary suspected as much and criticized Moses for accepting the presentation. He also castigated him for believing stories spread by Kirke and others that he was by-passing Moses' authority and dealing directly with staff.[62] The incident reflected manoeuvrings among ABC staff and highlighted some of the problems that inevitably attended the rapid expansion of the ABC bureaucracy. It was to sour what had been hitherto a good working relationship between Cleary and Moses.

Under the terms of the ABC Act, the Commission could 'appoint a general manager and such officers and such servants as it thinks necessary', and it could set their working conditions. ABC employees did not have the protection of the Public Service Act. This meant that the Commission could deal ruthlessly with inefficiency or incompetence (for example, demoting an announcer found drunk at the microphone).[63] Staff generally were kept ignorant about management decisions.

Moses personally could appoint staff whose position carried a salary of £422 per annum or less. Cleary often ventured opinions, and could if he wished override appointments, but usually had no reason to do so. Life could be made very unpleasant for an employee who failed to impress the general manager. Those staff fortunate enough to become 'Moses men' normally enjoyed rapid advancement, but those who were not in his favour or did not warm to his flamboyant, cocktail-party style often found their career ambitions frustrated.[64]

This was not quite what Cleary had in mind when he said: 'Work may be brightened, and made more interesting and personal, by the introduction of a more personal touch into the relations between workers, and supervisors, and the management'.[65] Yet he did nothing to improve ABC management–staff relations. In fact, he was an aloof leader and generally had no contact with other than senior colleagues.[66]

Much suspicion consequently surrounded ABC staffing arrangements. Some people feared that advancement required an 'establishment' background. The case of Moses himself, the grammar-school educations of many federal officers, and the appointment of Mrs John Moore (daughter of Mr Justice Owen) as talks adviser seemed ample proof.[67] Senator Collings labelled the ABC a 'paradise for social climbers', and told of a young man who had secured a position only because he was the son of a bishop. Investigations to check the story's accuracy found that the bishop was not a married man![68] But whatever their truth, such allegations reinforced the disquiet within and outside the ABC. Cleary only exacerbated the situation by admitting that the ABC preferred announcers with 'good public school educations'.[69] On general recruitment policy, he said:

> I do not think that in the long run a man can do any good in broadcasting if he has not the basis of a good education because

3 Cleary and the ABC

only in that way can he widen his view of national and social problems and be enabled to bring into better balance the conflicting claims that he will have to meet in this work, as, for example, between culture and entertainment.[70]

While preference was not deliberately given to non-Australian born, or to people with the correct accent, the ABC confessed difficulty in finding adequate numbers of Australians with the type of 'all-round' education so common in Britain.[71] The educational, sporting, and army record of someone like Moses fitted the ABC mould admirably. As well as the right background, a potential staff member was expected to have a particular view of the ABC's role in society and a commitment to national (as against commercial) broadcasting. To convince the skeptics of his qualifications to manage Australia's largest cultural institution, Moses played down his sporting record and emphasized that he was not a stranger to good music or other cultural forms.[72] The fact that he said these things indicates how closely the top ABC executives identified with the goals of the organization; and how, in turn, people inducted at the top, and to a lesser extent lower down the bureaucratic hierarchy, were expected to be part of the ABC's ideology and purpose. In this regard, the ABC mirrored the BBC where Reith ensured that staff worked 'in the same spirit' as he did, and only people who *wanted* to be members of the BBC were hired.[73]

Why did people want to joint the ABC, especially those in non-executive positions? The pay was good, but not better than the Public Service until July 1939, when the ABC put a £6 loading on the Public Service male clerk rate of £222.[74] There was, of course, an employment crisis in the 1930s, but there was something more positive about the large number of private inquiries regarding ABC positions. One of the management's justifications for not advertising vacancies was that applications for employment were received almost daily, and a large register of job seekers kept.[75] Many applicants possibly sought excitement; Ellis Blain confessed 'I felt I was part of the entrancing, glamorous world of entertainment of which radio was the newest and most glittering jewel'.[76]

Blain was an announcer, one of the most important positions in any broadcasting organization. That many sought the status and prestige of an ABC announcing job is evident from the fierce competition for places. Over the twelve-month period to September 1937, the ABC's New South Wales branch received 195 formal applications. At a first audition, applicants were awarded marks for knowledge of 'cultural' subjects and for voice presentation. A short list of candidates reached a second audition, twenty-one a further stage; but only two people were offered appointments.[77] These figures suggest that the ABC was very selective in its attempts to recruit the right type of person. In August 1938, there were moves by the programme controllers to re-classify the position of announcer to make the job even more attractive to 'the right type of man'.[78]

Cleary's personal influence on recruiting extended beyond Head Office. During 1936, he, Moses, and the other commissioners visited each state branch, examining the qualifications and performance of staff. As a result of the investigations, two state managers, E. J. Lewis in Queensland and C. M. Hosking of South Australia, were removed from office early in 1937.[79] Also, Cleary produced a document outlining the duties of state managers. He sent it originally to Conrad Charlton of Western Australia, but it became a standard guide for state managers in following years. By 1937, not a single staff appointment, even of typists and office boys, could be made in the states without Head Office approval.[80] This veto extended to various programme advisory committees which were not part of the official staff establishment: in October 1935, for example, Cleary refused to approve the appointment of Miss Sheila McClemans, a young lawyer and feminist, to the ABC's Western Australian Advisory Committee. He wanted 'someone more mature' with 'a different field of interests'.[81] In fact, the entire membership of that body, as recommended by the then state manager, Basil Kirke, shows how Cleary's standards filtered through even to Australia's remotest city. On the committee were Professors R. G. Cameron, Walter Murdoch, and H. W. Whitfield, Sir Walter James and Dr J. S. Battye of the University of Western Australia, W. Somerville, chairman of the University Adult Education Board, and other people prominent in West Australian educational and cultural circles. Despite the difference in nomenclature, Cleary was every bit a 'director-general' in the organization's formative years.

At the heart of Cleary's recruitment philosophies lay a belief that being permitted to work in the ABC was sufficient reward in itself. He was willing to give up financial rewards to perform what he saw as a public service and a mission of cultural enlightenment. Why should not others? Again, this closely paralleled the outlook of Reith, who with pride claimed that he and his BBC colleagues helped found 'a tradition of public service rather than public exploitation'.[82] The idea of public enterprise, of the public institution operating without profit motive, had gained popularity in Britain since the 1920s through the writings of people like Herbert Morrison, Sir Henry Bunbury, and W. A. Robson, and Fabians like

3   Cleary and the ABC

the Labor politician William Graham.[83] It related partly to the Fabian view that what really mattered was 'a life of fascinating interest to the exercise of faculty, and in the consciousness of service rendered.'[84] Moses, though no Fabian, was content with these rewards: he worked often to two or three in the morning, refused bonus payments, and rarely took a holiday.[85] Cleary did likewise. But how realistic was it to think that the majority of ABC employees, especially those in lower, less creative positions, would be similarly content?

Many general staff did make great sacrifices. At one stage, the New South Wales manager and his staff were working till 11.30 p.m. four nights a week, plus most Saturday afternoons.[86] But there were limits. By 1938, staff were beginning to react to the pressures of work with an increased assertiveness of their rights, or what they took to be their rights. Basically, they wanted the same privileges enjoyed by other government employees: no Saturday-morning work, classified positions with provisions for annual salary increments, and a superannuation scheme. In addition, they sought regular procedures for recruitment, promotion, transfer, and dismissal, and machinery for appeals.[87]

Lack of these benefits created ready support for the establishment of the ABC Staff Association at a meeting in Sydney on 5 May 1938. The timing is explained by the actions of a number of unions which approached the Arbitration Court purporting to speak for sections of ABC staff. Endless demarcation disputes threatened. Realizing this, a group of Head Office and New South Wales staff, including W. A. Alexander, R. J. O'Connor, Miss M. Skill, C. Wheeler, Heath Burdoch, and W. J. Beausang, took advantage of the office climate and used the arbitration machinery available to staffs of government agencies to form a house association.[88]

W. A. Alexander, a member of the administrative staff, was the Association's first president. Together with P. J. Sheehan, an industrial advocate, he drafted a constitution modelled on that of the Public Service Association. Early in April 1939, Alexander reported that all state branches had agreed to establish local Staff Association committees.[89]

Despite the Association's grassroots support, Moses and the Commission gave it little encouragement. Initially, they refused even the request to deduct Staff Association dues from pay packets.[90] Nevertheless, by the end of 1939, either as a result of the Association's representations or to forestall further staff activity, the Commission introduced a set of Staff Rules.

The Staff Rules were the first written exposition of working conditions in the ABC. Staff were classified as administrative, programme and public relations, clerical or manual. Within these divisions, all staff were graded with provisions for annual salary increments. Job vacancies were to be advertised, but the general manager could ignore this requirement for positions which carried more than £422 per annum. Moreover, the Commission reserved the right to fill such positions without notification. Women officers were required to resign on marriage (unless granted special permission by the Commission), and no married woman was eligible for a classified position. The branch managers, general manager, and the Commission could punish breaches of the Staff Rules. Striking was prohibited under penalty of dismissal.[91]

From the staff's point of view, the introduction of a set of rules was a welcome innovation, but few were satisfied completely. The Staff Association had been given very little time to study the Rules and offer comment, and some of its important suggestions had not been incorporated: in particular, there were no appeal boards or committees with appropriate staff representation to guard against unjustified appointments, promotions, dismissals, or punishments. The discretion allowed the Commission to fill vacancies without advertisement the Association considered 'dangerous'. But the most fundamental objection was the dubious legal status of the Rules and the lack of compulsion on the ABC to implement them fully.[92]

The new staff classifications took effect from 1 July 1939, but the Commission took several months to deal with anomalies and then refused to re-classify the positions retrospectively.[93] Filling of vacancies also remained unsatisfactory. When the Staff Association protested over the appointment, without prior advertisement, of the federal concert manager in December 1939, Moses replied that only 'less senior positions' would be advertised.[94] The Commission clearly intended to use its discretionary powers to appoint without advertisement as the norm, rather than as the exception. Above all, there was continuing dissatisfaction with the Commission's tardiness in considering matters such as cost-of-living adjustments or salary relativities.[95]

By this time, the ABC's senior executives had begun to express their grievances. They, too, were responding to pressures of work. Most worked ridiculously long hours and had annual leave accumulating in arrears.[96] They had no official gradings, no provisions for annual salary increments, and they were not covered by the Staff Rules. Most importantly, they had no security of tenure and held office at the pleasure of the Commission. What if an incoming Commission, for political or other reasons, decided to replace any or all of them? These issues prompted Molesworth and other Head Office executives to take advantage of the state managers' presence in Sydney on 8 November 1939 to hold a meeting at which the ABC Senior Officers' Association was formed. Dr Barry became the first president, with Kirke, Molesworth, and Clewlow committee members. The establishment of their own association brought one additional benefit, in that a senior officer would not find himself in the awkward position of having to deal individually with concerted action by the non-executive staff.[97] Cleary was surprised by the senior officers' actions, but accepted their decision with grace. Possibly to make their actions more palatable to the commissioners, the senior officers listed as one of their association's objects 'To improve the efficiency of the services of the Commission', and spoke of themselves as being moved by the wish to foster *esprit de corps*.[98]

Clearly, the Staff Rules did not go far enough. The senior officers had been ignored, and the general staff made few gains in the vital area of 'job regulation', that is, in gaining 'a measure of creativity and control' within the working situation (as against pure financial gains).[99] Perhaps the only answer, so the Staff Association believed, was to have ABC staff brought under the Public Service Act. Archie Cameron, the postmaster-general, supported the Association. In March 1939, he told Cabinet that there were 'strong arguments' for this course. Among other things, it would 'give a great measure of stability, would eliminate the possibility of patronage in the selection of staff, and the employees concerned would obtain certain security of tenure. The Commonwealth would therefore be assured of reasonable continuity of effort from the established staff.'[1] For the time being, no action was taken; but the problems associated with staffing which began during these years of rapid expansion were to occupy an increasing proportion of the Commission's time into the war years and beyond. In the meantime, having built up a professional staff and a suitable organizational structure, Cleary's prime concern was to improve ABC programmes.

One month after his arrival at the ABC, Cleary wrote to Brookes:

> The programme side of the organisation is anarchic. There is hardly a vestige of plan or policy in respect of the States' local programme, and in respect of Commonwealth control and coordination ... As a result of this absence of plan, there is no standard, no star to which our waggon may be hitched; and consequently, no development. We jump from this artist to that, from this feature to that, according to the whims of chance or managers.[2]

The formation of the Federal Programme Committee in 1936 overcame many of these problems, but it also snatched an area of responsibility from the state branch managers.

Moses was chairman of the Programme Committee. It comprised the Head Office controllers, and usually the state programme controllers for New South Wales and Victoria. State managers sometimes attended. The committee decided the time-slot of programmes, their content, the mix of national relays and local programmes, and so on; and it often spelled out basic philosophies, more properly the prerogative of the Commission.³ In September 1937, for example, it agreed to adopt, in a modified way, the BBC practice of programme contrasts. This meant that a military band could be featured on the same evening as a symphony concert. Hitherto, the ABC had tried to sustain the same mood for the entire evening's programmes on one station, while providing a different type of programme on the alternative network.⁴ The committee also made some definite assumptions about taste: in two-station states, for example, 'definitely "highbrow" ' items were to be confined to one station, and programmes on both stations were to be predominantly 'of medium standard'.⁵ Although the Commission was the final arbiter on such matters, most initiatives suggested by Moses and the Programme Committee were rubber-stamped.

The preponderance of regular features distinguished 1939 programme schedules from those of earlier years. Weekly plays and serials, the 'Children's Hour', celebrity concerts, the 'Symphony Hour', talks by 'The Watchman', the 'Diggers' Show', and many others came to occupy the same time-slot each week. This was true also of broadcasts from the BBC Empire Station at Daventry, such as 'World Affairs' on Thursdays and a special talk programme on Sunday afternoons. State managers were required to submit programme layouts to the Federal Programme Committee up to two months in advance. No new programme idea could be tried, and no timing changes made, without Head Office or Programme Committee's approval.⁶

65.77 per cent of the ABC's 1938/9 budget was spent directly on programme production. This did not include the 5.84 per cent spent on administrative staff salaries.⁷ Live broadcasts were expensive to produce, but they were still preferred over recordings and accounted for a large proportion of programme items: 233 367 out of 654 677 total programme items in 1938/9.⁸ Many more programme hours had to be filled by the late 1930s, partly because there were more ABC stations, but also as a result of extending the hours of transmission. In 1939, major ABC stations broadcast continuously from

3 Cleary and the ABC

6.30 to 10.15 a.m. and from 12 noon to midnight. Station 3AR's programme for 6 June 1939 illustrates the greater continuity, and is an accurate indicator of the regular time-slots of many features:

   6.30 Essential Services
   6.45 News
   7.00 Physical Exercises
   7.15 Music
   8.00 News
   8.15 Music
   9.30 Morning Story
 10.00 Religious Devotion

10.15 – 12 noon   Close

12.00 School Broadcast
12.20 Essential Services
12.40 'The Watchman'
 1.00 News and Essential Services
 1.15 Music
 2.00 Favourite Tunes
 3.45 'Over the Teacup'
 4.15 Classic Hour
 5.30 Tiny Tot's Corner
 5.40 Children's Session
 6.00 Dinner Music
 6.30 Market Report
 6.45 Sporting Session
 7.00 'Digger Doings'
 7.20 News
 7.40 National Talk
 8.00 Celebrity Recordings
 8.10 Orchestral Concert
 9.00 National Talk
 9.15 'The Colored Counties' by Edmund Barclay
 9.45 'Jim and Jitters'
10.15 Story
10.30 The Sydney Instrumental Trio
10.45 The ABC Wireless Chorus
11.00 Recorded Music
11.20 Dance Music
11.50 News and Weather

12 midnight   Close.

Technical advances helped to improve the quality of reception of these programmes. 2FC and 3LO's transmitters were boosted, as was 3AR's which relayed the National Programme. Better short-wave transmissions also enabled Australians to hear clear descriptions of, for example, the proclamation ceremony of Edward VIII and the *Queen Mary*'s departure on its maiden voyage from New York. Studio productions benefited from an ever-increasing choice of microphones. At first, the ABC had used carbon and condenser (electro-static) microphones almost exclusively; now, there were directional microphones, moving-coil microphones which gave good frequency response, or lapel microphones which freed performers from standing in a fixed position. There was also better recording equipment. A Marconi Stille steel magnetic tape recorder had been installed in Sydney by 1936, and both Melbourne and Sydney possessed Neumann disc recorders capable of instant replay. ABC record turntables were fitted with the latest pick-up devices, a far cry from the early days of broadcasting when microphones were positioned precariously in front of a gramophone horn. Refinements in the fidelity of radio sets ensured that listeners reaped the benefits of technological developments at the studio end.[9]

Faults in transmission were the responsibility of the Postmaster-General's Department which still controlled the ABC's technical services. Not all problems were 'technical'; for however technically competent a sound control mechanic, he might not have the musical ear necessary for correct tonal adjustment. Other difficulties arose when the mechanic attending a rehearsal was not available for the actual broadcast.[10] These were the grounds on which the ABC began its long campaign to have studio technicians brought under its control. Bearup did some of the early liaison with the Postmaster-General's Department, and J. W. Kitto, an ex-PMG official who replaced commissioner Wallace in June 1935, made what use he could of past connections. But neither man could match H. P. Brown's personal influence on government broadcasting policies. New stations opened when and where Brown and Cabinet decided. The ABC sometimes was not even consulted.[11] In these circumstances, Brown felt no compulsion to surrender control of broadcasting technicians.

Western Australia presented unique technical and programming problems. The two-hour time lag meant that programmes broadcast in the East at peak listening periods were rarely broadcast in the West where it was only late afternoon or meal time. For a while, this applied even to the very popular Sunday-night play. Moreover, the gaps in programme variety could not easily be filled locally, as Perth had only one ABC station until October 1938; and even then, although the West received the relayed National Programme, it could not reciprocate for want of a musical channel from west to east.

The Federal Programme Committee bore these difficulties in mind when planning programme schedules. Sporting programmes, for example, resisted central processing. Local loyalties ran high, and it was unlikely that listeners in Perth or Hobart would be satisfied with descriptions of rugby in Sydney. This partly explains why there was no federal department or federal controller of sport. However, A. N. ('Huck') Finlay did act as federal editor of sporting broadcasts, helping to co-ordinate relays of important national and international sporting events: Sheffield Shield cricket, the Davis Cup and Wimbledon tennis matches, boxing championships, Test cricket, or the English Football Cup Final; and especially occasions like the 1936 Berlin Olympics. State programmes did also feature a common sporting programme, 'Highlight in Sport', a review of the week's sporting events broadcast on Saturday evenings.[12]

Children's sessions lent themselves more readily to centralized control, and they were the subject of one of the first serious programme studies conducted by the Federal Programme Committee in 1936. Dr Barry presented a damning report, decrying the lack of policy to date.[13] In its search for an underlying philosophy of children's programmes, the Programme Committee, working closely with the Commission, looked to each of the states. Mrs Couchman was unimpressed by what she saw in Tasmania, whose Judy Lucke she believed had little knowledge of the child mind. Clewlow joined the criticism with reference to the 'sort of "B" Class complex' implicit in Judy Lucke's attempts to ape the commercial stations.[14] In Melbourne, Nina Murdoch's ideas survived, attracting particularly the attention of Bearup and Clewlow. Isobel Ann Shead had taken over 3LO's children session but retained an 'Argonauts Theatre' segment. This was the general approach adopted for the national children's programme finally introduced in 1939. All states except Western Australia received the 'Children's Hour'. Children contributed news, poems, stories or plays to *Mike,* the weekly magazine of the air. However, Nina Murdoch's 'Argonauts Club' as such was not incorporated into the session for a further eighteen months.

News programmes made little headway between 1934 and 1939, despite the appointment of a federal news editor, M. F. Dixon, in 1936. Dixon's previous experience of battles with newspaper combines while editor of various provincial newspapers, among them the

Maitland *Daily Mercury* and the Goulburn *Evening Post*, did not reduce the ABC's difficulties in negotiating a permanent settlement with the press. An impasse continued, with Herbert Brookes as late as May 1939 attacking the newspaper proprietors for their selfishness.[15] In an attempt to force the lifting of press restrictions, the ABC tried confrontation, moving the 7.50 p.m. news bulletin forward to 7.30, expanding the 200-word limit on overseas news cables into 1500-word bulletins, and threatening to establish an independent news service.[16] Dixon was allegedly told at the outset to 'start thinking along the lines of an independent service',[17] but apart from his being authorized to recruit a small news staff, there is otherwise no evidence of Commission plans for an autonomous news organization at this time. In any case, Lyons would never have agreed to it.[18]

There was nevertheless a discernible attempt to make news bulletins more compatible with ABC commitments on standards and impartiality. Sensational, inconsequential stories were no longer generally included. Sunday-evening bulletins, for example, ran less than their allocated five minutes if nothing more than weekend human-interest stories came to hand.[19] Head Office saw that bulletins were constructed in a factual, objective manner. One employee's reply to criticism from Dr Barry suggests that staff were becoming conscious that there was an ABC way of doing things:

> My difficulty has been that the paragraphs must be short, and that so much of each is skeleton—name, date, hour, stations, etc. —that I seemed to feel the need of wrapping a little more flesh on its bones than your experience decides is judicious. If you can bear with me a little I think I can rigidly discipline myself into ABC style.[20]

Musical programmes received Cleary's closest personal attention. The 1932 Act stated that the Commission 'shall endeavour to establish and utilize ... groups of musicians for the rendition of orchestral, choral and band music of high quality'. Both Cleary and Moses interpreted this clause broadly, deploying a very large percentage of ABC resources into orchestras and public concerts.

Bernard Heinze, the Commission's musical adviser, worked well with Cleary, Moses, and James (whose appointment he recommended). His personal contribution was such that in August 1935 the Commission more than doubled his retainer.[21] While his prime function was to tender advice on musical policy, he personally conducted for the ABC, becoming especially famous for his series of children's and youth concerts. From July 1934 to June 1935, 112 000

3 Cleary and the ABC

Sydney schoolchildren attended them.[22] The programme usually contained popular classical pieces: Beethoven's Fifth Symphony and his Concerto for Pianoforte and Orchestra, Dvorak's 'New World' Symphony, or Schubert's 'Unfinished Symphony', all of them aimed at sowing the seeds of a new generation of music lovers.

Cleary reasoned that the Australian adult population should also be exposed to the best in symphonic music, if they were to be persuaded that the ABC should spend large sums on it. Following the precedent of Sir Hamilton Harty's celebrity tour early in 1934, the ABC organized visits by the Budapest String Quartet, the Spivakowsky-Kurtz Trio, Lotte Lehmann (soprano), Dr Malcolm Sargent (conductor), Bronislaw Huberman (violinist), Professor Georg Schneevoigt (director and conductor of the Finnish National Orchestra), Howard Jacobs (dance-band leader and saxophonist), and many others. There were also tours by Australians who had achieved success abroad, such as Eileen Joyce (pianist), Dorothy Helmrich (soprano), and Essie Ackland (contralto).[23]

John Curtin, among others, attacked the extravagance of celebrity tours, especially the 'lavish' welcome afforded artists. Yet he was surprised to learn that the cost of entertaining artists at the Menzies Hotel over a two-year period was only £89.[24]

The entertainment industry attacked the ABC for different reasons. Some musicians believed that their work opportunities were lessened by the presence of foreign performers. Bernard Heinze expressed their views when he criticized suggestions that Dr Malcolm Sargent was to be appointed ABC musical director:

> Radio is one avenue of public appearance and in fact employment for our Australians. For heavens sake don't take that away from them. Have your visiting conductors and artists by all means but let it be understood that they are visitors . . . We are in danger of becoming a dumping ground for the unemployed of the old world otherwise.[25]

The musicians' criticisms were not fully justified. ABC orchestral activities provided work for many of them, and the Commission continued to hold composers' competitions. From the mid-1930s, composers could submit works at any time. During the 1936/7 year, twenty major works were accepted for radio, including an opera, a symphony and a string quartet by Clive Douglas, a musical by Alfred Hill, and various songs by Fritz Hart. During the same year, 92 per cent of artists' fees paid by the ABC went to Australians.[26] But there were always those who missed out and who joined the critics' condemnations.

More serious resistance to ABC musical activities came from the private concert agencies. On 20 July 1934, the entrepreneur E. J. Tait expressed his concern that the ABC should attempt to compete with private enterprise.[27] Artists brought out under the auspices of the ABC seemed to enjoy greater prestige, and the private firms feared that their artists would be considered secondrate. Both J. C. Williamson Ltd and Taits argued that the ABC, though supposedly a broadcasting organization, organized many concerts which were never broadcast. Were listeners who paid annual licence fees to receive broadcasts in their homes, expected to subsidize the ABC's exploits as a concert agency?

From July 1936 to June 1937, the ABC sponsored 193 public concerts. The following year's figure was 258.[28] The private firms argued that the ABC had unfair advantages: it paid no rates or taxes; it could advertise free of charge; and it could give away free tickets, whereas private enterprise relied on ticket sales to break even.[29] Cleary and Moses were unmoved and remained determined to see that the ABC was not forced out of the concert business. In response to complaints that only parts of concerts were broadcast, Moses replied that no artist would be able to hold a radio audience for an entire evening. Cleary added that if concerts were broadcast in full, people might not attend the concert itself.[30] Their stance reflected the broad interpretation of the 1932 Act. Perhaps, too, they were influenced by the exorbitant fees demanded by the private firms for the right to broadcast their concerts. On one occasion, £1000 had been demanded for a single broadcast of the violinist Menuhin.[31] But such commercial considerations took second place to the belief of Cleary and Moses that concert production was a proper function of a cultural organization such as the ABC.

Matters became more serious in February 1938 when J. C. Williamson Ltd took out an injunction to restrain the ABC from sponsoring public concerts, arguing that the ABC had no constitutional right to exist. Cleary realized that if he did not defeat the challenge, his cultural mission was doomed.[32]

The Lyons administration applied no pressure on the ABC to cease competing with the private firms; on the contrary, the postmaster-general, A. J. McLachlan, expressed complete agreement with Cleary's opinion that 'as Williamsons are the aggressors, it is highly undesirable that anything should be done which might suggest that the Commission is afraid of the threatened test of its powers, and can be driven into a bad bargain by any vested interest which attacks it, rather than face that test'.[33] In addition, the government was adamant that no one firm or group of firms should establish a monopoly.[34]

5 Cleary the bushwalker

6 Bernard Heinze, Cleary, and Moses at work

7 Cleary, Moses, and the British conductor, Dr Malcolm Sargent

8 Adelaide schoolchildren during a 'Music through Movement' broadcast

9 Jim Davidson (conductor) and Peter Finch (compère) of 'Colour Canvas', October 1937

Cleary's perseverance resulted in triumph. Just as the writ was about to be heard, J. C. Williamson's leased its amusement business to another company, Australian and New Zealand Theatres Ltd. After consultations, the new firm decided to co-operate with the ABC, fearing that even a victory in court would be costly and hollow.[35] Cleary's conditions for full co-operation were absolute: all pending actions must be withdrawn unconditionally, so dissuading the press or the commercial stations from launching a similar challenge.[36] The firm's compliance was a tremendous victory for Cleary. He had successfully carved out a piece of ABC territory in an area of the entertainment world hitherto dominated by a few powerful interests, and he had virtually legitimated the ABC's role as a concert agency, indeed, its very existence.

Much less controversy surrounded the ABC's establishment of symphony orchestras, perhaps its most significant act of musical patronage in the 1930s. The Commission opted for separate state orchestras, rather than a single national orchestra, taking advantage of the small combinations already present in a number of cities. Broadcasting ensembles of piano, violin, and cello had grown into permanent bodies of fifteen players in both Melbourne and Sydney by 1932. The ABC supplemented these groups, and in 1934 purchased broadcasting rights from the New South Wales State Orchestra, the Melbourne Symphony Orchestra, and the South Australian Symphony Orchestra. Two years later the ABC's goal was achieved: Sydney and Melbourne had permanent bodies of forty-five and thirty-five players respectively; Brisbane, Adelaide, and Perth had seventeen permanent players; and Hobart had eleven. These were supplemented as required. By June 1937, the ABC employed 155 orchestral musicians full-time, and 255 on a casual basis.[37]

There had been no widespread public demand for the establishment of permanent orchestras. Dr Edgar Bainton, director of the Sydney Conservatorium of Music and a close personal friend of Cleary, publicly urged the formation of a full-time orchestra, as did a very active group of Sydney music enthusiasts which included Mrs Walter Swinson (pianist), Lady Gordon, and Mrs Hubert Fairfax.[38] There were similar pressures from people in the other states.[39] But these calls did not necessarily reflect majority opinion. As the *Sunday Sun and Guardian* put it: 'Musical people might like the Director of the Conservatorium to be chairman of the ABC, but 400 000 people with radio sets have a wider and more vulgar variety of preference.'[40] The Commission was anticipating, not responding to, public demand. In this, it was some twenty to thirty years ahead of world trends. The Philadelphia Orchestra managed only nine months per annum at full strength, and of the many orchestras in London, only the BBC's offered anything like the continuity of employment in the ABC's orchestras.[41] By persuading the Australian public to accept official patronage of the arts in the 1930s, the ABC contributed to expectations that such patronage should continue in later years.

The heavy concentration on concert-giving did not mean that musical programmes were neglected. A new weekly session of contemporary music featured the compositions of Debussy, Stravinsky, Ravel, and the like, while another session concentrated on Australian composers. South Australia and Western Australia introduced a 'Music through Movement' programme in 1938. This session aimed to 'lead children through a variety of rhythms and movements connected with their daily life, to the foundation of a time appreciation of music'. Dance-band broadcasts also continued, featuring some new personalities. Jim Davidson's Dance Band's success in Melbourne from 1934 to 1936 ensured a further ABC contract in Sydney from 1936 until the opening years of the war. The band formed by Howard Jacobs during his 1936 tour was taken over by Al Hammett, and Harry Bloom's Tango Band could be heard on ABC radio from 1937. Military band music also figured regularly. Stephen Yorke conducted the ABC's National Military Band, formed originally for the visit by Captain H. E. Adkins of Britain in 1933/4. Overall, musical programmes still accounted for more than half of ABC programme time; in fact, 60.08 per cent for the year ended 30 June 1939.[42]

Addressing a parliamentary committee of inquiry in 1942, Cleary said that his aim in the 1930s had been not to foist music upon people, but to expose them to it, in the hope that they would avail themselves of the opportunity for cultural improvement.[43] On the surface, people seemed to respond. The number of ABC concert subscribers in Brisbane more than doubled from 1937 to 1939; in Sydney they more than trebled between 1936 and 1940. This trend was national: 5900 people subscribed to ABC concerts in 1939 compared with 3675 in 1937.[44] But subscribers were a small percentage of those who finally attended a concert or listened on the radio; and public responsiveness was more complex than concert attendance figures or estimates of listener numbers might reveal. Cleary would cite these figures as proof that the ABC was changing people's taste: good attendances implied an increasing appreciation of fine music.[45] Yet how many people attended ABC concerts merely because it was the right thing to do? In March 1935, Bernard Heinze estimated that Melbourne had, at best, only 2000 'constant music lovers'.[46] ABC celebrity tours were glamourized by the press who displayed a preoccupation with the high-society cocktail parties held for the visiting artist.[47] Did people attend concerts out of social snobbery, knowing that their photograph might appear in the social pages of the morning newspaper? Alternatively, did they only attend concerts by the famous, thus reducing Australia's musical culture to a matter of personalities?[48] On the one hand, it would be wrong to assume that everybody attended ABC concerts out of a love of music; on the other hand, it is impossible to ascertain individual motives for attendance, just as one cannot determine a listener's reasons for choosing a particular broadcast. Cleary and Moses argued that, whatever people's original motives for attending, once exposed to the possibilities of music most people came again. They added that one had to be unusually dedicated to tolerate the conditions in most Australian halls, which were cold and draughty, and had seats that were 'instruments of torture'.[49] Nevertheless, ABC claims of success in uplifting musical tastes must be treated with caution.

Drama programmes were another important ABC cultural activity. Leslie Rees has written of a 'professional vitality and competence' which began to characterize Australian drama in the 1930s.[50] The ABC contributed to this development by sponsoring play competitions. Generous monetary rewards and the possibility of having one's play broadcast were welcome incentives to inspired amateurs as well as an additional source of income for the professionals. In the 1936 competition, over 400 entries were received;[51] a response which suggested that if there were talent in Australia the ABC would unearth it.

The setting up of a federal department of productions in 1936 gave drama another boost. Frank Clewlow, the controller of productions, was a forceful personality who took his job very seriously. One Melbourne actress remembers him affectionately: 'The other radio producers were pretty ordinary by comparison, but it was never dull working with F.D. He had a star quality to him'.[52]

Clewlow's closest assistants were Max Afford, Edmund Barclay, Lawrence Cecil, and Leslie Rees. Afford had written extensively for commercial stations in Adelaide and became known to the ABC after winning first prize in the 1936 competition with his play, *Merry-go-Round*. He adapted the Father Brown stories for radio, and received acclaim for his thriller-serials. Barclay wrote many successful series of plays, among them *Khyber, Shanghai,* and *As Ye Sow*.[53] He based some of the plots on his father's recollections of life in the Indian army. *Khyber,* for example, contained a mixture of characters, ranging from the cool, often flippant regimental officer with his Cockney orderly, to the courteous, dignified Indian officer; a talkative Bengali clerk and one Chunder Lal's attempts to speak 'mostly correct' English added touches of humour.[54] Lawrence Cecil produced most of Barclay's plays, and Leslie Rees, who later told his own version of the history of Australian drama, assisted as federal play editor.[55]

Writers were invited to submit scripts to the central drama staff at any time. The scripts were examined, and either accepted for broadcasting or returned with suggestions for improvement. Even outright rejections were returned with advice on the requirements of a radio playwright. Of 1367 plays received between July 1936 and January 1938, 363 were accepted immediately, and 500 letters of detailed criticism and advice were dispatched. Altogether, 459 straight plays and serials, 150 musical comedies, and 1107 children's plays and serials were purchased from June 1936 to July 1939.[56]

Although the commercial stations bought some 4000 plays a year, the majority were ten- to fifteen-minute serials, and they were purchased from a limited group of authors, whereas the ABC's buying market was unlimited.[57] However, both commercial and national broadcasters brought the popularity of the radio play to a height warranting continued investment. 'The broadcast play has come to stay', commented Cecil in January 1936. 'It is an entity in itself, and through it artists will rise to fame who otherwise might never have been known'.[58]

Radio plays presented special production problems. Whereas in a theatre the audience is captive and everybody sees the same thing, the radio play must build up a clear image in the listener's mind, or have disastrous results. Cleary once illustrated the difficulties by describing the production of a play about two old men, each in love with the other man's daughter, and each of their daughters in love with the other man's son. The two old men were indistinguishable over the air, as were their daughters and the two young men. 'Add to this', said Cleary, 'the failure to announce the coming in and going out of characters, and by the time the play was half-way through I would defy anyone to know who was who and which old man was addressing which girl'.[59]

Despite the problems, radio drama thrived, especially serials. In the late 1930s, two main classes of serial were in vogue. One centred on well-known historical figures, and two very popular examples, *The Loves of Henry VIII* and *Coronets of England,* were broadcast on commercial stations. The ABC answered this demand with Barclay's *As Ye Sow,* but it reacted strongly against the other class of serial, the very popular soap-operas of *Dad and Dave* fame. In fact, it purposely eschewed 'family-life' serials until the launching of the *Lawsons—Blue Hills* saga during the war.[60] Nevertheless, it was during these formative years of ABC programming that many Australian families adopted the weekly ritual of assembling around the lounge-room radio set to hear the Sunday-night play.

The numbers of people who attended orchestral concerts, or who listened to radio plays, reveal little about overall community response to the ABC's cultural initiatives. People talked or wrote to individual commissioners, and there were comments in the press, but otherwise the ABC had few means of ascertaining this response. Did it really care? The results of listener surveys undertaken by the press were usually dismissed out of hand, not because, as Cleary insisted, the sample was too small,[61] but because the ABC had a fundamental aversion to audience research consistent with the belief that it had a duty to give public leadership; to cater for community needs, not wants. Volunteers sometimes completed ABC questionnaires about their listening habits, but the numbers involved were so small as to render the exercise pointless.[62] All this illustrates the ABC's paternalistic attitude: what was the point of eliciting listeners' opinions until they had been educated in the art of critical appreciation and had gained a cultural awareness that gave credence to their views?

Even had the ABC taken more interest in listener reaction, it would still have faced problems of interpretation; for there was no monolithic public with a unanimous opinion, but rather a conglomerate of groups making competing demands. While one group of listeners complained that ABC programmes were too 'highbrow', another would decry the 'rubbishy recordings' and 'tin-can crooning' broadcast.[63] The so-called average listener's views were of no assistance. As William Macmahon Ball said:

> Until all broadcasting authorities are wholly convinced that there is no 'average listener' but different groups of listeners, each with its own interests and needs, broadcasts with a serious intellectual purpose will tend to be regarded as too dull, with a consequent effort to brighten them up. The high-brow will be irritated and the low-brow will not be amused.[64]

Arguments concerning 'highbrows', 'lowbrows', and even 'middlebrows' dominated community discussions of ABC programmes. Cleary personally never used these terms, but he did speak of 'improving', 'uplifting', and 'raising', which in themselves suggest a degree of cultural arrogance.[65] This enabled the press to level accusations of 'highbrow' bias, and there can be no doubt that the ABC's cultural preference would have been considered 'highbrow' by large numbers of Australians. To many people, 'highbrow' meant simply 'serious' and referred to programmes which required intellectual effort or concentration. Others used the term loosely to describe all those cultural activities outside their own personal experience.[66] Dance music or jazz would have satisfied the cultural aspirations of many Australians, but the ABC men, clinging to their belief in the superiority of 'high culture', steered programming in that direction. An experimental jazz programme was introduced in the late 1930s, but this type of music received little official encouragement until after World War II, when there was a fundamental shift in ABC attitudes towards 'light' entertainment.[67] Meanwhile, even programmes designed for a popular audience usually fitted into the overriding desire to raise cultural standards: observe, for example, Moses' comment on the Saturday night variety programme, 'Hotch Potch', in March 1937: 'the essential point in it, the one or two highbrow items, are the most important of all. By them it is hoped to show the lowbrow listener that there is something worth listening to in good music and good class entertainment generally.'[68] Cleary might have used less patronizing language, but the statement accurately reflected the strategy of ABC programming during his term of office.

The 'highbrow'–'lowbrow' debate was not dampened by Cleary's claims that the ABC presented a balanced diet of cultural experiences. To many Australians, the ABC was still a faceless, dull, authoritarian, culturally pretentious organization. 'The trouble with the Australian Broadcasting Commission', wrote one listener, 'is not that it is wrong in any particular department, but that it is so impeccably correct. It goes forth in spats, and carries a stick'.[69] Moses periodically attempted to improve the ABC's image, and instructed announcers on one occasion to be 'a little brighter and friendlier without being objectionably intimate'.[70] Sometimes the ABC did reach its audience. For example, there was an enormous public response when H. M. Watts ('Watto'), the Sydney morning announcer, died at the microphone in 1937. Thousands attended his funeral while many more people contributed £2200 to a *Daily Telegraph* appeal for his widow and children.[71] Yet this was one of the rare occasions when it is possible to find tangible evidence of deep empathy between the public and the ABC which, in general, discouraged personality cults like those surrounding the commercial radio stars such as Jack Davey or Si Meredith. More commonly, the ABC distanced itself from the bulk of society, singularly unable to shed its 'highbrow' image.

3 Cleary and the ABC

Perhaps the ABC men were out of step with the dominant cultural mores of the 1930s. They certainly regarded what they believed were the materialistic and unintellectual preoccupations of Australians as one of their major obstacles; but how realistic was it to think that the ABC could change this? How many people, for example, even listened to the ABC's programmes? Country listeners might have no choice, but the majority of city people—by most contemporary accounts[72]—listened to the commercial stations. Notwithstanding the didactic bias of ABC programmes, could they possibly influence people to the point that they would abandon long-held preferences and values?

The contemporary essayist, Walter Murdoch, insisted that radio was 'the most powerful instrument ever devised for propaganda and for education'.[73] All statements by the ABC controllers reflected a similar unqualified belief in the potency of radio as a social force. But as Asa Briggs pointed out in his history of the BBC, it is very easy to exaggerate the influence of radio. 'For the most part', he wrote, the BBC 'reflected the society and the culture in which it developed rather than reshaped them'.[74]

In the Australian context there might be grounds for attributing greater influence to radio (not only the ABC). For example, the BBC was a monopoly organization which broadcast programmes approved of by Reith and his associates. Dislike of a BBC broadcast would often induce a listener to switch off his set, whereas the choice of both national and commercial stations in Australia probably encouraged longer listening hours and produced a greater attachment to radio as a medium. This hypothesis is necessarily tentative; for no one has as yet evolved an acceptable way of measuring intangible 'influence'.

The question of the ABC's possible influence is complicated by the presence of commercial radio. Did this presence hinder or help the ABC's self-proclaimed mission? A recent study of the BBC notes that the old spirit of public service broadcasting—identified with needs rather than wants—died once commercial stations appeared: the style of programmes changed; ratings began to matter.[75] Though it is difficult to draw conclusions about Australia from experiences in Britain, the two societies being so different, the circumstances decades apart, Burns' study does point to a need to consider the commercial stations as more than an appendage to the national system. In October 1935, acknowledging the power of the commercials and the dangers of monopoly control of commercial networks, the Lyons government introduced anti-network regulations which prevented any one interest from owning more than five stations. The actual number of commercial stations by 1940 was

100, as against twenty-six ABC stations, though the latter had more powerful transmitters. To maintain their position *vis-à-vis* the ABC, the commercial stations had a national organization, the Australian Federation of Commercial Broadcasting Stations.[76] Yet there was no competition in the purest sense between the commercials and the ABC, apart from the most basic competition for survival. Commercial stations were business undertakings out to make a profit. They did not seek to enlighten or to improve cultural standards, but aimed rather to maximize their audience by providing acceptable entertainment.[77] By helping to establish radio's popularity, they may have heightened the influence which any broadcaster, including the ABC, could have. As well, their activities partly released the ABC from the task of satisfying a popular audience, allowing it to cater for minority interests.[78] On the other hand, the commercial stations reinforced popular standards and increased the likelihood of the ABC being viewed as extraordinarily dull, even stuffy.

Cleary had the great advantage of possessing a clear view of the ABC's role in society. Neither the inertia of the apathetic, nor the resistance of the complacent, caused him to redefine his basic goal— that Australia should become more 'cultured'. Within the ABC organization, his conception of national broadcasting went as yet unchallenged. Staff activity, though on the increase, was directed at obtaining better working conditions; it was not directed towards questioning ABC values. However, some groups outside the ABC did question these values. Cleary's attempt to promote ABC talks and political commentaries ran into obstacles created by a Commonwealth government bent on crushing political dissent, and a community which was unavoidably conditioned by this official intolerance.

4
The Politics of Broadcasting

It was Cleary's expressed hope that Australians might become 'more and more interested' in talks and commentaries, 'even and indeed especially about controversial matters'.[1] However, the Lyons government, equally hopeful of maintaining the docility of the Australian electorate, was prepared to interfere with ABC programme content to prevent criticism of government policy or even general discussion of politics, international affairs, and current intellectual controversies. Thus the ABC developed a formula for survival based on its conception of what the government would regard as acceptable broadcasting.

For advice on talk programmes, the ABC drew on the expertise of talks advisory committees in each state and its National Talks Advisory Committee. The latter comprised Molesworth, Barry, and Bronner, plus a number of academics chosen by Cleary, among them W. J. Dakin, W. G. K. Duncan, G. V. Portus, G. L. Wood, and H. Alcock. Molesworth personally examined the minutes of each state committee. Items requiring further attention were passed on either to the National Talks Advisory Committee or to Moses, who if he wished could forward them on to the Commission.

The main speakers of these years were usually from the universities. William Macmahon Ball, from the University of Melbourne, delivered talks on politics and foreign affairs. Other academic speakers included advisory committee members Duncan, Dakin, and Portus. One of the most popular broadcasters was Professor Walter Murdoch of Western Australia. His name became almost a household word.[2] So, too, did 'The Watchman', the pseudonym used by the ABC's most controversial political commentator in the 1930s. Most national talks were delivered between 7.40 and 7.55 p.m., Monday to Friday, though on Tuesday nights a more topical talk was given between 9 and 10 p.m. On Thursdays at 10 p.m., the BBC's commentator on international affairs was rebroadcast, and part of Sunday afternoon's 'BBC Hour' was devoted to talks.

By 1939, the lecture style of talk programmes was being supplemented increasingly by the interview and the debate. Both provided scope for the ABC to create its own presentation rituals, many of which are still in use. As well, the ABC began to bring out 'celebrity speakers', such as the author H. G. Wells and Dr R. A. Millikan, the noted physicist. But the occasional good interview or famous name did not sufficiently offset the most common feature of ABC talks—dullness.³ This dullness sprang not from the topics themselves but rather from the manner of presentation. Some university professors, such as G. V. Portus, were excellent broadcasters; most were not. Even people with good delivery were constrained by ABC attitudes about objectivity. For example, a debate on the subject 'Is the United States a menace to culture?' failed to take off because all the participants were too polite and too scared to advocate an extreme position over the ABC.⁴ The Commission promoted this approach. One Commission directive, for example, forbade speakers to discuss the notorious Mrs Freer case, and only allowed discussion of the general problems involved; in this instance, the state of the law on prohibited immigrants.⁵ By this type of action, Cleary institutionalized rules about permissible political topics, in effect evolving a 'play-safe' ideology that came to be embraced by many ABC officials. Keith Barry, for example, ordered the elimination of 'political' content from the national children's session;⁶ Molesworth would not allow anybody to broadcast an attack on government policy unless another speaker presented the opposite point of view,⁷ a policy which could theoretically make for interesting debate, but which in practice usually led to dull, 'balanced' programming. In Ellis Blain's words: 'To express no view, to give no opinion is to reinforce the image of a prissy old aunty, out of touch with life as it is.'⁸ Cleary's approach to talks sessions, therefore, was somewhat ambivalent. He wished to stimulate public discussion on controversial issues, but he had constantly to guard against the touchiness of the government.

Obscurities in the ABC Act encouraged government interference. ABC control over political broadcasting was limited to election 'speeches' until a wartime amendment in 1942 granted it control over 'any matter relating to a political subject'. Before the 1942 amendment, the postmaster-general could prohibit or order any broadcast, or the government could interfere more subtly by inserting government propaganda into a 'non-political' ministerial broadcast. From January 1935 to August 1936, there were seventy-five ministerial broadcasts on the ABC, compared with six broadcasts by opposition members.⁹ The ABC could object to the use of the ABC as a government public-relations station and could sometimes block a broadcast,[10] but it could not escape the irritations of outright ministerial instruction. During the 1932 debates, ministers gave assurances that ministerial powers *vis-à-vis* the ABC would not be used for party-political advantage.[11] In October 1936, one minister, R. G. Menzies, again assured the House that 'Neither this Government, nor any member of it, has given any direction to the Broadcasting Commission. The decision is reached by the Commission as to the nature of the broadcast to be made and the identity of the person who may make it.'[12] But the government's actual record was a complete abrogation of these guarantees.

Political interference was inseparable from control of ABC finances. Licence fees, the main source of ABC revenue, were not an independent source of income: they were collected by the postmaster-general, who then paid the ABC's share into a trust fund. The ABC received its income in monthly installments from this fund. Each year, the ABC was required to present an annual report and balance sheet to Parliament, and the Commonwealth auditor-general could inspect its books. On more than one occasion, the auditor-general's criticisms found their way into the press, exposing the ABC to large amounts of unwanted publicity, and placing it in the invidious position of having to justify its programme expenditure—something not required of any commercial station proprietor.[13] At other times, the ABC's freedom of action was limited by the postmaster-general's veto powers. A proposed £700 000 building programme, to which the ABC would contribute £400 000 and Treasury the balance, was rejected in 1938 by both the treasurer and the postmaster-general who argued that the ABC must be financially self-sufficient. Indeed, the postmaster-general directed the ABC to set aside a greater percentage of its revenue for future building projects. As a result, 15 per cent of the ABC's revenue for 1939 was 'tied' to building funds.[14]

The government's most powerful financial weapon was control of the listener's licence fee. Throughout the 1930s, reductions in the fee were merely threatened,[15] but in 1940, the new postmaster-general, H. V. C. Thorby, using the ABC's £250 000 building reserves as a pretext, persuaded Cabinet to cut the licence fee and reduce the ABC's share by two shillings. The ABC was not consulted: Cleary first learnt of the cut while reading the morning newspapers.[16] Thorby acted mainly for reasons of electoral expediency, without regard to the severe financial difficulties the cut caused the ABC. Immediately afterwards, the government threw ABC finances into further disarray by imposing £10 000 pay-roll tax, hitherto not collected. These actions had more than financial significance. Thorby told Cleary at their first meeting that he intended to change the ABC Act to provide for full ministerial control.[17] Unilaterally reducing the licence fee was a means of demonstrating who was really in charge. The ABC, moreover, could expect no help from the Labor Party: John Curtin disapproved of the personnel of the Commission, and on that ground alone raised no objection to the cut in ABC revenues.[18] While ABC revenues remained so vulnerable to political manipulation, there was always a better chance that the Commission would be politically compliant, either by succumbing to government pressures *vis-à-vis* a certain broadcast or by imposing strict self-censorship.

ABC independence was further weakened by the choice of postmaster-general in the 1930s. J. E. Fenton steered the ABC Bill through Parliament in 1932 but did little else afterwards to further ABC interests. R. A. Parkhill and A. J. McLachlan also did not push ABC matters in Cabinet. Archie Cameron, postmaster-general from November 1938 to April 1939, had little but contempt for the ABC. Cleary's report of his first meeting with Cameron illustrates the mentality he was up against:

> He is a countryman, thick set, appears to have a very suspicious disposition, very impulsive, jack-blunt, proud of being impulsive, proud of being jack-blunt, proud of his ignorance of things. Greeted us with—'I know nothing about broadcasting. I am not interested in it. If I had my way I would stop all broadcasting. No time for these mechanical things. Don't know anything about music. As for people who give talks and commentaries over the air ... [I] would bring them under the Vermin Act'.[19]

When Cleary later said that he believed the ABC was entitled to work within its charter, Cameron allegedly replied: 'Forget your charter, I don't believe in boards or commissions—I believe in ministerial control'.[20] It was thus with some justification that Cleary spoke to Brookes of the 'black and abysmal ignorance and prejudice which envelopes the ill-fated seat of broadcasting'.[21] There was faint optimism over the appointment in April 1939 of E. J. Harrison, in Cleary's words 'the first Minister to take a keen and intelligent interest' in ABC affairs,[22] but this interest gave way to straight interference with the outbreak of World War II.

The ABC's ability to resist interference was seriously reduced by the uncertainty surrounding the future of individual commissioners and the ABC itself. Various new broadcasting Acts were drafted but allowed to lapse, to the confusion of everyone, and to the advantage of the government which could exploit the uncertainty to obtain political compliance. From 1937 onwards, speculation about changes in the ABC's structure centred on the positions of chairman and general manager: the two positions would be merged; one or the other would be abolished; the general manager would become a member of the Commission; and so forth.[23] In the meantime, the government recognized the extra responsibilities temporarily being shouldered by Cleary and awarded him an honorarium of £2000. But even this was used by some politicians to step up their scrutiny of ABC members. 'As a representative of the taxpayers', said Senator Collings, 'I, and my fifteen colleagues, intend to constitute ourselves watchdogs on such matters.'[24]

None of the political parties clearly stated their plans for the ABC. The Australian Labor Party was opposed to a full-time chairman on the grounds that the job could become a political sinecure.[25] John Curtin emphasized public control of broadcasting, but he would not go on record as supporting nationalization of the broadcasting system.[26] The public remained uncertain about what the Labor Party was advocating. Nor was there any lead from the United Australia and Country parties. Discussions at a joint party meeting on 6 October 1938 were followed by Parkhill's recommendations to Cabinet on 11 October that the general manager become the vice-chairman of the Commission.[27] After some hard talking, Cleary managed to thwart this proposal.[28] In March 1939, Archie Cameron produced another set of draft amendments, this time recommending an expanded Commission of seven members; again the Bill was not proceeded with. By this time, events in Europe were receiving higher Cabinet priority, and Cameron did not push for the passage of the legislation.[29]

While the government procrastinated, the terms of commissioners were extended and extended again. Cleary's initial five-year term was extended for four months, two months, and three successive terms of six months. Protests to government proved fruitless.[30] In Cleary's words, the commissioners had been granted extensions of office 'much as a condemned man's date of execution might have been postponed!'[31] This uncertainty of tenure was hardly conducive to the smooth running of the ABC, already strained by increasing staff activity and the ministerial attention ABC staffing policies were attracting. It also weakened the ABC's bargaining power with outside interests.

Cleary would not bend easily to government demands. In June 1936, he answered A. J. McLachlan's request for greater internal ABC censorship of talk sessions with the comment that open discussion was a 'characteristic of British communities which should be jealously preserved', and said that the ABC had special responsibilities to maintain this against the 'narrow or one-sided presentation of important public issues by the press in Australia'.³² At a similar meeting with Archie Cameron, in November 1938, he argued that the ABC must be independent of political interference if it were to be viewed as a reliable safeguard against the influence on public opinion of 'vested interests'.³³

He was, on the other hand, a pragmatist and a realist, who was willing to compromise to ensure the ABC's survival. A policy of balanced programming was virtually mandatory during a decade in which the government banned some 5000 books, including Huxley's *Brave New World*, James Joyce's *Ulysses*, Norman Lindsay's *Redheap*, and any writings by Trotsky, Stalin, and Lenin. Contemporary visitors like H. G. Wells were appalled by the book and radio censorship they found in operation.³⁴

To some extent, the government was reflecting Australian philistinism; for there were groups of citizens which shared government narrow-mindedness and encouraged the censorship of anything 'which in any way—cleverly or stupidly, wittily or pompously—questioned, betrayed or attacked what they took to be values of the patriotic family man and woman'.³⁵ A government ban on forty-eight different magazines in 1938 was applauded by more than thirty organizations, among them the Father and Son Welfare Movement, the Western Australian Housewives' Association, the Australian Women's National League, and the Council of Churches of New South Wales.³⁶ The Sane Democracy League was another organization which urged tight political censorship. On one occasion, it labelled as 'subversive propaganda' an ABC broadcast in honour of the USSR's National Day and sent a complaint to the government. The postmaster-general asked the ABC to explain this 'unpardonable' broadcast.³⁷

Cleary took up the cause of groups in society which were determined to challenge the apparent narrow-mindedness of the government. He rejected arguments that radio should be more closely scrutinized than the printed media.³⁸ Many of his talks advisers, in addition to actually broadcasting, belonged to bodies which tried to provoke debate, such as the Australian Institute of Political Science or the Institute of International Affairs, and were active in anti-censorship campaigns. William Macmahon Ball, for example, helped to found the Book Censorship Abolition League in 1934. In addition, he criticized Lyons' attitude towards radio censorship, arguing that national broadcasting systems should not be used for the 'propagandizing' of democracy.³⁹ The government claimed that it left the ABC alone except on party-political issues where it believed it should censor statements 'not of a definitely National character'.[40] Unfortunately, the interests of the nation were usually equated with the interests of the Lyons government.

During the 1930s, the ABC insisted on its rights to control political broadcasts only in respect of election broadcasts. Federal politicians had used radio extensively for electioneering purposes as recently as the 1931 campaign. In the name of impartiality, the ABC adopted a policy for the 1934 federal elections of granting equal air time to the leaders of all established political parties—that is, those with representation in Parliament. Cleary incensed all parties in 1937 when he attempted to divorce the ABC from political campaigning by refusing any party air time until after the election. John Curtin began to advocate ministerial control of the ABC.[41] Lyons also criticized the ABC for going too far, especially when it refused to broadcast his own speech and that of Forgan Smith (the premier of Queensland) at the Brisbane Show.[42] After proddings from Moses and other commissioners, the ban was modified to allow broadcasts by politicians provided they did not speak in support of any political party or candidate; but general policy on the allocation of air time remained intact.

Other political broadcasts were usually censored within the ABC in anticipation of an unfavourable government response. Such censorship could be political, in that an ABC official might be motivated by personal political preference to censor an item, but the general impression given by the ABC's records for the 1930s is that, at the level of the Commission at least, people acted with impartiality. As a joint parliamentary committee of inquiry (the 'Gibson Committee') found in 1942:

> There is no evidence to lead us to believe otherwise than that the Commission has exercised its great powers with calm judgment and measured impartiality, and such difficulties as it might have encountered could only have arisen through an itching desire on the part of Ministers to assert their authority in a manner that Parliament never intended and never should sanction.[43]

However, it is clear that the quest for impartiality was taken to extremes on matters of both domestic and international political significance. In September 1936, for example, a planned discussion between Norman Lindsay and Max Montesole on the banning of books was deleted from the evening's programmes.[44] Colin Badger abandoned a talk on 'Machiavelli and the Modern Dictators' in July 1937 after the ABC manager for Western Australia insisted on the elimination of two paragrphs which referred disparagingly to Hitler and Mussolini.⁴⁵ On 8 July 1938, the *Labor Daily* carried the headline, 'HITLER—THE UNSEEN CHAIRMAN OF THE ABC' when a talk by Anne Caton (international social worker) on the German destruction of a Basque town was censored on the grounds that it would be unpleasant hearing for Germans in South Australia.⁴⁶ Perhaps the most notorious case of self-censorship was that in May 1938, when Judge A. W. Foster's talk on 'Freedom of Speech' was so heavily censored by the ABC that he refused to deliver it. Foster's talk included references to the government's treatment of Egon Kisch and the Commonwealth Crimes Act.⁴⁷ That the ABC should consider such ruthless self-censorship necessary for the maintenance of good relations with the government and the wider community is an indication of the extent of its 'politicization'.

But even though self-censorship was so pervasive, the Lyons government found numerous opportunities for interfering in ABC programming. This interference was nowhere more obvious than in the case of 'The Watchman'. His broadcasts were the occasion of the first outright ministerial proscriptions of ABC programme content.

'The Watchman', really Edward Alexander Mann, was born in Mount Gambier on 11 August 1874. He was educated privately and at the University of Melbourne, after which he worked in Western Australia as a government chemical analyst, then as chief inspector of explosives and as an agricultural chemist. In 1902, he served on the royal commission into ventilation and sanitation of mines, and as president of the Civil Service Association in 1920 he helped lead a civil servant strike. In 1922 he entered the Commonwealth Parliament as the Nationalist member for Perth, and remained there until defeated in 1929, having helped to bring on the election by siding with W. M. Hughes against the Bruce government's Maritime Industries Bill. His next move was into broadcasting, and in January 1932 he broadcast his first session of 'News Behind the News'. When the ABC took control in July 1932, his duties were extended to include two additional 'At Home and Abroad' sessions.⁴⁸

'The Watchman's' two sessions were different in content and approach. 'At Home and Abroad', a daily session, dealt briefly with national and international affairs. It was relayed at lunchtime and sometimes repeated in the evening. 'News Behind the News' was a more thoroughly researched weekly programme which examined issues in greater detail. 'The Watchman' displayed a preaching style in this session, championing causes like freedom of speech, the rights of minorities, or the need for improvements in public transport. He also discussed the jury system, child neglect, the White Australia policy, working conditions, unemployment, and many other issues.⁴⁹

4 The Politics of Broadcasting

E. M. Andrews argues that the government would not have attempted to suppress 'The Watchman' had it not believed his talks were effective;[50] but the extent to which this was so is difficult to assess. Popularity is not synonymous with influence, although there is no doubt that his talks were popular. In country hotels, conversation usually dropped during 'The Watchman's' lunchtime session. It was claimed that he had won people's respect for his 'sincere and independent presentation of news: something different from the syndicated paragraphs of the daily Press'.[51] In September 1936, listeners in Horsham district complained when 'The Watchman's' talks could not be heard easily in their area.[52] City people often gathered on footpaths outside shop windows to catch his commentaries. They liked his simple, straightforward style.[53] Mail from listeners was often complimentary: his commentaries were 'an education and provocative of right thinking'; they had not been 'so stimulated and re-energised for years'; the ABC must 'Let him go on with the good work of enlightenment'.[54] Australians had few other sources of information on international crises apart from 'The Watchman'. Some snippets of overseas news were to be found in the press, and S. H. Roberts, William Macmahon Ball, R. M. Crawford, and Kurt Offenburg gave the occasional broadcast on ABC radio, but generally Australia's reporting of overseas affairs could accurately be described as 'very poor, fragmentary and inadequate'.[55] The volume of listeners' letters received by 'The Watchman' suggests that he was at least informing, if not influencing, a sizeable audience.[56]

Despite his popularity, there were complaints that 'The Watchman' was abusing his position by advancing personal opinions through an authoritative medium like the ABC. Some complaints stemmed from ignorance, or from mishearing what 'The Watchman' actually said. Others came from people who could tolerate no point of view other than their own. But a large number of people based their concern on mistaken associations of the ABC with government. 'The Watchman', although he frequently attacked government initiatives, was viewed as a 'Big Brother' figure propagandizing the community with government notions.[57] The ABC pointed out that 'The Watchman's' opinions were his own, not those of the Commission or the government, but 'The Watchman's' anonymity seems to have confused the issue.[58] 'If the ABC is a national service,' wrote one listener, 'then let us have a national expression of opinion and let the listening public be the judges'.[59] In response to this criticism, the ABC introduced a weekly session, 'I Don't Agree', in which listeners could express objections to points made by 'The

Watchman' or other commentators. But the complaints continued. Possibly some listeners' complaints stemmed from a deep distrust of anything even vaguely authoritarian. The forceful nature of 'The Watchman's' presentation is attested by those who heard him, the ABC manager for New South Wales, H. G. Horner, suggesting that he proclaimed his views more like a town crier than a radio commentator.[60] What better seeming manifestation of authoritarianism than a regular, anonymous, forcefully presented political commentary?

A common criticism of 'The Watchman', as of other commentators, was political bias, but the universal nature of the criticism precludes the possibility that he pushed a consistent line.[61] Most allegations of bias surfaced around election times. 'The Watchman' eschewed comment on party politics just before elections, but he did offer an opinion on the results.[62] In 1940, following the Corio by-election, he offended some Labor voters (whose candidate won) by claiming that the issue of a motor-car monopoly agreement was more important in deciding the vote than the UAP's general handling of the war effort.[63] Another time, he attacked the communist influence in the Labor Party,[64] but it would be wrong to accuse him of consistent anti-Labor bias. He often referred to rifts within the Country Party,[65] and he certainly criticized UAP policies.

The most worrying complaints for the ABC were those from the government. Mostly, they concerned 'The Watchman's' talks on foreign affairs, and were often accompanied by blatant political direction. Lyons was particularly upset by 'The Watchman's' failure to support a traditional British line on foreign policy. In September 1936, his government signed a convention in Geneva binding Australia to broadcast only in the interests of peace. Australia was one of the first governments formally to ratify the agreement.[66] Lyons used the agreement as an excuse for stifling any viewpoint which differed from his government's. Commercial radio stations were threatened with non-renewal of their transmitting licences should they fail to comply with the terms of the convention, and confidence was expressed that the ABC would not contravene the provisions.[67] This pressure reinforced ABC self-censorship tendencies, but it did not eliminate clashes between Cabinet and the ABC over the words of 'The Watchman'.

One of the first big controversies involved 'The Watchman's' comments on the government's trade diversion policy. Adopted from 1936 onwards, this policy plunged Australia into a virtual trade war with Japan and the United States.[68] High duties were imposed on Japanese textile products and on American motor-vehicle bodies. On 17 May 1937, 'The Watchman' criticized what he saw as an

4 The Politics of Broadcasting

attempt to give preference to British goods, noting 'the growing conviction everywhere that economic hostility is the background of war, and that trade obstacles are the seedbed of international political conflicts. So long as such economic hostility exists, political pacts will have but a transitory value'.[69] The trade diversion policy, he argued, went against this conviction. He hoped that Australia would eventually open her 'restricted markets', recovering any losses incurred through her share of the increased world trade.[70] On the question of motor vehicles, he alleged that £27 had been added to the price of every non-British car at a total cost to Australians of £1 500 000 per annum. This, he claimed, 'instead of creating closer bonds between Britain and Australia as intended, may leave the opposite effect, because it gives the impression that Imperial sentiment is being exploited for group commercial interests.'[71] He also told of an Adelaide firm's suspension of five hundred employees because of steel shortages which it attributed to the government's trade policies. This, 'The Watchman' suggested, was 'a case of protection causing unemployment, instead of removing it as it is calculated to do'.[72]

'The Watchman's' comments on trade policy were in direct conflict with the government view. As a commentator, he should have been entitled to give an opinion, but neither the government nor some of the public could accept this. The Australian Industries Protection League continually wrote to the ABC complaining about 'The Watchman', and once suggested that he be debarred from discussing all 'economic or social questions'.[73] Cleary answered government inquiries in general terms: 'The Commission, unless it is to assume a purely propagandist role, must not be concerned with a commentator's viewpoint, but rather with his fitness by education, experience, reputation for fairness, character, and qualities as a broadcaster.'[74] Moses was more responsive to government complaints. After the minister for trade and customs, Colonel T. W. White—a man whom Peter Coleman labelled 'one of the most determined censors in the history of Australian Customs'[75]—complained that 'The Watchman's' broadcasts were 'first-class propaganda for the disgruntled section of the motor trade', Moses asked the Commission to instruct 'The Watchman' to leave out personal opinions on political issues.[76] He also sent a message to the ABC manager for Victoria, from which state 'The Watchman' broadcast, asking that there be greater scrutiny of the scripts, so as to 'avoid giving offence to listeners who support a Protectionist Policy'.[77] It had not been necessary for the government to issue a written directive. In January 1938, the *Radio Retailer* reported that

Cabinet had applied censorship to the ABC over 'The Watchman's' comments on trade policy;[78] but it was through the use of ministerial pressure, not powers. The disturbing thing is that the government considered it proper to shield itself from public criticism and silence dissentient opinion in this way — despite its continued pronouncements that the ABC would be free of political direction.[79]

'The Watchman' also aroused hostility for his comments on the Spanish Civil War. Overall, he maintained a fairly neutral attitude, but on occasions favoured the Republicans. Archie Cameron quite blatantly stated to Moses: 'The Commonwealth is maintaining an attitude of neutrality in the Spanish Civil War. The ABC men should observe a similar neutral attitude.'[80] In this instance, Moses defended 'The Watchman' against public attacks and took no action in relation to Cameron's remarks except to pass them on to the Commission for consideration.[81] After discussion, the Commission decided that while news services should be impartial, commentators should be given an opportunity to advance definite points of view, provided someone had right of reply.[82] 'The Watchman' continued to give his talks on Spain relatively unhindered, despite the clear government pressure, but he soon incurred even greater Cabinet anger for his stance on the Munich settlement of 1938.

E. M. Andrews has claimed that 'The Watchman' was the 'most outspoken, bitter, and possibly influential opponent of appeasement, both before and after Munich'.[83] While Lyons expressed full support for Prime Minister Chamberlain's appeasement policy, 'The Watchman' attacked the Munich settlement as a ghastly mistake, and argued that the troubles supposedly ended by Munich were only beginning.[84]

The *Age* attacked 'The Watchman' for his views, published letters criticizing him, and in its editorials urged the appointment of a new ABC foreign affairs commentator.[85] The *Bulletin* joined the campaign, expressing annoyance that Australians should be subjected to the 'cockeyed' views of 'The Botchman'.[86] Yet it is interesting that in one batch of 133 listeners' letters on Munich received by the ABC, 112 expressed unqualified support and admiration, 11 were appreciative but disagreed on some points, and only 10 were sharply critical. Among the appreciative remarks were statements of joy that there was at least 'one honest man in the British Empire'. Others, in contast, regarded 'The Watchman' as 'pale-pink' and wrong for not showing gratitude to Chamberlain.[87]

'The Watchman' stated his lack of confidence in Chamberlain long before the signing at Munich. His eagerness to point out any signs of support for the policies of R. A. Eden worried M. F. Dixon, who thought that 'The Watchman' might be instructed to modify his anti-Chamberlain stance.⁸⁸ Dixon's concern was noted just one month after the Australian minister for defence, H. V. C. Thorby, in the wake of Eden's resignation as British foreign minister, asked 'all loyal Australians' to refrain from 'unnecessary' criticism of leaders of the Empire.⁸⁹ The request was heeded, for 'The Watchman' complained in April 1938 that recent restrictions placed upon talk topics meant the elimination of political comment from his sessions.⁹⁰

Cleary was ambivalent towards 'The Watchman's' commentaries on Munich. On the one hand, he personally supported Chamberlain's efforts to negotiate with Hitler. In November 1937, he informed 'The Watchman' that 'all peace-desiring peoples should avoid provocative statements or actions which might inflame public opinion of our own people, or unnecessarily or unwarrantably offend the peoples with whom Great Britain is endeavouring to arrive at friendly understandings.'⁹¹ On the other hand, his commitment to freedom of opinion prevented him from ordering 'The Watchman' outright to alter his line of comment, especially when most of the pressure for this action came from outside the ABC, and in peacetime. But by October 1938, other ABC officers were beginning to question the extent to which attacks on British government policy should be permitted in a time of international crisis. Barry voiced his concern, as did members of the National Talks Advisory Committee which early in 1939 resolved that 'In view of the International situation and the extraordinary importance of getting another daily point of view other than the "Watchman's", this Committee feels it a matter of urgency that the "Watchman" should not be permitted daily to advance an unchallenged point of view.'⁹²

Lyons was at the limit of his patience. Despite warnings from the secretary of the Commonwealth Department of External Affairs that the government should be careful not to be seen to interfere with free speech,⁹³ he asked his postmaster-general, on 24 October 1938, to look into the comments being broadcast on the Munich crisis and to discuss with him 'the possibility of the Commonwealth taking some action to prevent the broadcast of any matter which is inimical to the State or unduly disturbing to the peace of mind of listeners'.⁹⁴

The issue assumed new significance with the declaration of war by Britain on Germany in September 1939. 'The Watchman's' statements on British policy were tolerated even less by the newly formed Menzies government. When, on 21 September 1939, 'The Watchman' criticized Britain's delay in giving assistance to Poland, ministerial interference was swift and absolute. The new postmaster-general, Harrison, telephoned instructions to Cleary that 'The Watchman' must refrain from any further criticism of government policy. Unless he confined himself to 'factual observation', the government would cut him off the air. When Cleary asked whether 'The Watchman' could still criticize the Labor opposition, Harrison replied that Cabinet was not concerned about that, but he must not criticize the government![95]

'The Watchman' reacted to the censorship instructions with 'extreme indignation'.[96] He asked for them to be put in writing, and for their source, voicing at the same time his belief that the ABC had issued them of its own volition.[97] This, of course, was not true. Cleary believed that, even in wartime, occasional adverse criticism of government 'would give listeners greater confidence in the National service and re-assure them that it was not purely a Government propaganda service', and he put this view to Harrison at a private meeting two weeks later. Harrison admitted privately that he agreed, but whatever his personal feelings, Cabinet insisted on the original instructions being carried out.[98] On 11 October, Moses informed 'The Watchman' that the instructions were confirmed and must be obeyed.[99] William Macmahon Ball, now the acting controller of talks in the ABC's Victorian branch, protested that he could not in all conscience apply such exceptional rules of censorship to 'The Watchman's' scripts;[1] but it was wartime, and ultimately the government's wishes prevailed.

Controversy surrounding 'The Watchman' subsided quickly after his resignation from the ABC in October 1940. Although his identity had been forced out into the open late in 1939 during question time in Parliament,[2] the ABC decided to continue his sessions, but 'The Watchman' made this impossible by nominating for the seat of Flinders in the 1940 federal election. His programme was eliminated immediately. When, subsequently, his election bid proved unsuccessful, the ABC offered to let him resume broadcasting but only as one of many commentators, not with his own regular session. Mann refused the offer and wrote a bitter letter of resignation.[3] After leaving the ABC, Mann worked for commercial station 3UZ in Victoria, then transferred to 6ML in Perth. However, the Perth station soon replaced him with another commentator. Without the prestige of the ABC, and with his loss of anonymity, Mann's sessions gained no significant following in the West. Even allowing for a different response from a Western Australian audience, there seems some truth in the local ABC manager's summation: 'It is certainly a win for us. I readily think that once people who have made a name in the National Service transfer their affections

4 The Politics of Broadcasting

elsewhere, they seem to fade out of the limelight altogether, and National broadcasting still stands supreme.'⁴ But for all the ABC's jubilation over this 'win', the ready acceptance of 'The Watchman's' resignation in part amounted to a surrender to the increasingly heavy-handed approach of the government in relation to his commentaries.⁵

'The Watchman' was merely one ABC political commentator, but his case reveals much about the ABC's handling of political pressure and public controversy in the 1930s. Despite pretensions to independence, the ABC avoided a fuss wherever possible: thus someone like 'The Watchman' was never permitted to advance a point of view that could offend government opinion. This was a conservative approach,⁶ but to a large extent it was an unavoidable and realistic approach, and it guaranteed institutional survival in a political atmosphere that might otherwise have allowed the ABC's destruction. 'The Watchman' was certainly provocative, lively, and informative, but he enjoyed independence only within the parameters set periodically by the commissioners whose decisions were made with one eye on the government to whom the ABC owed its continued existence. The extent to which independent political commentary was possible thus depended on the ability of leading ABC figures to influence Cabinet, but even Cleary could not sway the men of Lyons' and Menzies' ministries. Compromise was necessary to reduce the attacks of ministers who believed it was their prerogative to dictate to the ABC. It was also necessary, if ministerial interference were to be reduced, to woo listeners who disagreed with 'The Watchman' or with other commentators. This was attempted by devoting meticulous attention to answering letters, issuing press statements in defence of ABC initiatives, and introducing programmes to enable opposing points of view to be put; in other words, by adopting a public relations approach and aiming for 'balance' in programming. Viewed in the widest sense, therefore, government pressure on the ABC was fairly successful. The ABC's most common approach became not confrontation but the expedient of self-censorship. It was thus a politically compliant institution during its formative years, and its compliance created a tradition, even an institutional ideology, that has continued to affect ABC operations to the present day.

5
Wartime Programming

Throughout the 1930s, Cleary had challenged, with varying success, the cultural and social mores which hindered his attempt to encourage cultural uplift. He had been less successful in challenging political interference. But neither of these challenges quite equalled the threat posed to ABC philosophies, indeed, to ABC survival, by the outbreak of World War II. The ABC's record in the late 1930s guaranteed that it would remain politically compliant in a time of national crisis. At the same time, it made a very positive and distinctive contribution to the Australian war effort from 1939 to 1945.

The presence of private radio sets during World War II brought the war effort, both military and civilian, into the lounge-rooms of Australians. By 1939, approximately 1 132 000 or about 60 per cent of Australian homes possessed a licensed radio; two years later 77 per cent did so.[1] Few people, except those who had actually fought in the last war, had any conception of the realities of front-line combat, and intimate subjection to government radio propaganda was a new experience for everyone. Menzies' historic broadcast of 3 September 1939, stating that because Britain was at war, Australia was also at war, marked the first occasion on which ordinary Australians heard their prime minister declare war on another nation. This broadcast was the ABC's first 'act of war'.

In April 1940, during the so-called phoney war period, Moses expressed the view that the ABC should attempt 'to counteract the public's apathy and lack of interest in the war and to give publicity to the manner in which Australian resources must be organised'.[2] Soon after, the urge to get back into uniform proved irresistible and on 27 May he informed the Commission of his decision to enlist for active duty. Presented with a *fait accompli*, the Commission appointed Bearup to act as general manager.[3] By this time, however, the ABC was beginning to perform the propaganda function Moses envisaged for it. For the rest of the war it was involved in the dissemination and the production of propaganda both for domestic and overseas consumption. Propaganda for domestic consumption was

5 Wartime Programming

designed to promote the national war effort and to build and sustain civilian morale. When Japan entered the war there was an increase in overseas propaganda. The objectives were to separate Japanese troops from their officers, persuade them to treat Australians more sympathetically (or at least less barbarously), and to sap Japanese morale, if possible, by stressing Australian strength and determination.

At least one senior officer, Frank Clewlow, at the outbreak of war threatened to leave the ABC rather than 'subordinate art to propaganda'.[4] Dixon, on the other hand, had no such qualms: in January 1942, he even urged a greater injection of Australian sentiment and 'stirring patriotic music' into programmes.[5] ABC management realized from the outset that in all probability, it would be called upon to spread propaganda,[6] and by 1942 it had accepted that such a task was a proper activity for the ABC. Hence Bearup's comment in 1942: 'We should have no inhibitions about the use of the word "propaganda" if we are satisfied with the worthiness and the integrity of the ideas which we use it to disseminate'.[7]

Any account of ABC wartime programmes must include reference to the Department of Information (DOI). The Menzies government created the department immediately after the outbreak of hostilities, installing Sir Henry Gullett as its first minister. It was to be purely 'a wartime instrument' to distribute information about the war and to boost morale, and it was to be disbanded with the return of peace.[8]

The ABC devoted from 20 to 27 per cent of domestic air time to programmes directly connected with the war.[9] Throughout 1940 and 1941, the DOI used the ABC network mainly to broadcast war information, propaganda as such being confined to overseas transmissions. Hasluck notes that during these first two years Australians were 'subjected to far more persuasive statements to the effect that the Government was bungling, that monopolists and profiteers were making a good thing out of the war and the ordinary man was getting nothing, and that Britain was making Australia bear the brunt of the fighting'.[10] Things had begun to change by mid-1941, after a paper prepared for Cabinet recommended 'Immediate and double time propaganda by the Department of Information to educate the public'.[11]

Most early DOI domestic propaganda took the form of two-minute morale-boosting talks at 6.43 and 7.58 p.m. daily. There were, among others, 'Eat more Lamb', 'Petrol Saving', 'Anti-complacency', 'Vegetable Growing', 'Nutrition', 'Absenteeism', and 'Anti-Gossip' campaigns.[12] The department also produced advertisements for both ABC and commercial radio, inviting listeners to purchase war savings' certificates or to enlist in the Forces. An 'Australia at War' series included 'actuality' broadcasts of ship-board life on troop carriers between Melbourne and Fremantle, broadcasts from military camps, broadcasts portraying the nature of work performed in the Lithgow small-arms factory, and many others. There were also talks designed to stimulate production in programmes like the 'All Australia' session, broadcast on Sunday evenings.[13]

Sometimes the DOI preferred to assist in propaganda production without public acknowledgement. It did this, for example, for the serial *Dad and Dave* on commercial radio, and later for an ABC series, *When Tomorrow Comes*. This was probably a wise move, for the public could receive instruction on war matters—such as how to black-out chimneys—without any suggestion of government direction.[14] Policy decisions about the propaganda content of broadcasts were firmly in the hands of the DOI and there is no evidence that the ABC saw this as a slight to its autonomy. On the contrary, the ABC readily accepted government advice on the content of war effort talks. For example, it abandoned a talk on how to make an air-raid shelter after learning that the script conflicted with government advice on the use of the home as an air-raid shelter and on the use of building materials in short supply.[15]

The events of 7 December 1941 brought a new sense of urgency to the war in Australia. On 17 February 1942, two days after the fall of Singapore, the new Curtin Labor government announced a complete mobilization of resources, emphasizing that there was no more time for leisure or for domestic political squabbling. The Opposition leader, A. W. Fadden, pledged full support.[16] This new climate was accompanied by an increase in DOI/ABC domestic propaganda talks.

Some of the early anti-Japanese propaganda directed at civilian Australians was amateurish and crude. A series begun in March 1942 entitled 'The Jap as he really is' so outraged many intellectuals that they lodged protests with the government, demanding an end to the 'hate broadcasts'.[17] One broadcast began: 'An ugly crowd of blood-stained, intriguing Japanese rascals control the policy which has plunged the Pacific into war and brought Japan to the door-step of Australia.'[18] An earlier talk included a quote purportedly from a Japanese schoolboy magazine: 'It is clear that we Japanese have tolerated for too long the white plague which infects New Asia. The time is at hand when Japan will crush out once and for all the memory as well as the substance of the so-called white civilisation.'[19] Yet another talk asked listeners: 'do you know that the enemy we

5 Wartime Programming

are fighting today is moved by creeds and dogma far more perverted than those of the dark ages?'[20] The DOI no doubt believed that radio was a novel form of inculcating perceptions of the enemy, and that the ABC was the ideal vehicle, but these crude broadcasts were bound to offend some of the ABC controllers. In the ABC's report for 1941/2, Cleary noted that there had been some 'difference of opinion' between the ABC and the government over the series. Eventually, after continued protests, the series was abandoned.[21] It was probably only the fear of Japanese invasion which saved the government from more widespread condemnation.

An equally controversial series of domestic propaganda talks was that delivered by trade-union leaders on the labour movement's contribution to the war effort. The talks began during Menzies' prime-ministership and continued under Fadden and now Curtin. But by late 1942, the ABC expressed its concern that the talks were taking on a partisan political character. In October, it refused to broadcast a talk by T. Nicholls, secretary of the Adelaide Labour Council, when part of the script read: 'The essential basis of our planned democracy must be production for use and not for profit. . . . The post-war world will have the choice of two paths, one leading to a New Order on a socialist basis, the other leading to the end of our civilisation.'[22] The DOI, significantly, rejected Bearup's claims that the talk was 'party-political' and 'propagandist', and indeed reminded the ABC that it could invoke the National Security (Information) Regulations and compel the ABC to broadcast the talk.[23] The three stages in this dispute, first, that the ABC tried to stop the broadcasts, second, that the DOI refused to allow this to happen, and third, that the trade unions threatened to challenge any attempt by the ABC to drop the series,[24] all indicate the importance attached to access to ABC facilities, and indicate, too, the widespread recognition of the role that the ABC could play in influencing, or at least in informing, attitudes about the war.

The ABC initiated a number of wartime projects on its own. One of these was concerts and competitions for the troops. Prizes were offered for songs, plays and short stories composed by members of the Forces. In April 1942, the lord mayor of Melbourne proclaimed the Sunday-night troop concerts an outstanding success,[25] but within the ABC there were some reservations about their content. Keith Barry said of the singer Thea Philips: 'I would not have engaged her at a concert for soldiers. Great artist as she is we must be blunt and acknowledge that she's a woman of 50 and looks it'.[26] Apparently her rendition of 'Ave Maria' failed to impress the boys. But the concerts continued for the duration of the war, and, despite the occasional poor choice of programme, were generally well received. Unfortunately, no attendance figures were kept, but it is reasonable to assume that the free admission resulted in full or near full houses. One indicator of the popularity of the concerts is the number performed: in Melbourne alone they rose from twenty in 1942 to forty-four in 1944.[27]

The ABC also helped to raise patriotic funds. It broadcast daily appeals from accredited war charities like the Red Cross, Salvation Army, RSL, and Queen Victoria Hospital, and held one fund-raising concert per month in each state. Local committees organized these concerts which featured the ABC's orchestras and dance bands and artists who volunteered their services. Because of international travel restrictions, performances by overseas artists were few, but Cleary noted in 1942 that the results of using almost exclusively Australian performers had been 'gratifying'.[28] Half of the proceeds of the concerts went to the Red Cross and half to the Patriotic (Comforts) Fund, 20 per cent of which was used to purchase radio sets for military camps.[29] War-fund concerts proved extremely popular with the public; however at one concert in Martin Place, Sydney, things got out of hand when Jim Davidson's ABC Dance Band was mobbed by an ecstatic audience. The bandstand almost collapsed, women fainted, and police had to appeal through loud-hailers for the 9000-strong crowd to keep back![30]

Technological advances enabled the ABC to make some particularly compassionate contributions to the war effort. In one series, children evacuated to Australia took part in radio-telephone conversations with their parents in England. Known as the 'Children Calling Home' session, the broadcasts contained purely personal messages and no direct propaganda. One reader of the *Sydney Morning Herald* believed that the broadcasts merely upset both parents and children,[31] but the keenness of potential participants suggests otherwise. There was one broadcast every eight weeks, arranged between the ABC, the BBC, and the Amalgamated Wireless Radio-Telephone Service. The children were selected by the BBC and the New South Wales Child Welfare Department, and were assisted at the Australian end by the ABC's James Pratt. Parents did most of the talking, asking their children about their experiences: what they had learnt about 'typical Australian conditions and scenery', about native bears and kangaroos, and whether they had done much surfing.[32] A similar programme, 'Wives Calling Husbands', enabled women evacuees from Hong Kong to send messages home.[33]

Children were given an opportunity to forget the war by listening

5 Wartime Programming

to the ABC's Argonauts Club, established in January 1941. A special committee comprising Bearup, Barry, and Clewlow had recommended that this feature, firmly based on Nina Murdoch's original ideas, should become a regular segment of the national children's session.[34] Membership was open to all children between the ages of seven and seventeen. Each member became one of fifty rowers in a ship named after a Greek hero. Those children who sent in literary contributions could receive the 'Order of the Dragon's Tooth' and, ultimately, the 'Golden Fleece' award. Throughout the Argonauts Club's existence, many well-known people helped in its production, among them A. J. Marshall ('Jock'), Frank Harvey ('Nestor'), and A. D. Hope ('Anthony Inkwell').[35]

Though basically escapist in nature, the Argonauts Club also gave children a chance to contribute directly to the war effort. To celebrate a membership of 10 000 in September 1941, the Club launched an appeal to purchase a mobile canteen for the children of blitz-torn London. Club members raised the money by a variety of means, some 'selling vegetables', others 'coming top of the class', 'collecting snails for Dad', or 'having 5 teeth out'![36] By June 1946, a membership figure of 40 000 ensured that the Club would continue well into the post-war period.[37]

Ida Osborne ('Elizabeth'), who ran the national children's session, was one of many women to be heard on the ABC during the war. Nine months into the war, Bearup had written to all commissioners: '... I think we must look in the face the possibility that within a measurable space of time public opinion might strongly object to youthful male voices coming from the loud speakers and we may have to use women announcers, or men well over military age.'[38] Some of those who achieved fame during these years were Beryl Coles and Margaret Denholm in Perth, Mollie Broadbent in Hobart, Mary Herbert in Brisbane, Gladys Millar, Betty Higgins, and Judith Halse Rodgers in Sydney, and Dorothy Crawford, Mary Ward, and Jean Davis in Melbourne.[39]

Many Australians were more interested in the male voices they heard in the programme 'Voices from Overseas', produced by the ABC's mobile broadcasting unit which accompanied the Second AIF overseas. The 'voices' were those of Australian soldiers sending messages to relatives back home and those of war correspondents recounting the latest war news. Both the BBC and the NZBC sent similar units overseas with their troops. For some unknown reason, the Australian unit's departure for Palestine had been delayed until June 1940, but it soon made up for lost time under the expert guidance of Lawrence Cecil.[40] Assisting him, as commentator-journalist, was Chester Wilmot, released from the DOI for this purpose. Wilmot had a grammar-school background, degrees in arts and law from the University of Melbourne, and was widely travelled. He was in Europe during the Nazi takeovers of Austria and Paris. William Macmahon Ball once described him as an 'ace' broadcaster. He was to become especially famous for his lively, accurate reporting of the war in New Guinea.[41] The three other members of the unit were R. Boyle (engineer), and G. Gallway and W. T. MacFarlane (both mechanics), all from the Postmaster-General's Department. Like other interdepartmental wartime agencies, the unit had demarcation disputes. Boyle's refusal to acknowledge Cecil's authority in January 1941 forced General Blamey to request his return to Australia.[42] Yet the unit provided Australians with firsthand accounts of overseas events and in no small way helped to give a sense of immediacy to the war. Wilmot and Cecil took considerable personal risks, on one occasion nearly losing their lives when enemy shells began to explode around them. There is a story that they were the first Australians to enter Sidon. Somehow they overtook the army advance, and on arrival had to reassure an enthusiastic though puzzled crowd that the general would be arriving shortly![43]

Though not purely a 'war programme', the ABC's 'Listening Groups', established in 1939, helped to stimulate interest in current issues. The groups listened to specially prepared broadcasts, afterwards forwarding reports of their discussions to the ABC for comment.[44]

The Commission contemplated the introduction of 'Listening Groups' as early as 1935, but did nothing until 1938, when one member of the National Talks Advisory Committee, J. C. Proud, raised the subject at a meeting of the executive of the Australian Institute of International Affairs. A sub-committee of that executive designed a scheme similar to that eventually adopted by the ABC. However, the AIIA took no part in its formal organization. The University of Melbourne Extension Board was similarly of little help until the arrival of Colin Badger who secured the use of the University Extension Board Library for group members.[45]

A few experimental broadcasts in Victoria in June 1939 led eventually to the formation of fifty-seven groups.[46] In July, Proud produced the results of a questionnaire which suggested that the broadcasts were tapping different sections of the community from those covered by the University Extension and the Workers' Educational Association, notably isolated country listeners. Country groups contained as many as twenty-five members, some of whom were illiterate.⁴⁷ Proud's findings, together with evidence of the successful introduction of a similar scheme in Britain, persuaded the ABC to launch a full-scale 'Listening Groups' series in August 1939, though for the time being confining it to Victoria and New South Wales. G. Parry was appointed full-time organizer of the groups.⁴⁸

The talks offered to the 'Listening Groups' centred on general contemporary issues, such as 'Slum Clearance and its Problems', but a number bore direct relation to the war—'What Happened at Versailles?' or 'What Shall we do with Japan?'.⁴⁹ The scheme was not an outstanding success, it never really extended significantly beyond New South Wales and Victoria, and its successes were confined largely to the war years. Yet it did prove popular in the countryside, where by 1943 more than half of the 343 active groups were located, and the number of regular listeners, estimated at just under 5000 in August 1944, compared favourably on a population basis with Britain where 11 000 people were enrolled in groups.⁵⁰ Moreover, it did possibly reach a new type of listener. A survey of 500 group members in August 1940 revealed that the largest occupational group was manual workers: librarians, university lecturers, and journalists, all traditionally part of the educated elite, were very few in number.⁵¹

A serious problem for the wartime ABC was how to reconcile its commitment to uplifting cultural standards with complaints that ABC programmes were too dull for soldiers and civilians anxious to forget the present crisis.⁵² This was partly a continuation of the old 'highbrow' versus 'lowbrow' debate, but with a new twist: during wartime, public morale had to be maintained at all cost. The ABC did what it could to cater for public demand by employing popular entertainers such as Paul Jacklin, Dick Bentley, and Wilfrid Thomas to host after-dinner variety programmes.

Bentley is possibly the ABC's best-remembered wartime comedian. An Australian by birth, he had played the saxophone in 3LO's dance band in the late 1920s, and appeared in a number of radio revues and musical comedies in the 1930s. From 1938 to 1940, he toured Britain doing cabaret work, delighting audiences with his 'breezy, impudent, and chuckling comedy'.⁵³ In 1940 he returned to Australia, and for the next five years appeared frequently on both ABC and commercial radio. He became famous for his performances in 'Out of the Bag', 'Merry Go Round', and later in his own 'Dick Bentley Show'.⁵⁴ 'Merry Go Round' was one of the ABC's first audience-participation sessions, consisting of short plays, musical items and quiz segments, though after 1942, for security reasons, the quiz segment was eliminated.

Light entertainment received higher ABC priority in 1943 following Moses' return from active duty. Both Curtin and General Blamey pushed for more light entertainment, particularly in programmes for the Forces, and were instrumental in bringing Moses back to the ABC to do something about it.[55] Even before his return, in July 1942, a programme controllers' conference had recommended the establishment of a light entertainment department.[56] Wilfrid Thomas was appointed acting director of light entertainment in August 1943, but he failed to make an impact on ABC policy. Clewlow said of a report Thomas compiled in December 1943: 'it seems to say nothing but express pious hopes, which I seem to have heard on every occasion when light entertainment has been discussed.'[57] In March 1944, Moses directed Thomas to resume his job as a full-time broadcaster and replaced him with Harry Pringle (originally of the BBC).

The Forces programmes underwent a fairly drastic transformation as a result of these administrative adjustments. Bentley's and Thomas's variety programmes replaced some segments of 'serious' music and 'academic' talks, as did the 'Jack Benny Show', the BBC's 'Regimental Flashes', or performances by Gladys Moncrieff, the comedian Mo, and others.[58] But there was no revolution in ABC attitudes towards light entertainment. Programmes like the 'Amateur Hour', so popular in America and on Australian commercial radio, were considered unsuitable for the ABC because of the 'commercial' way they were presented.[59] There were also never any doubts that, for example, the 'crooning' of Bing Crosby and others was inappropriate for the ABC. When the BBC placed an embargo on 'crooning' in favour of more 'robust and virile' music, Clewlow said in support: 'I have long felt that the sentimental lyrics which seem so much a part of dance numbers were frankly aphrodisiac in character and often full of sexual argot.'[60] W. G. James, the federal controller of music, seems to have been the only senior executive to argue, on the grounds of listener popularity, that some 'crooning' should be retained in ABC programmes. Among other senior officers, support for more culturally uplifting programmes remained as strong as ever.[61]

Rural broadcasting was something of an anomaly. The new 'Country Hour' which began in April 1941 fitted ABC philosophies of public-service broadcasting, but the most famous segment of the programme from the beginning of 1944 was Gwen Meredith's serial, *The Lawsons,* undeniably of popular appeal.

The Lawsons was the ABC's first five-days-a-week serial. It gave glimpses into the life of a 'typical' Australian country family, partic-

5 Wartime Programming

ularly as they were affected by the war. In addition, it highlighted some general social issues, such as the marriage of a divorcee, and the marriage of Sue Lawson to an older man, Max Ralston. This last-mentioned event caused such great listener interest that Meredith had to compose lengthy expositions to be delivered by Sue, Max, and Sue's parents justifying the marriage.[62]

Meredith was a graduate of the University of Sydney who began writing plays as a member of the Chelsea Theatre Group in 1937, and who received her first taste of broadcasting success when listeners voted her play, *The Opportunist*, the best in an ABC play competition.[63] Her original contract, signed in 1943, directed that she should produce five episodes weekly of a 'Farm Hour' serial for a trial period of six months, but the amazing audience response ensured its continuance.[64] Nobody would have predicted that *The Lawsons*, later to be absorbed into the *Blue Hills* story, would continue for more than thirty-three years, reaching episode number 5795 on 30 September 1976!

General ABC radio drama remained during the war much as it had been during the 1930s. Listeners still heard large numbers of BBC recorded plays, and the standard thrillers and historical sagas of Barclay and Afford continued. Naturally a number of productions had war themes: Alexander Turner's *Wheat Boat*, for example, linked the arrival of Greek ships in Geraldton (Western Australia) with the ancient Greek fleet. Another of Turner's plays, *Neighbours*, told the story of Geraldton's evacuation, while his *Westward Journey* described the return of a soldier to his home town, Perth. Catherine Duncan's later famous *Sons of the Morning*, set in Crete during the German invasion, was broadcast in its original form first on the ABC. Other productions of these years, though not on war themes, established themselves as all-time classics. This was true, for example, of Douglas Stewart's account of the Scott Antarctic expedition, *The Fire on the Snow*, first broadcast on 6 June 1941. Stewart's other wartime successes included *Ned Kelly* and *The Golden Lover*.[65]

Plays roughly maintained their share of programme time from 1939 to 1945,[66] and they could, like some other sessions, serve both an escapist and a patriotic function. However, if there were any strong Australian nationalist literary responses to the 1939–45 war, they were not obviously reflected in ABC dramatical productions.

Perhaps more than anything else, Australians looked to the ABC during the war years for frequent, accurate, and objective news bulletins. A survey conducted by the *Broadcaster*, Western Australia's radio journal, in December 1939, revealed a clear preference for news broadcasts and information about the war above all other programmes.[67] Continued bickering between the ABC and the press delayed the conclusion of a permanent news agreement, but some gains were made: indeed, Dixon nowadays believes that there would have been no independent ABC news service had it not been for the war.[68]

On the night of 1 September, Moses had summoned senior officers to Broadcast House to discuss the ABC's responsibility for war news bulletins should Britain declare war on Germany. Rumours that the military might take control of all radio news services reached the ABC the following day, but this never happened.[69] Instead, to ensure adequate coverage of the war, Sir Henry Gullett called a conference between representatives of the ABC, the Postmaster-General's Department, the Federation of Commercial Broadcasting Stations, Australian Associated Press, and Consolidated Press. Among those to attend were Cleary, Brookes, Moses, Dixon, Sir Keith Murdoch, and H. P. Brown. All speakers indicated their willingness to co-operate in the production of good war news broadcasts; Murdoch gave assurances that the press especially would not stand in the way. It was agreed that both ABC and commercial stations could relay BBC news sessions, and the ABC agreed to pay AAP and CP £2500 and £500 per annum respectively for the right to broadcast 200 cabled words of overseas news per day. For the first time, the ABC was permitted to broadcast its evening news bulletin at 7 p.m.[70]

The ABC extended its contacts with BBC news operations by sending R. C. McCall, then ABC manager for Victoria, to London to help with the production of the BBC's overseas news services. A. Mason, since 1932 on retainer to the ABC in London, was appointed full-time ABC representative.

Murdoch abandoned his assurances of co-operation upon his appointment as director-general of information in July 1940. He transferred the production of the 7 p.m. news bulletin to Melbourne, under the direct control of the DOI, and used newspaper men to compile the bulletins. Cleary was furious, as were many of the public who complained of deteriorating standards in news bulletins. Public outcry plus continued representations from Cleary finally resulted in the transfer of news production back to the ABC. For a short while, Murdoch still insisted on the material being prepared in Melbourne, but eventually everything was returned to Sydney.[71]

The news service arrangements were reviewed in February 1942, to take account of the changed war situation and the Curtin government's greater independence of outlook. On 16 February, the ABC

5 Wartime Programming

prefaced its 7 p.m. news session with 'Advance Australia Fair', replacing 'The British Grenadiers'. This was just one of the changes to result from a conference called earlier that month. Other initiatives included the introduction of a national news session from Canberra. It was to be broadcast by the ABC three times daily and relayed by all commercial stations. The ABC's federal roundsman, Warren Denning, was to conduct the 'Canberra Calling' session, which would precede the BBC news.[72] Denning was the author of several books on political history. He had worked previously on the Melbourne *Star*, the *Herald*, the *Daily Telegraph*, and other newspapers, and at the outbreak of the war was the Canberra representative of Australian United Press as well as being on retainer to the ABC.[73] The press viewed Denning's new appointment as an unwelcome intrusion of the ABC into the field of news gathering, but before the war was over Denning came to be accepted by the other journalists and gained election to the Parliamentary Press Gallery Committee.[74]

There was always a danger in wartime that only news favourable to the government would be broadcast. It was easy to justify censorship on the grounds of national security, but the temptation for the government to use the national news bulletins for its own ends was overwhelming. On 21 September 1939, Curtin declared his hope that there would not be a repetition of the censorship abuses of the last war;[75] but inevitably they occurred.

In the first two months of 1940, 5½ per cent of news sessions comprised ministerial statements.[76] Under the Labor government, things became almost impossible for a time. Too many Labor ministers, especially H. V. Evatt and Beasley, treated the Canberra news session as a forum for eulogizing themselves and the work of their departments. On 4 January 1942, Beasley demanded that the ABC interrupt a radio play to broadcast his statement, omitted from the 7 p.m. news bulletin, on the new Allied command. The statement was not broadcast until the following morning, with the result that Cleary and Bearup were summoned to a fiery meeting with Beasley, Evatt, and W. P. Ashley. Yet the only outcome of the meeting was a direction to inject more Australian and south-west Pacific content into ABC news sessions.[77] On 28 January, Molesworth explained to the National Talks Advisory Committee the need to avoid any criticism of the government's attempt to awaken Britain and America to the importance of the war in the Pacific. The Committee responded by asking the Commission to continue news commentaries only so long as government direction was confined to the exclusion of 'hostile comments on Government war policy';

should the government go so far as to 'dictate comment', the ABC might 'consider the desirability of advising the transference of the News Commentaries to a Government Spokesman announced as such'.[78]

When one listener complained that ABC news sessions were no longer objective—for example, they constantly highlighted attacks on Churchill—Bearup's reply suggested that the government was influencing the content of news broadcasts. The ABC, he said, was not 'entirely responsible' for all broadcasts: the minister had overriding authority, but he added that it would be improper to indicate whether such authority had been exercised.[79]

The UAP-Country Party opposition derived political mileage from Labor's abuse of ABC news sessions, condemning the 'Canberra Calling' programme as government propaganda.[80] By July 1942, the government censor could write: 'the people are becoming distrustful of official news disseminated by press and radio';[81] however ministers' eagerness to have their statements in news bulletins eventually subsided, and ABC news was still considered more reliable than news from other sources.

In July 1944, feeling the financial strain of wartime, the ABC asked for payment and acknowledgement from commercial stations for the right to continue taking ABC news bulletins.[82] No new agreement was reached then, nor at a later conference in January 1945. The commercial stations had ideas of substituting for the ABC news sessions one provided by the newspapers, but the government thwarted their plans by refusing to supply land lines for anything other than the receipt of ABC news. Menzies called the government's decision 'socialism by force, with a vengeance'.[83] The *Sydney Morning Herald* alleged that this was merely censorship in a new guise.[84] Maybe it was, but Labor's decision to back the ABC at this point was consistent with its desire to see, ultimately, the establishment of an independent ABC news service.

A corollary of the ABC's continuing fight with the press was the conflict over the publication of an ABC programme journal. On 27 January 1939, the *Sydney Morning Herald, Daily Telegraph, Sun*, and *Daily News* notified the ABC that, as of 1 February, they would cease to publish free of charge ABC programme schedules. Rather than pay the high cost of advertising, the ABC decided to publish its own journal, something along the lines of the British *Listener*.[85] There were no legislative obstacles to this action, but the newspapers embarked on a vicious campaign against the journal. *Smith's Weekly* denounced it as a 'socialistic' enterprise.[86]

5 Wartime Programming

The press urged Cabinet to intervene. Although government approval was neither required nor sought, the matter was discussed by Cabinet on 15 March. Menzies, under pressure from the press, tried hard to block the project, but the postmaster-general, Harrison, himself in favour of the journal, persuaded Cabinet to approve the scheme.[87]

When questioned in the House two months later, on 24 May, Harrison said that no decision on the journal had yet been reached.[88] Menzies probably prevented a public announcement at this stage, hoping still to stop the publication ever reaching the streets. But despite a further letter from newspaper proprietors to Menzies in June, the first edition of the *ABC Weekly* appeared in December 1939.[89]

The press eventually played down their propaganda campaign against the *Weekly* (or '*Weakly*' as *Smith's Weekly* called it) after realizing that this merely served to advertise it,[90] but through their powerful network they did manage to disrupt its distribution and sale. Booksellers and newsagents did not push the journal, and sales fell far short of the estimated 100 000 per week.[91] There were other problems, especially costs. The journal received very little advertising, even from the DOI. Heavy losses were an embarrassment for the ABC which had to justify such expenditure during the austerities expected in wartime. Some politicians had argued from the start that it would have been cheaper to advertise programmes in the press than to publish a separate journal.[92] The ABC thought otherwise, especially Moses, and considered some loss was justified since the journal was the ABC's main advertising outlet and was, in addition, a public service. This view was accepted by the Gibson Committee which suggested that a loss of £30 000 per annum was not unreasonable.[93] The press continually misrepresented the journal's financial standing and put losses as high as £60 000 per annum, but actual losses were very close to the Gibson Committee's figure: £32 807 for the year ended 30 June 1941.[94] Nevertheless, the financial aspect was worrying for the ABC. It was rumoured that another reason for Moses' decision to enlist was to avoid further fighting with Cleary over the size of the *Weekly*'s losses.[95] Cleary had resisted the idea of a journal in 1936, but had been persuaded of its merits by 1939. Once committed there had been no stopping him, but he was concerned that the sales figures differed so markedly from Moses' estimates.[96] Perhaps therefore, Moses wished to be out of the government firing line as the financial losses continued to climb.

On 6 June 1941, Cabinet decided, on financial grounds, to direct the suspension of the *ABC Weekly* for the duration of the war, but the journal received a reprieve following considerable opposition in the House. Within the ABC, few doubted that the decision to suspend had been taken in response to further pressure from newspaper interests.⁹⁷

The journal limped on for the remainder of the 1940s and into the 1950s when it was replaced by the *TV Times*. As a programme guide it was adequate, but it never approached anything like an Australian *Listener*. Various radio talks were reprinted, but much space was taken up by advertisements from commercial stations, a necessary evil that had to be included to keep the *Weekly*'s losses within reasonable limits. The publication of the journal was, above all, an exercise in standing up to interference in ABC affairs.⁹⁸

Censorship and political interference posed constant threats to ABC independence during the war. When war first broke out, amateur radio operators had their transmitting licences withdrawn, and all national and commercial radio stations were placed under tight security censorship. The government, after some hesitation, did not close down the commercials, though in January 1941 it revoked the licences of four stations—5AU, 5KA, 4AT, and 2HD—because of their affiliation with the Jehovah's Witness Church, itself declared an illegal organization.⁹⁹ Some ABC utility broadcasts, such as weather reports, were eliminated, and the mandatory pre-recording of audience participation sessions fourteen days in advance created new costs. The Commission contemplated eliminating German-language and Italian-language broadcasts, and did for a very short period, but there were no attempts to delete 'enemy' classical music from programmes. ABC stations closed earlier during the war, and at one stage the state of hostilities in the Pacific caused the suspension of ABC broadcasts in northern Queensland.¹

It was hard to avoid the occasional breach of censorship restrictions. In 1941, the ABC was reprimanded for broadcasting news of the sinking of HMAS *Sydney*. The circumstances illustrate the difficulties of wartime broadcasting. On the day in question, the ABC arranged to broadcast from a school in Melbourne. The headmaster, having learned of the *Sydney*'s loss from elsewhere, urged his pupils to sing 'God Save the King' with increased feeling in view of the tragedy. Censorship authorities had placed a radio ban on the incident and the ABC was thus caught red-faced. To cover itself with the government, the ABC decided to discipline the manager for Victoria, C. C. Wicks, for allowing the breach to occur, and did so by transferring him to South Australia!²

5 Wartime Programming

In view of the ABC's experience with 'The Watchman' during the 1930s, it is not surprising that a policy of extreme caution was adopted in relation to talks delivered during the war. The close liaison with government departments, such as the DOI, also increased the opportunities for political direction or influence. In July 1941, for example, the ABC decided to remodel the 'All Australia Session', hitherto a joint production of the ABC and the DOI. K. T. Henderson was appointed editor of special talks and placed in charge of the new series, now called 'Tomorrow's World', which was to include talks comparing Allied aims with those of Hitler. The change displeased the DOI which ceased to share control of the series from that time. However, the DOI again offered its assistance six months later when the series was reoriented more to discussing 'what's happening now' than to speculation about the future.[3] It is interesting that this reorientation took place during the Gibson Committee's deliberations. As Henderson wrote to Clewlow in February 1942: 'while the relations between the Government and the Commission remain uncertain, it would be necessary, I think, to seek for "harmless" themes when discussing war changes in the light of their future possibilities.'[4]

There is evidence that ABC officials were too cautious. Moses was to complain late in 1944 that the Talks Department, under Molesworth, had adopted an 'unduly conservative attitude' towards the deletion of contentious material.[5] A War Talks Register was installed at all ABC branches to record the essential details of every talk delivered, and all scripts had to be submitted to Molesworth's office for approval, regardless of whether they related to the war effort or touched on a political subject.[6]

Even precautions such as these did not prevent public criticism. The complaints of the 1930s, that people should not be permitted to express personal opinions over ABC stations, grew louder in wartime. In February 1940, *Century* condemned the ABC for allowing a Communist Party member to speak on the Soviets and the inevitability of world revolution. In what can only be described as an astounding conclusion, the editorial observed: 'If ever proof was required of the collusion between the UAP and the Communist Party it is surely provided by the action of the Commission in permitting this remarkable and insidious broadcast.'[7] This statement was typical of much of the ill-informed and naive criticism which was levelled at the ABC.

Greater government control over the media was to be expected in wartime, but the ABC's main concern was the use of security censorship for partisan political purposes. With the outbreak of war, the postmaster-general's power to prohibit or command broadcasts was extended to permit the censorship of any item 'if it appears to a Minister to be necessary or expedient so to do in the interests of public safety, the defence of the Commonwealth or the efficient prosecution of the war, or for maintaining supplies and services essential to the life of the community'.[8] In March 1941, Cabinet also approved an amendment to the broadcasting Act which read: 'The Minister may from time to time by notice in writing direct the Commission to refrain from any action taken or proposed to be taken under the powers conferred by this Act'.[9] However, the amendment lapsed due to other wartime priorities. Cleary was determined to resist any abuse of ministerial wartime powers, and stated in his annual report for 1941/2 that the ABC would not become 'merely the mechanical mouth-piece of war-time agencies or government departments'.[10] But the pressure from government was fierce.

Paul Hasluck claims that the extension of censorship to political items and the increase in ministerial interference came only after the change to a Labor government late in 1941.[11] Certainly, some of Curtin's ministers did seem to regard the ABC as their personal publicity station, but the record of the Menzies government was little better. A broadcast by R. W. G. MacKay, a member of the British Labour Party, was abandoned in March 1941 after the government censors emasculated the script. The ABC, in accordance with regulations, had submitted the script, 'The Kind of Peace Britain is Fighting For', to the state publicity censor, H. A. Rorke, who had returned it with twelve major deletions. Two of the offending passages were 'the causes of war must be recognised as being the responsibility, not of one nation alone, but of the international conditions in which all people live and of which the Germans, like ourselves, are equally the victims' and 'people want to be assured that, having won the war, we shall not waste the victory by ruining the peace'.[12] While the ABC considered whether to appeal to the chief publicity censor, both Menzies and his minister for information, H. S. Foll, denied in Parliament that the censorship was political.[13] Rorke's explanation to the chief publicity censor suggests otherwise. He told his superior:

> When a man stands on the hustings and tells people to be sure that they know what they are fighting for, and that if they do fight it should be with a view to obtaining better conditions—such statements being along Communistic lines—then I am of the opinion that such matter is not political, but subversive.[14]

Rorke was entitled to this opinion, but in judging the talk to be

5   Wartime Programming

subversive he was making a judgement of political philosophy rather than one of national security. It is significant that when a copy of the script was presented to another state censor, C. Burns, he could uphold only two of the twelve deletions on security grounds.[15]

In July 1940, again when the UAP-Country Party government was in office, the ABC had to defend a talk by C. Barclay-Smith on Douglas Social Credit, part of a series entitled 'This Tangled World —Ways Out'. The government complained that it could hinder attempts to raise finance for the war effort and demanded that the series be stopped.[16] Postmaster-general Thorby's actual instructions were that 'anything in the nature of talks cutting across the grain of Government policy was not to go over; there were to be no talks on controversial political subjects against the Government.'[17]

There was also some significance in the fact that, in March 1942, Curtin could quote Cleary as saying 'No instruction has been given by the present Government to the commission that criticism of domestic and political policy or actions should be suppressed'.[18] That was more than could be said for the non-Labor coalition government which, on 21 September 1939, had threatened to cut 'The Watchman' off the air.[19]

Yet there is no denying that a number of Labor ministers abused their positions by demanding to broadcast statements ostensibly connected with the war. Some ministers were merely making up for the frustrations of the 1930s when, so they believed, the Labor Party had been denied access to ABC stations.[20] But this does not excuse an amazing incident involving the minister for the army, F. M. Forde, in February 1943, when the minister for information invoked his powers to enable Forde to broadcast a talk, 'The Australian Army'. The ABC did not see the script beforehand, and the request for time came more in the form of an order. In the event, the talk turned out to be a statement in support of the government's militia Bill currently being debated in the House. Cleary was furious and protested in the strongest terms.[21]

The Forde incident occurred even after the publication of the Gibson Committee's report which criticized the high number of ministerial broadcasts, and which recommended that only the prime minister and the leader of the opposition should deliver statements free of censorship.[22] The point to be emphasized is that while political interference was frequent during the war years, it had occurred before, and it continued after the war was over; and despite Hasluck's assertion, the political colour of the government made little difference.

Controversy was not confined to political items. Because public outcry could be just as great on matters of morality, the ABC refrained from broadcasting a number of popular songs in 1940, including 'She had to go and lose it at the Astor' and 'No wonder she's a blushing bride'. If anything adventurous were broadcast, the ABC had to answer to the government and to bodies such as the Good Film and Radio Vigilance League. In September 1941, the secretary of the Vigilance League complained about the 'Salacious and erotic matter' in camp concert programmes, which allegedly was undermining national morale. Mrs Eleanor Glencross, the League's president, attacked the 'immoral' content of Sunday-night plays, and the vice-president, the Rev. A. E. West, condemned the broadcasting of sacrilegious jokes. West particularly objected to a recently broadcast song, 'The 'Ole in the Ark', which began 'The Ark sprang a leak and Noah sat on the 'ole until the Ark reached Ararat'.[23] Fortunately for listeners, Cleary had a sense of humour. Before the Gibson Committee he said:

> If one were to try to tone down all broadcasting, so that there would be no rough edge anywhere—I do not mean indecency, but that everything should be uplift; the sort of thing you could say only in front of God or the vicar—broadcasting would suffer. Life has to be balanced; it is a mosaic. ... I think that dullness is in many ways a greater menace to intellectual progress, sometimes to spiritual progress, than so-called sharpness or roughness of edge or wit.[24]

He gave the above defence specifically in relation to Dick Bentley's jokes on 'Merry Go Round', which he sometimes had to defend even against the attacks of ABC officers, particularly Clewlow and Bearup who disapproved of his 'infantile indecencies' and reliance on 'smut'.[25]

The largest controversy during the war years related to a debate on birth control in August 1944, presented as part of William Macmahon Ball's series, 'Nation's Forum of the Air'. Entitled 'Population Unlimited', the debate had as its principal speakers, Dame Enid Lyons, a Mr Clarke, and at the centre of the controversy, Dr Norman Haire. Haire advocated greater use of contraception in Australia, citing the problem of his own mother who had aged prematurely after giving birth to eleven children. Clarke had then countered with the assertions that acts of contraception were 'filthy, vicious, and disgusting', that they constituted 'one of the worst forms of sexual immorality', and that contraception 'had always been recognized as a moral wrong by the natural instincts of all decent men and women'. Haire replied that Clarke's views were 'determined by the peculiar religious superstitions of the church to

5 Wartime Programming

which he belongs'.[26] The next day, the ABC found itself in the midst of a sizeable controversy. Moses defended the broadcast, as did Cleary,[27] but a number of listeners and politicians were not satisfied.

Most of the complaints received by the ABC came from predictable sources. Some were from clergymen, but the majority came from organizations such as the Women's Christian Temperance Union and the League of Catholic Women.[28] The latter considered Haire's views an insult to all women, and, together with the Rev. W. Hobbin, objected that people with such beliefs were given a hearing on the ABC.[29] Yet of the letters received at ABC Head Office, there were fourteen protests and thirty-two statements of approval.[30] The ABC managers for Western Australia, South Australia, Tasmania, and Queensland all reported favourable reactions to the broadcast in their respective states,[31] but this did not spare Cleary from some eight months of public odium.

The parliamentary debate on Haire's broadcast was opened by Senator Nash who inquired whether Haire's views were 'offensive to decent-living citizens' and 'calculated to undermine family life, which is the basis of order in society?'.[32] Some members expressed indignation at the fact that Haire had sunk 'so low as to discredit his mother'.[33] Of course, he had done no such thing: he merely pointed out her suffering. But the senators were convinced that Haire was a dangerous, undesirable type—his attacks on his mother proved that —and argued that he should be denied further access to ABC facilities. Senator Amour noted, irrelevantly, that 'Some of our finest women are the mothers of large families'; Senator Cameron called Haire 'despicable'; Senator O'Flaherty labelled him 'not human'; and Senator Foll, though forced to admit he had not actually heard the broadcast, voiced his disagreement with it all the same, and suggested that the government should use the ABC to encourage people to increase the size of their families.[34]

The issue did not end there. Cleary was called to give evidence before a parliamentary inquiry in February 1945. He repeated the point, made *ad nauseam* since the beginning of his chairmanship, that views expressed over the air were those of the speaker and not those of the ABC, but his well-argued defence fell on deaf ears. That the politicians missed the point became obvious when Senator Nash asked whether Cleary was implying on behalf of the ABC that contraception should be practised in Australia.[35]

The ABC's defence of Haire was a brave act and indicates that the Commission was more willing to challenge government interference on matters of morality and taste than it was on items more obviously political. At the same time, it is understandable, in view of the reaction to Haire, why the ABC continued, indeed hardened, its resolve not to create a fuss if possible.

Religious broadcasts brought their share of trouble for the ABC. Air time had always been allocated to churches according to their number of adherents as revealed by the Commonwealth census. The ABC rejected the idea of an advisory committee to allot time to each church, out of fear that sectarian squabbling would prevail.[36] There were fifteen-minute devotional broadcasts each weekday on the ABC and live broadcasts of a church service each Sunday at 9.30 and 11 a.m. Cleary, personally, had no interest in increasing the number of purely devotional style broadcasts, but his main concern was the fact that the scripts were not subject to ABC scrutiny. In the early years of the ABC's history, the Rev. T. Ruth took advantage of this situation to denounce from his pulpit ABC cocktail parties, which he believed promoted a bad image. Cleary, powerless to prevent a repetition of the incident, could do little except fume privately.[37]

On some religious programmes it was possible to have more say. In November 1942, Professor H. A. Woodruff attempted to use the 'Pleasant Sunday Afternoon' session to denounce the evils of drink. Unlike the devotional services, this session was subject to ABC editing. The Commission rejected the script because it attacked the use of liquor, not just the abuse. Station 3DB later broadcast the talk after prompting from the Rev. Irving Benson who also complained to the press about the power of liquor interests in the ABC, an unfair reference to Cleary's former associations with Tooth's Brewery. The press and the churches attacked the ABC's veto, but Cleary stood firm, on this occasion scoring a victory for the ABC's power to control programme content.[38]

Cleary once dismissed a government suggestion that the ABC should accommodate itself to the wishes of the churches rather than vice versa.[39] An additional problem of leaving broadcasts entirely in church hands was that few clergy knew much about the ingredients of a good broadcast. Many clergy spoke with 'parson's voice', an intonation that sounded artificial and monotonous to some listeners.[40] From 1943 to 1944, Henderson toured all state capitals discussing with church leaders, among other things, presentation problems, but there were limits to what the ABC could do in this area. More importantly, Henderson concluded an agreement with the churches granting the ABC control over 15 per cent of religious broadcasts, the remaining 85 per cent being left to the heads of recognized denominations.[41] But Cleary could do nothing about Sunday devotional broadcasts, for his hands were tied by the govern-

5 Wartime Programming

ment's support of the Gibson Committee's comment: 'Any question of providing an alternative entertainment programme at this generally recognized hour for religious observance is surely unworthy of consideration in the national broadcasting service of a Christian country.'[42]

The ABC had its most sustained contact with government departments while involved in the production of overseas propaganda, which unlike that for domestic consumption, served a specifically military function.

AWA had experimented with overseas shortwave broadcasts since 1927. Cabinet refused to grant the company a licence to operate a permanent overseas service, and when war broke out cancelled even the experimental licence.[43] On 18 October 1939, after British government requests for Australia to help counter German radio propaganda, Cabinet agreed to set up an official shortwave broadcasting service, but it did not settle immediately the problem of control.[44]

As the established national broadcasting authority, the ABC wanted full responsibility for the service. Cleary put this view to the postmaster-general, Harrison, in October 1939. Harrison concurred and drew up a submission for Cabinet. But it was Sir Henry Gullett who persuaded Cabinet that, for the duration of the war, primary responsibility should rest with his department.[45]

At a conference in December, Gullett devised a 'co-operative' plan for the production of shortwave transmissions. The DOI would prepare all the material to be included, the ABC would present the programme, providing announcers and translation services as required, and the Postmaster-General's Department would provide technical assistance.[46] In addition, the DOI was to operate a 'Listening Post' in Melbourne, to monitor and transcribe broadcasts from overseas on a 24-hour basis.[47]

Australia's overseas shortwave service was officially inaugurated by Menzies on 20 December 1939. 'The time has come for Australia to speak for herself' he began, and then pointed to the need to counter foreign propaganda.[48] Following the precedent set by AWA, 'Australia Calling' broadcasts were introduced with the laugh of the kookaburra. The service began on an ambitious scale with transmissions in English, French, German, Dutch, and Italian being beamed to parts of Europe, the Americas, India and South Africa. These arrangements, especially the number and destination of the broadcasts, were reviewed throughout the war, according to the military situation.[49]

The struggle for control of the service had not ended. In January

1940, the ABC produced a document outlining the shortcomings of dual responsibility for overseas broadcasts. It criticized the unnecessary duplication and emphasized that ABC staff were 'experienced broadcasters and better able to devise interesting programmes'.[50]

The DOI did not agree. William Macmahon Ball, appointed controller of the shortwave division of the DOI in February 1940, resented suggestions that ABC staff were more competent at producing broadcasting material than he was, and argued that the writing, translation, and presentation of propaganda should be one process under the control of one authority, preferably his division. He conceded that there was probably less chance of political interference with the ABC in control, but said the real problem was money. The ABC, he argued, received no special grant for overseas broadcasts and would be unwilling to sacrifice the interests of Australian licence-fee payers by spending their money on the development of shortwave programmes.[51] While the ABC did not view finance as an obstacle, it did consider that there should be some reimbursement from Treasury if it assumed full control of the overseas service.[52]

The government's decision, in June 1941, to concentrate shortwave operations in Melbourne (where DOI headquarters were located) seemed to strengthen the DOI's case for control. Ball was even authorized to second ABC staff to work in Melbourne with him.[53] But the ABC received an opportunity to attack the move to Melbourne in giving evidence to the Gibson Committee. At the inquiry, it criticized the DOI's 'invasion' of the practical broadcasting field, which created the prospect of a national broadcasting department with a vested interest in survival after the war.[54]

The control issue became more heated after the fall of Singapore in February, when shortwave propaganda assumed increased significance in Australian defence strategy. A few weeks earlier, when Japanese victory had appeared imminent, Cleary, Bearup, Ball, and C. H. Holmes (the director of information) were summoned to a meeting with Evatt, Ashley, and Beasley and subjected to considerable verbal abuse. Holmes walked out of the meeting and soon after tendered his resignation. The ABC was accused of carrying on as if it were still peacetime. Out of the meeting emerged a modified form of dual control: shortwave news bulletins were to be the ABC's responsibility; propaganda as such would remain the responsibility of the DOI. Ball suffered no loss of responsibility. He retained his status as controller of shortwave broadcasting and, for all practical purposes, remained responsible to Calwell and Evatt.[55]

5 Wartime Programming

Evatt had no intention of allowing the ABC to opt out of the propaganda field altogether. He told Cleary that the government expected the ABC to counter BBC 'Atlantic first' propaganda with ABC 'Pacific propaganda'.[56] Cleary transmitted these instructions to his senior officers, which suggests that he was prepared to tolerate direction on matters of war policy, but his co-operation might also have related to fears about the ABC's future should he resist. The Gibson Committee's report was due in just over one month's time, and for all Cleary knew it might recommend the abolition of the ABC or full ministerial control of broadcasting.

The ABC could contribute little to propaganda production without a policy lead from the government. Few leads were forthcoming until, in July 1942, the government established yet another body, the Political Warfare Committee, to co-ordinate the propaganda war against Japan. The committee comprised representatives of the Australian chiefs of staff, and the departments of Defence, Information, and External Affairs. Like other government wartime agencies, it had its share of departmental and personal rivalries, but it did effect the creation of a Political Warfare Section within the Department of External Affairs which, among other things, serviced the Political Warfare Committee. Geoffrey Sawer, one of Ball's staff, frequently acted as the DOI's representative on the Political Warfare Committee. Some years later, he described his responsibilities on that Committee as being to ensure that the directives of the government 'duly blossomed' into appropriate propaganda broadcasts.[57]

At times, it was difficult to know exactly which responsibilities lay with the DOI, which with the ABC, and which with the Political Warfare Committee or the Department of External Affairs. Even the ABC had to ask for clarification.[58] Ball was rather disappointed with the Political Warfare Committee (of which he was a member) and soon tired of all the bureaucratic manoeuvrings. On 2 September 1942, he wrote to a colleague:

> Off the record, I get a bit annoyed with all these discussions about the right machinery for political warfare. We have in our own way, and often in a pretty poor and amateurish way, been carrying on political warfare for two and a half years. If we had waited till we had got the right machinery we would never have done anything.[59]

The problem of control of overseas propaganda was not solved before the end of the war. The Gibson Committee and a later parliamentary standing committee on broadcasting recommended that full control be vested in the ABC, but on 25 March 1944 the government transferred full responsibility back to the DOI. As the war drew on, the Department of External Affairs began to desire a greater say in the content of shortwave broadcasts;[60] however the big clashes with External Affairs did not take place until after the war. The ABC, never quite sure where it stood in this complex bureaucratic struggle, emerged the ultimate victor in 1950 when it gained permanent control of 'Radio Australia'.

In the meantime, the overseas propaganda service had to operate under a number of handicaps besides divided control. Money was short, and a few people had to do the work of many. Ball himself handled a huge workload. From the outset, the service lacked qualified staff, especially foreign-language experts. Ball had to engage staff from Britain to produce Thai and Mandarin broadcasts in July 1942.[61] Similarly, after the commencement of transmissions in Japanese to New Guinea and the Pacific, the government had to engage D. Tokamasa, an American citizen and former attaché to the Japanese legation in Canberra, and Sgts J. Masuda and P. Sumida from the United States Army.[62] The situation for European-language broadcasts was not as critical. The ABC had Dr Kurt Offenburg, former correspondent for the *Frankfurter Zeitung* in the Far East and a naturalized Australian. Offenburg's proficiency in both English and German was exceptional. He had translated Chaucer's *Canterbury Tales* and had written several novels in both languages. Early in 1940, he was engaged to write talks directed at Germany, and he also wrote propaganda for inclusion in overseas news bulletins. Ball was glad to accept his offer to write propaganda for the DOI.[63]

The propaganda service had technical problems. Until 1942, only three shortwave transmitters were available: VLR in Victoria and VLW in Western Australia, both of a mere 2 kw power, and VLQ in Sydney (belonging to AWA) still only of 10 kw power. There was little point in preparing high standard material for overseas listeners if the broadcasts were never heard, or if so only faintly or with interference. Ball urged the government to construct a 100-kw transmitter, claiming in February 1941 that the time had come for Australia to decide whether or not propaganda was to be a major part of the war effort. The recently inaugurated shortwave broadcasts from Tokyo and from Shanghai needed rebuttal, he argued, and there was also the possibility of damage to BBC transmitters during the imminent blitzkrieg, which could place new responsibilities on Australia.[64]

The government finally agreed to build three 100-kw transmitters, later reducing this to two when the United States offered to

5 Wartime Programming

make available a 50-kw transmitter at Shepparton, Victoria. But slow action meant that for some considerable time, Australia would continue to counter enemy transmitters of 100 and 50 kw with Australian transmitters of 10 and 2 kw.[65]

Censorship was a further restraint. There is no evidence that Australia's censorship was more restrictive than that imposed overseas,[66] but it is true that the chief censor, E. G. Bonney, was an extremely zealous public servant. A confidant of senior government ministers, he used his position to protect the government's reputation as much as that of Australia. Curtin gave him power to initiate prosecutions, which led to a number of controversies, but most of them are outside the scope of this book.[67] The instructions Bonney issued in relation to broadcasting were invariably vague, with neither the ABC nor Ball's division knowing how to interpret them.[68] Ball also thought the censors frequently overstepped the mark. 'The basic question', he wrote in 1942, 'is whether the Government desires Censorship or this Department to be responsible for determining the propaganda lines of overseas shortwave broadcasts'. He raised no objections to cuts on security grounds, only those meant to 'improve' the propaganda.[69]

Despite all the obstacles to smooth programming, by the end of 1942, DOI/ABC propaganda broadcasts were being carried out in French to Indo-China, in Mandarin to Chungking, in Malay and Dutch to the Netherlands East Indies, in Thai to Bangkok, and in Japanese to New Guinea and the South Pacific (these last broadcasts were also received in Japan and on the coast of China).[70]

The broadcasts mostly comprised news bulletins and short talks. The Political Warfare Committee suggested propaganda lines which were derived mainly from the British and American 'Plan for Political Warfare against Japan', aim one of which was 'To weaken the foundations of the Japanese war machine—military, economic, political and psychological'.[71] Unlike the racist anti-Japanese propaganda broadcast to civilian Australians during the early stages of the Pacific war, overseas propaganda talks emphasized two themes: first, that the Japanese could not hope to win the war because of their faulty and dishonourable leadership; second, that defeat and surrender were consistent with national and personal honour.[72] The propaganda was meant to help Australian and American military operations and to counter Japanese broadcasts proclaiming the ability of the peoples of Asia under Japanese leadership to throw off European rulers, the encouragement Japan would give to old cultural and religious traditions, and Japan's destiny to bring prosperity and peace to Asia.[73]

One of the dilemmas facing Australian propaganda writers was how to emphasize Japanese weaknesses without simultaneously weakening Australian demands for more American military assistance. As Ball put it:

> If, in describing the situation in the South-West Pacific, we broadcast only the grave warnings of Japanese strength, and Australia's weakness, we cut at the roots of our political warfare campaign in East Asia; if we broadcast news and comment about increasing success in this area and Japanese increasing difficulties, this policy may run counter to the Government's efforts to gain more aid from U.S.A.[74]

Every effort was made to ensure that propaganda levelled no criticisms at ordinary Japanese soldiers, in case they were discouraged from surrendering. For similar reasons, any suggestions of revenge were excluded.[75] Hence a broadcast on the treatment of Allied prisoners-of-war, rather than focus on the excesses of Japanese prison guards, was presented thus:

> We ask Japanese soldiers to consider carefully a statement recently made by your government. Your government has threatened to punish severely, even by death, American or Australian or British airmen who are taken prisoner after having bombed Japanese cities or areas occupied by your forces. We ask you to consider whether this policy is consistent with the honour of the Japanese army and with the precept of the Emperor Meiji.[76]

Unlike the Japanese, at no time did the Australian government use prisoners-of-war for propaganda purposes. General MacArthur rejected this approach, fearing that the Japanese command might believe the broadcasts were made under duress and carry out retaliations.[77]

Was Australia's propaganda effective? Did the ABC's contribution help to win the war? Such questions are virtually impossible to answer. It has been suggested that

> short-wave radio as a propaganda medium is too fraught with technical and other difficulties and is beamed from too remote a source ever to be of outstanding success as a moulding agent of public opinion. Even in peace-time the short-wave audience is too small; in war-time, the conditions too abnormal.[78]

Briggs has argued that German propaganda, usually regarded as brilliantly successful under Dr Goebbels' guidance, actually had 'relatively little effect' except when it was 'closely geared to the operational needs of military campaigns'. He has dismissed even the

5 Wartime Programming

notorious broadcasts of 'Lord Haw-Haw' as being 'largely a failure'.[79] But what of Australia's broadcasts, specifically? It was reported, during the war, that American listeners regarded Australia's shortwave service as 'perhaps the spiciest in the world, better even than Hitler, when he really goes to town'; in Noumea and in New Caledonia, nine out of ten houses were said to tune in to Radio Australia. But there is no means of determining exactly why people listened, or whether they were influenced by what they heard. Many letters received from shortwave listeners were from enthusiastic fans who wrote to obtain a listener's certificate from Radio Australia.[80] Yet we should not dismiss overseas propaganda broadcasts out of hand. Certainly they were 'fraught with technical and other difficulties', but by August 1944, largely because of the efforts of the Political Warfare Committee, the 50-kw transmitter at Shepparton was in use and this wattage seems to have been adequate for transmissions to Asia.[81] There were also various testimonies to the good reception and alleged usefulness of the propaganda. After the war, MacArthur paid tribute to the role Australia's 'Philippine Hour' played in encouraging resistance to the Japanese.[82] And in September 1945, Sgt Masuda, a prejudiced but nonetheless intelligent observer, wrote from the Philippines:

> I hear that the Japanese garrison in Manila used to listen to Japanese language broadcasts from Melbourne with great interest. The words 'Melbourne Broadcast' are often mentioned in their paper 'Shimbu Shudan'. Melbourne broadcasts in Japanese were apparently well regarded by the Japanese garrison because they avoided the use of words such as 'enemy' and reference to the Emperor.[83]

It might be argued that the ABC's role in the Australian war effort was irrelevant because the willingness of Australians to adapt to total war conditions stemmed more from fear of Japanese invasion than from home-front propaganda. And even if the latter were important, perhaps it was the commercial stations to which most people listened and which therefore ultimately had the most impact. These are powerful arguments which cannot be dismissed, and they only underline the fact that it is difficult to reach definite conclusions about radio's 'impact' on the community, during war or at any other time.

The importance of the Japanese invasion threat *vis-à-vis* Australian mental adjustments to the war is undeniable. Nor would there be any point in denying the hold which commercial radio had gained on the Australian community during the 1930s and which probably increased during the war years: the rise in licensed listener households, despite shortages of radio parts, reflected a growing attachment to radio generally, not just to the ABC.[84]

Nonetheless, we can at least infer that ABC broadcasts informed Australian opinions, thus helping to maintain, perhaps improve, the war effort. During all wars there is an almost insatiable thirst for news. Given the ABC's rising reputation for impartial and accurate news bulletins, it is not unreasonable to assume that people relied, perhaps increasingly, on ABC news sessions during these anxious years. The doubling of time occupied by news bulletins and commentaries between 1939 and 1945 might well have reflected growing attachment to the ABC as a reliable disseminator of information.[85] As well, ABC radio was the only medium for some listeners in the Australian outback, and it was often the sole source of entertainment and information for Australian troops overseas, particularly those stationed in the Pacific. Finally, trade unionists, government departments, and politicians would not have been so anxious to gain access to ABC facilities had they not believed it capable of influencing attitudes about the war; perhaps there was substance in their beliefs.

But while the question of 'impact' or 'influence' is interesting and important, it is not central to the theme of this chapter. It has been my concern not to establish causal connections between ABC programmes and wartime achievements, but rather to analyse the type of contribution made by the ABC, given the nature of its leadership, its philosophies, and its modes of dealing with outside interests.

Thus it is more significant to note that ABC programming underwent no radical or fundamental changes. Certainly, the demands of wartime impinged on regular ABC programming. The percentage of air time devoted to sport, for example, decreased from 7.3 per cent in 1939 to 1.8 per cent in 1943, in line with the general curtailment of sporting activities after 1942.[86] Probably the biggest single challenge to ABC traditional programmes was manifested in the programmes for the Forces with their emphasis on light entertainment. Dance music was a prominent feature of these sessions and occupied 15.7 per cent of air time in 1944, compared with just 6.4 per cent at the outbreak of war. The Forces programmes indeed foreshadowed the post-war devotion of the second ABC network almost exclusively to light entertainment. But while this type of programme challenged ABC beliefs about the educative responsibilities of broadcasters, the programmes for the time being supplemented rather than supplanted ABC programme staples, the more

5 Wartime Programming

serious cultural forms: classical music, talks, and drama. Serious music, for example, more than maintained its position against the inroads of other types of music between 1939 and 1945. Table 5.1 gives the exact figures.[87]

TABLE 5.1
Analysis of Music Broadcast by the ABC, 1939—45

Type of Music	Percentage of Programme Time for year ended 30 June						
	1939	1940	1941	1942	1943	1944	1945
Serious classical	5.99	4.10	4.82	6.04	7.06	6.19	6.73
Popular classical	17.18	13.13	13.21	15.75	16.51	14.84	16.13
Light	30.52	29.36	25.66	22.45	19.87	20.90	19.13
Dance	6.39	7.48	6.61	7.97	9.92	15.69	12.98
Total	60.08	54.07	50.30	52.21	53.36	57.62	54.97

Criticisms of ABC highbrow bias continued but did not noticeably increase. Perhaps, as A. Marwick has suggested for the British, 'the monotony of much of wartime life created a willingness to attend any entertainment offered, even a symphony concert'.[88] General talks and talks on special subjects (excluding sport and religion) occupied a constant 11—12 per cent of programme time from 1939 to 1944 and rose during the 1944/5 year to 15.12 per cent. Drama also maintained its position.[89] In general, the ABC's most fundamental philosophy of exposing Australians to quality programmes, thus providing opportunities for cultural betterment, survived the challenge of wartime.

6
The Other Side of War

Continuity of programme policy during the war years to some extent concealed important changes in the character of the ABC. Lack of funds, an increasingly assertive staff, departmental rivalries, and the general exigencies of wartime all had an impact on the organizational structure Cleary had evolved.

At the outbreak of war, the Commission itself faced an uncertain future. New broadcasting Bills continued to be drafted but were allowed to lapse. On 19 December 1939, as a tentative measure, Cabinet reappointed Cleary and Mrs Couchman for another term. Brookes, Orchard, and Kitto were replaced by, as Cabinet put it, 'more active and virile members': E. C. Rigby, S. J. McGibbon, and R. J. F. Boyer.[1]

Herbert Brookes' retirement was a substantial loss for the ABC, though it is doubtful whether, as R. Rivett suggested, his refusal to become the first chairman in 1932 was one of the reasons for the ABC never enjoying complete independence.[2] There are no grounds for believing that he possessed a greater commitment to ABC autonomy than Cleary did. Moreover, his health was never good and he was already in his mid-sixties when Cleary, aged forty-nine, assumed the chair.[3] Nevertheless, his contribution to Commission meetings had been substantial, and it was difficult to replace fully eight years of experience.

The press displayed no enthusiasm for the new appointments, realizing that they were partly a 'stop-gap' measure until the government reviewed the ABC seriously. Rigby, the new vice-chairman, was a solicitor from Victoria who had been mayor of Hawthorn three times running. McGibbon was an accountant with interests in Rotary. The one appointment of significance was Boyer: a Queensland grazier, he would eventually succeed Cleary as chairman.[4]

The war so absorbed the government's attention that, in December 1940, it merely extended the commissioners' terms for another year. A new set of amendments to the Broadcasting Act lapsed. The proposed changes had included increasing the number of commissioners to seven, staggering appointments to ensure continuity, granting the ABC power to conduct public concerts, and new controls relating to political broadcasts.⁵

Another reason for government inaction was the precarious political situation. Menzies' UAP government, in order to survive, was forced into coalition with the Country Party in March 1940, and retained power after September 1940 only with the support of two Independents. In June 1941, still procrastinating over the ABC, Cabinet re-appointed all commissioners for another six months and opted for a committee of inquiry to examine all aspects of broadcasting in Australia.⁶

The Gibson Committee, as it came to be called, was chaired by a 72-year-old Country Party senator, W. G. Gibson, and had as its other members Sir Charles Marr and Dr A. Grenfell Price from the UAP, and S. K. Amour, W. J. F. Riordan, and A. A. Calwell from the Labor Party. Warren Denning, the ABC's federal roundsman, was appointed liaison officer between the committee and the ABC. The Commission welcomed the inquiry: it was the commercial stations which, despite their past desires to expose the ABC's inadequacies, lobbied (unsuccessfully) to limit its scope.⁷

Before the Gibson Committee had completed its work there was a change of government. In a desperate bid to hold office, the coalition had made A. W. Fadden prime minister in August, but in October, John Curtin became prime minister when the two Independents crossed the floor and voted with Labor.

The change of government produced cautious optimism within the ABC. It was hoped that Labor would clarify the Commission's responsibilities, and take a more long-term view of broadcasting's place in society. McGibbon believed Labor was also likely to 'increase the avenues available to the Commission rather than to retard them as [had] been done for some years through the intervention of commercial interests'.⁸

Labor's actual intentions were not clear. On 26 March 1941, Calwell had moved in Caucus that the Labor Party oppose all amendments to the Broadcasting Act proposed by the Menzies government 'in accordance with the Party's policy to move for the abolition of the Commission'. However, this motion had later been withdrawn and a committee comprising Scullin, Calwell, and Evatt had been formed to report on the government amendments.⁹ In keeping with this more pragmatic approach, Curtin allowed the Gibson Committee to proceed, its composition and terms of reference unaltered.

Cleary was the first person to appear before the Gibson

Committee and immediately won respect for his forceful, competent presentation. He argued that the current broadcasting system should remain intact, but with some changes: there should be longer terms for commissioners, the ABC should be given authority to determine the salaries of its senior officers, and there should be checks on the minister's power to influence programme content. He suggested that ministerial instructions should always be in writing and be reported to Parliament.[10]

Altogether the Gibson Committee heard 156 witnesses. It presented its report in March 1942. The seventy-one separate recommendations were signed by all members of the committee, with the three Labor members adding an endnote: 'We have signed the above Report and desire to state in amplification of our views that we believe that the whole of the broadcasting system should be nationalized.'[11] The Broadcasting Act of 1942 was a compromise which embodied most of the important recommendations of the Gibson Committee without replacing the Commission with the departmental type of administration desired by the Labor left.[12]

The new Act raised the chairman's salary from £500 to £1250 and authorized the general manager to attend Commission meetings, though at the Commission's pleasure. There was no alteration in the basic structure of the Commission, except that in future one member would have to be a woman. Curtin rejected suggestions that the Commission should include a representative from each state, and accepted the Gibson Committee's recommendation that members 'should not be specialists or representatives of particular interests or localities. They should be persons of acknowledged capacity, experience and judgment, imbued with high ideals, and sensible of a responsibility to contribute to the moral and intellectual well-being of the community.'[13] The Act authorized the ABC to hold public concerts, restored one shilling of the two-shilling cut in licence fees of 1940, and stipulated that 2½ per cent of all music broadcast must be Australian. Two final but important changes were the requirement that ministerial instructions be noted in the ABC's annual report and the creation of a parliamentary standing committee on broadcasting.[14]

Apart from the creation of the standing committee, Cleary could look with satisfaction at the terms of the Act. The position of chairman remained, as he wished, part-time. His request that ministerial directions be made public had been met, though not so his request that the ABC be attached to a portfolio other than that of the postmaster-general.[15] Moses was also pleased. He had persuaded Menzies to move an amendment (accepted by the government) stating that the general manager was the chief executive officer of the Commission. The clause removed his fears that the Bill would reduce his position to that of an office boy,[16] though whether it had any real significance is doubtful: Cleary claimed the new clause 'would not in the slightest degree affect the powers of the Commission or of the Manager.'[17] The ABC seemed set for further progress, its position and powers more clearly defined and its record publicly vindicated.

The new Act became law in June 1942. On 10 June, Curtin announced the composition of the new Commission, the first to be appointed by a Labor government. Cleary was re-appointed chairman for a further five years. Boyer's term as commissioner was also renewed for four years. The terms of Mrs Couchman, Rigby, and McGibbon were allowed to expire. P. G. J. Foley, secretary of the Railway Workers' Union and formerly secretary of the Western Australian Timber Workers' Union, became the new vice-chairman. The other appointees were Ernestine Hill, author and journalist, and J. D. B. Medley, vice-chancellor of the University of Melbourne. These appointments gave the Commission its most mixed political complexion since 1932.[18]

The Standing Committee on Broadcasting performed a watchdog function on this new Commission. During the Committee's first year, under Calwell's chairmanship, it tended to ignore even its own words: 'In relation to the ABC, it is not the Standing Committee's function to interfere with day-to-day administration. ... The function of the Committee is to report on those matters of policy which are referred to it by Parliament or the Minister.'[19] At one stage, the Commission complained that too much time was being absorbed answering the Committee's questions, and that the ABC was being subjected virtually to daily supervision.[20] The real pressure began after Labor's return to power in 1943. A split in the opposition in March helped Labor to obtain landslide victories in both Houses at the August elections. Senator S. K. Amour became the new chairman of the Standing Committee and resurrected the old 'highbrows' versus 'lowbrows' argument about ABC programming, much to the annoyance of Cleary who replied: 'It would be a national tragedy ... if the Commission accepted the jargon of the commonplace and forgot the fine minimum of people who wanted better things'.[21] Other subjects to be investigated by the Standing Committee included staff regulations, news services, finance, administration, the *ABC Weekly*, the broadcasting of parliamentary debates, the use of overseas programme material, and broadcasts on sex and venereal disease. Even though very few of the Standing Committee's reports resulted in legislative action, its 'nark' role inhibited ABC freedom of action throughout the 1940s.

Shortages of funds also undermined ABC attempts to grapple with the organizational pressures of wartime. Cleary complained that the cut in the ABC's share of the listener's licence fee in 1940 reflected 'far too light an attitude' on the part of the Menzies government, yet in February 1941 the same government deprived the ABC of a further £450 per annum when it revoked the licences of 2000 enemy aliens.[22] The government also failed to intervene in the longstanding dispute with the Australasian Performing Rights Association. Since an arbitration decision in October 1937, the ABC had agreed to pay a copyright fee of sixpence per listener's licence in force. For the year ended 30 June 1941, this amounted to £37 436, a substantial slab of the ABC's increasingly scarce resources. The Gibson Committee merely suggested another temporary formula for copyright payments, and copyright fees remained an unresolved issue throughout the period covered by this book.[23] Another rising expense was salary increments. From 1940 to 1942 inclusive, increases in salary payments absorbed £22 602 of ABC income.[24]

Unfortunately, the new Labor government did little to relieve the ABC's financial problems. It did adopt the Gibson Committee's recommendation and restored one shilling of the two-shilling cut in licence fees, but this still left the ABC in a poor position. The demand for war programmes, especially documentaries, and more light entertainment, caused expenses to climb at a higher rate than income. As a result of the initial licence-fee cut, the ABC's income had fallen from £773 865 in 1940 to £729 968 in 1941; for the year ended 30 June 1942 it fell to £700 639.[25] The restoration of one shilling made little difference because few new licences were now being issued. Many potential licence holders were with the Forces overseas, and restrictions on manufacturing led to shortages of spare parts and working radios within Australia. Although the number of licensed households increased by 29 per cent from 1939 to 1945, this was a significant easing of the rate of increase in the 1930s: from 1932 to 1939, licensed households had increased by more than 120 per cent.[26] The Labor government rejected requests for the restoration of the second shilling, and instead made a grant to the ABC of approximately £70 000 for the 1944/5 year, based on the number of licences in force on 30 June 1944.[27]

The ABC welcomed this boost to its coffers, but it disliked the insecurity of the grant. Bearup was directed to write to the postmaster-general, expressing the ABC's wish to see the restoration of the second shilling. When Cabinet reviewed the question in June 1945, it decided merely to renew the grant for a further twelve months.[28]

6 The Other Side of War

The consequences of government action were readily apparent. Besides the wider implications for ABC autonomy, a reduced budget immediately resulted in, for example, reductions in the employment of casual artists, a halving of the number of celebrity concerts, and the decision, later reversed because of public reaction, to dispense with Jim Davidson's ABC Dance Band. There were also deleterious effects on co-operation between ABC programme departments and on staff morale.[29]

Shortly after Bearup became acting general manager, he foreshadowed the departmental rivalry which lay ahead by noting that in New South Wales alone, £900 per week was spent on music compared with £200 on all other programmes. He suggested that the ABC was due for a 'revolutionary change' in the distribution of programme funds.[30] There was no 'revolutionary change' during the war years, nor was there any prospect of one while programming continued to reflect the personal preferences of Cleary, but within the wider ABC organization competition between departments noticeably intensified.

The most determined competitor for more funds was the Talks Department under Molesworth. At a meeting in August 1942, the National Talks Advisory Committee recorded its belief that talk programmes were entitled to a greater share of ABC revenue than had hitherto been received, but neither special pleading by Molesworth nor comments by the Gibson Committee that expenditure on music seemed unusually high persuaded the Commission to allocate more staff and money to the Talks Department.[31]

Curtin may have influenced this decision. After bringing back Moses from the army to 'liven up' ABC programmes, he maintained pressure on the ABC to reduce the number of serious talks broadcast in the evenings.[32] The National Talks Advisory Committee believed that there had been a 'marked deterioration' in the Talks Department's position ever since light entertainment replaced other peak-hour items.[33] Curtin's pressure was probably one consideration behind an attempt to move the Monday-evening 'Listening Groups' broadcast to Sunday afternoon, a move which the Talks Committee labelled yet 'another indication of what we regard as the cavalier attitude towards talks which this Committee finds so disquieting'.[34]

Late in 1945, the Commission approved an increase in expenditure on talk sessions of £50 per week, but for financial reasons this was later cancelled.[35] There is evidence that Moses helped to keep the talks budget down. During discussions on finance, he produced statistics to 'prove' that the ABC spent more of its income on talks than did either the Canadian Broadcasting Corporation or the BBC. After the cancellation of the decision to increase talks expenditure, Molesworth pointed out the meaninglessness of the statistics Moses had produced, primarily by demonstrating that 'talks' meant different things for the ABC and for the BBC. For the ABC, the word covered news commentaries, documentary programmes, all outside and actuality broadcasts, talks given during women's and children's sessions, and stories. It was pointed out, too, that whereas Moses used yearly figures for the ABC, he used quarterly BBC figures. Moses eventually agreed to write to the BBC for clarification of the statistics, but this was only another delaying tactic.[36] Moses' behaviour during this episode showed the lengths to which he would go to get his own way within the ABC organization.

Inter-departmental squabbling was also a symptom of the continual redefining of responsibilities within the ABC as it tried to accommodate new production requirements. A reorganization in 1943 maintained the centralized administrative structure, at the same time drawing new lines of authority within Head Office. There were four new classified divisions: Programmes, Public Relations, Administration, and Shortwave Broadcasting. Each division was headed by a controller and each department within that division was headed by a director. The Programmes Division, under Barry, controlled all programme departments except News and Talks. S. H. Deamer's Public Relations Division encompassed the departments of News and Talks, publications (such as the *ABC Weekly*), and general public relations tasks. The Administration Division, led by A. L. Holman, dealt with accounts, staff, public concert management, statistics, legal matters, and office management. William Macmahon Ball controlled the Shortwave Division. Head Office remained the supreme 'planning and regulatory' body, while the operating staff continued to be attached to the six state branches.[37] The reorganization was not, as claimed by Moses, a delegation of authority:[38] in all important matters Head Office remained supreme.

A further change of designations in 1944 brought all ABC activities under just two divisions: Programmes and Administration.[39] Distinctions between programme and administrative staff were artificial and of questionable benefit to the ABC in either the short-term or the long-term. The Federal Programme Committee urged the elimination of rigid staff classifications, but there is no evidence that its pleas were heeded during the war years or immediately after.[40] Moses went so far as to express concern that Wilfrid Thomas, classified as acting director of light entertainment, an administrative job, was still performing in programmes.⁴¹ To accommodate people who did not fit precisely into either category, the Commission adopted the term 'auxiliary staff', defined as 'officers who occupy an intermediate stage in functions and in status, between permanent administrative officers and contract artists. Their talent is artistic, either executive (as with an accompanist), or creative (as with a script writer).'⁴² Cleary reinforced the dichotomy between programmes and administration by granting tenure to those staff who made the switch from the former to the latter. He told a meeting of Staff Association representatives in September 1941:

> once we see that a man or a position becomes administrative, depending upon the man's administrative ability rather than upon his skill as a musician, etc., then we are inclined to put him on the permanent staff. Even if he gets older, we are not depending upon his always having a supply of 'gags'.⁴³

Announcers were one group which despite having tenure was very conscious of divisions between different types of staff. Ellis Blain lamented: 'an announcer is a broadcaster and nothing else from his first day. This is the essence of the tight *esprit de corps* which exists between announcers, and of their traditionally cool relationship with the rest of the staff.'⁴⁴ From 1935 onwards, repeated requests that announcers be permitted to state their names at the commencement of a session were continually denied by the Commission.⁴⁵ This policy fitted the ABC's wish to present an impersonal, impartial face to the community, but it did little for the morale of possibly the most important single group of ABC employees. Those announcers who desired a greater role in the programmes they introduced had but one choice: abandon announcing and become purely an administrator. Moses is the most obvious example of how a 'programme person' had to turn to administration to rise in the ABC hierarchy.

Most criticisms of organizational structure from outside the ABC centred on the degree of centralization.⁴⁶ Why, for example, had all talk scripts to be vetted by Head Office? To this particular query Cleary replied: 'certain Ministers had made Commissioners personally responsible for seeing that comments of a particular type were not made, especially those relating to political matter'.⁴⁷ More generally, he defended the centralized structure by pointing out that only a central organization could produce the increasing number of 'Australian' contributions required for international relays, that there had been a mushrooming of regional stations whose programmes had to be co-ordinated, and that centralized purchasing of programme material helped keep costs down.⁴⁸ But he also attempted to appease his critics by establishing advisory committees in each state, as recommended by the Gibson Committee.

State advisory committees already existed in Western Australia and South Australia. The Western Australian Advisory Committee was created in 1935, partly to calm Western Australian paranoia about distance from ABC Head Office. South Australia's much less successful counterpart had been established in 1937. In both cases, the state manager had taken the initiative. Cleary saw little role for the committees, but acting on the *Gibson Report* established committees in the remaining states during 1942.⁴⁹

It is difficult to gauge the effectiveness of these state committees or of the many other programme advisory committees scattered throughout the country. In September 1941, the Western Australian Advisory Committee questioned whether it should continue; Walter Murdoch believed that the Committee had not done any 'great work'.⁵⁰ Many of the programme committees wasted energy fighting with each other. For example, there were clashes between the Federal Music Advisory Committee and the Educational Broadcasts Committee, and between the Kindergarten Advisory Committee and the National Talks Advisory Committee, each accusing the other of intruding on its territory.⁵¹ The minutes of their meetings were passed on ultimately to the Commission, but their ability to influence ABC policy seems to have been limited by their lowly place in the estimation of Cleary, the other commissioners, and Moses.⁵²

In any event, the advisory committees were good public relations. A further indication that the ABC, as an organization, was becoming more conscious of public relations during these years was its decision, late in 1943, to allocate £15 000 for the establishment of a listener research section similar to that of the BBC's recently formed division.⁵³ The ABC also renewed its subscriptions to the audience research surveys of the two organizations, Anderson's and McNair's, although in February 1945 it dropped its subscription to the latter.⁵⁴ Cleary's agreeing to establish some machinery for listener research did not reflect a new willingness to give way to public demand. Rather, it pointed to a realization that in times of financial stringency, the deployment of resources into public relations could, especially in the long-term, aid institutional survival.

The increasing complexity of the ABC bureaucracy brought with it the unavoidable problems associated with an increase in staff numbers. Between 1939 and 1945, Head Office staff increased by 118 to 229, and total staff numbers almost doubled from 500 to

6 The Other Side of War

976.[55] Yet this expansion of numbers hardly kept pace with the expanded wartime functions of the ABC. As a result, there was considerable staff dissatisfaction with general working conditions, heavy work-loads, long hours, pegged salaries, and the continuing tardiness of the Commission in dealing with these matters. In June 1941, the Staff Association informed Bearup of its belief 'that dissatisfaction and a sense of injustice are rapidly becoming general among members of the staff, and that these are likely to lead to a falling off in efficiency'.[56]

At the beginning of the war, ABC management created some of its own staff shortages by encouraging staff to enlist for active duty. Moses' own enlistment in 1940 set a precedent which could make life uncomfortable for those staff who, if eligible, failed to enlist. The Commission adopted a policy of employing (wherever possible) people not eligible for war service, and as an inducement to present staff to enlist, established a fund to supplement their Forces salary.[57] The *ABC Weekly* fed the enlistment fervour within the organization by, for example, carrying a full cover photograph of Captain Moses in military uniform. Moses' example was followed by A. N. Finlay, manager for Queensland, E. K. Sholl, New South Wales programme executive, Jim Davidson, the actor Peter Finch, Talbot Duckmanton (then news reader and present general manager of the ABC), and many others: the number of ABC staff on defence leave reached its peak, 153, in 1944.[58]

By early 1942, this policy had changed radically. The extra demands of wartime broadcasting, particularly after Japan's entry into the war, made Cleary reluctant to release key staff. It became so difficult to obtain defence leave from the Commission that in March the Staff Association protested against the refusal to grant permission to enlist with the AIF.[59] Moses' return to the ABC in March 1943 possibly accounts for the rise in enlistment over the following two years, but the Commission was not pleased with the result. In February 1945, Cleary even complained to the Parliamentary Standing Committee on Broadcasting that ABC operations had been severely affected by the absence of experienced staff.[60]

Cleary's statement was an indirect admission that staff had been working under great pressure. In July 1942, a meeting of programme controllers expressed its concern about the staffing position:

> The Committee feels it cannot be stressed too strongly that successful radio is largely a matter of adequate and expert personnel rather than Star performers. . . . It is felt that a simile may be drawn between the number of ground staff necessary to keep a

pilot effectively in the air and the number of radio 'ground' staff necessary to keep an artist effectively in front of a microphone.[61]

Some of the staffing gaps were filled by women, but under discriminatory conditions. At first, any female who married had to resign forthwith. This policy could not even be bent to accommodate the case of a machinist whose marriage plans were brought forward because her fiancé had been called up for military service.[62] As staffing problems became more acute, the policy was modified slightly: women already employed whose husbands enlisted for military service could remain on the regular staff with full rights, including that of promotion; single women who married civilians need not necessarily resign, but they were transferred to the temporary staff.[63] The retention of married women was a deviation from normal Public Service practice which Cleary had to fight for against later opposition from the Standing Committee on Broadcasting.[64] It was a practice not fully appreciated by the junior male staff who, on at least one occasion, complained that it reduced their opportunities for promotion.[65]

The presence of more women in the office was one of a number of changes in the physical working environment of ABC employees brought about by the war. Broadcast House, Sydney, fitted out its basement as an air-raid shelter, equipped with stretchers, medicines, and thirty pounds of chocolate![66] At a recently acquired site in Forbes Street, Sydney, a special blast-proof and gas-proof studio was constructed by tunnelling into solid sandstone.[67] Staff were not moved to regional centres for the duration, but a plan was drawn up in conjunction with the Postmaster-General's Department and defence authorities which provided for the widest possible dispersal of broadcasting facilities in the event of enemy attack. Emergency premises were built at Crystal Brook and Prospect in South Australia, at Wagin in Western Australia, in Lonsdale Street in Melbourne, at the School of Arts, Burwood (Sydney), and so forth.[68] As it happened, the southern cities of Australia were neither invaded nor bombed, but the precautions were clearly wise.

Many staff would have preferred physical changes of a different type: new buildings in which to work. The ABC still operated mainly from rented premises, most of them built for purposes other than broadcasting, and few with adequate staff 'club' facilities. Staff recognized that there was no prospect of any new buildings while almost all the ABC's reserve funds remained tied up in government war loans, but they made it known that with the return to peace they would expect more in the way of staff canteens, recreational facilities, and other amenities.[69]

10 The ABC Dance Band entertains the troops, June 1940

11 James Pratt helps evacuee children speak with their parents in England

12 Chester Wilmot records Scottish troops at Tobruk, 1941

Meanwhile, staff maintained their campaigns in relation to cost-of-living adjustments and wage relativities. ABC salaries compared favourably with those of the Public Service until July 1941, when public servants received a £12 per annum rise in their base salary in lieu of child endowment allowances.[70] However, it was difficult to draw exact comparisons. Only about twenty ABC adult employees filled positions directly comparable with Public Service positions in 1942. Even typist salaries differed, partly because the ABC required 'cultural inclinations' as well as typing expertise, for which it was prepared to pay extra.[71] Clerks in the ABC were worse off after July 1941, though by February 1945 middle-ranking officers at least enjoyed similar salaries to their Public Service counterparts. Had it not been for the promptings of the Staff Association, it is doubtful whether these wartime adjustments would have come about.[72] Of course, the ABC's hands were partly tied by government wage-pegging requirements, but this did not placate many of the creative staff who believed that their professionalism went unappreciated. These staff compared their salaries not with the Public Service but with the commercial stations, which, on the whole, paid considerably higher rates. In September 1944, two leading ABC orchestral musicians, Haydn Beck and Lionel Lawson, resigned in protest at the size of their salaries. Four months later, Heath Burdock (now chief news announcer), Bryson Taylor (now head studio supervisor), O. Lansbury (sound effects chief), and K. Keavney (staff script-writer), all resigned for similar reasons.[73] While attending the Commonwealth Broadcasting Conference in London the following month, Moses admitted that five members of the New South Wales staff had recently been offered positions at two to three times their ABC salaries.[74] The ABC certainly received its 'pound of flesh': John McLeod each week wrote scripts for 'Out of the Bag', 'Colour Canvas', 'Tonight We Dance', and 'For Valour'; in contrast, Mark Makeham left the ABC to work for the commercials at a higher salary, writing the script for one half-hour show per week.[75]

Arrangements for filling staff vacancies also remained unsatisfactory. In theory, the 1939 Staff Rules introduced a regular procedure: vacant positions were advertised first within the ABC and then outside, and a committee comprising Bearup, Molesworth, and Holman then recommended an appointment to the general manager who advised the Commission. In practice, many important vacancies still were not advertised. Cleary spoke of a 'fine mesh' through which no appointments by favour could find their way, but the Staff Association cited many instances of appointments by personal selection. Two of these were the appointment of a federal concert manager late in 1939, and of F. W. Simpson to the Head Office talks staff late in 1941.⁷⁶

One way the Commission circumvented the Staff Rules was by making 'temporary' appointments, which did not require prior advertisement, and later reclassifying them as 'permanent'. Almost always, the original occupant was confirmed in the 'new' position. This practice was especially unpalatable during wartime, when the appointment of permanent officers was considered detrimental to those staff away on active service.⁷⁷

It was therefore not surprising that the trend towards public service unionism, begun in the late 1930s with the establishment of the ABC Staff Association and the ABC Senior Officers' Association, gathered momentum during the war.

Membership of the Staff Association grew steadily. In January 1942, 500 or 58.4 per cent of the total staff belonged to the Association; in November 1944, 658 or 72.2 per cent of the staff did so.⁷⁸ Some employees still belonged to other unions such as the Australian Journalists' Association, the Musicians' Union of Australia, Actors' Equity, and the Australian Theatrical and Amusement Employees' Association, but by 1945 all members of the regular (permanent) staff were members of the Staff Association, the Senior Officers' Association, or the AJA.⁷⁹

ABC journalists remained a separate group for two reasons: the AJA opposed the idea of 'house unions' and discouraged its members from joining the Staff Association,⁸⁰ and journalists worked under quite different conditions from other ABC staff. Journalists were not required to retire at age sixty-five, received more generous leave provisions and overtime payments, served no probationary period, suffered no nationality restrictions, and did not have to pass a medical examination. At the same time, they were rarely given permanency to age sixty-five.⁸¹ The Staff Association tried to co-operate with the AJA, but to no avail. In 1941, it was even excluded from negotiations on conditions for news staff between the AJA and the Commission.⁸²

In July 1941, the Staff Association made Concannon, hitherto acting as industrial advocate on retainer, the full-time secretary of the Association. His first brief was to draft the Association's submission to the Gibson Committee.⁸³ Shortly afterwards, there were some other changes in the Association's executive. Alexander was replaced as president by F. G. Scott. Then followed a rapid succession of presidents caused mainly by service enlistments: Scott was succeeded by A. Gordon in April 1942, and he in turn by A. Jose in August 1943.⁸⁴ Leadership changes were accompanied by changes in the Association's constitution at the first Federal Conference held in September 1944. From this time onwards, the Federal Conference became the governing body of the Association with a Federal Council having power to make decisions between conferences. Federal Council consisted of the president, vice-president, secretary, and one representative from each branch of the Association. In October 1944, the first election of federal office bearers by plebiscite of all members resulted in the election of D. Bennett as president and Nancy Sheehan as vice-president.[85] Staff were kept informed of these changes in *Aerial*, an information bulletin which appeared for the first time in October 1943. Prior to that, since 1941, *The Open Mike*, a house publication, had been one of the few sources of staff news.

ABC staff were not operating in isolation. Within the wider Australian community, support for unionism generally grew during the war years: by 1945, 54.2 per cent of wage and salary earners belonged to trade unions compared with 47.6 per cent in 1939.[86] This trend derived partly from the extra burden placed upon workers during the war which caused many to look more closely at their working conditions, and partly from the positive encouragement given to unionism by the Labor government. Finally, perhaps most interestingly, the euphoria created in the atmosphere of a national war effort may have persuaded people that co-operation and unity could help to produce a better world.[87]

The Senior Officers' Association's activities were not nearly so obvious as those of the Staff Association, but they maintained their demands on classification of positions, salary ranges, and especially the introduction of a superannuation scheme. After the government deferred action on the postmaster-general's recommendation to bring ABC staff under the Commonwealth Superannuation Scheme in 1939, the Staff Association and the Senior Officers' Association made a joint submission to the Gibson Committee.[88] The Committee urged prompt action, and with the concurrence of the Commission, ABC staff were brought under the Commonwealth Superannuation Act in October 1942.

Cabinet action on the general question of ABC staff conditions was much slower. A broadcasting Bill drafted by Harrison in 1939 overturned A. G. Cameron's plan to bring ABC staff under the Public Service Act, and gave power to the Commission to make regulations for all staff except those on salaries of £1000 or more. The latter's conditions of work were still subject to the approval of the governor-general. This Bill lapsed, as did another drafted by Postmaster-General G. McLeay in 1941 which contained similar provisions.⁸⁹ Cabinet's excuse for inaction was the war. It believed that to amend the Broadcasting Act at this time 'might lead to justifiable criticism that in a period of national emergency the time of the Government and the Parliament is being diverted to a matter of purely domestic interest when the concerted efforts of all should be directed towards winning the war.'⁹⁰ After July 1941, the question was left to the Gibson Committee to resolve.

Concannon was authorized to appear before the Gibson Committee to push three main issues for the ABC staff: representation on the Commission, and, failing that, representation on all matters affecting the staff; superannuation; and staff representation on the appointments and appeals advisory committees. The aim was no longer to have staff brought under the provisions of the Public Service Act, but to achieve the machinery of a Public Service working environment, plus security of tenure, under a set of statutory regulations.⁹¹ In some areas, such as travelling allowances and some meal allowances, ABC conditions were superior to those of the Commonwealth Public Service: ABC staff obviously wished to preserve these distinctions while simultaneously enjoying the greater opportunities for 'job regulation' accorded public servants. There were also a number of more specific things which the Staff Association hoped to achieve through a set of staff regulations: promotions and appointments by merit (and then seniority), automatic annual salary increments, the advertising of all vacancies (which were to be filled from within if possible), proper overtime rates, three weeks' recreation leave as an entitlement (not a privilege granted by the Commission), meal allowances in addition to overtime, preferential chances of re-employment for retrenched officers, temporary and auxiliary staff who were made permanent to have their previous service counted, and no officer to drop in salary as a result of a promotion or transfer.⁹²

The Staff Association demand for a staff commissioner again was consistent with the mood of the early 1940s. Much union activity of this period was directed towards gains in 'job regulation' rather than towards purely financial rewards. The staff of the Commonwealth Public Service were prepared to make some financial sacrifice as 'their contribution to the war effort in lieu of military service',⁹³ although they and workers in other industries used this same sacrifice as grounds for increased militancy when the war was over.⁹⁴ For the duration, they concentrated on achieving a greater say in the regulation of the working environment. Employees' representation was requested and obtained on, for example, the Stevedoring Industry Commission, the Maritime Industry Commission, and the

Commonwealth Coal Commission.⁹⁵ A more appropriate comparison with the ABC might be the school-teacher federations of New South Wales which stepped up their campaign for an education commission with teacher representation.⁹⁶ In the event, Concannon failed to impress the Gibson Committee on this point. Indeed, staff representation on the ABC was not achieved until 1975.

The Gibson Committee did accept Staff Association arguments for a set of staff regulations. Curtin inserted a clause to this effect in the 1942 Act, but the governor-general's approval was still required for the salaries of the general manager and the 'next six most highly paid executive officers'. In September 1942, the first task of the Parliamentary Standing Committee on Broadcasting was to comment on the draft regulations compiled by the ABC.

In his submission to the Gibson Committee, Cleary had opposed the idea of a staff representative on the Appointments Advisory Committee. His arguments foreshadowed the difficulties encountered in the next three years in reaching agreement with the Staff Association on this issue and over the introduction of the staff regulations.⁹⁷ The Staff Association wanted the regulations to include provisions for staff representation on both the appointments and appeals advisory committees. Both these committees had existed since 1939, but they consisted solely of senior officers. The Commission showed signs of compromise on the appeals committee, but not on appointments. Cleary believed that the Commission, as the body responsible for the efficient running of the ABC, should have the prerogative on staff appointments. He also believed that senior officers were the best qualified to advise on appointments, junior officers being more subject to prejudice or moral suasion.⁹⁸

In an attempt to break the deadlock, the Parliamentary Standing Committee called both parties together in March 1943. The Commission indicated that it had had a change of heart, and in November it notified the Standing Committee that it would agree to the Staff Association's request. There were further delays, however, when in June 1944 the Standing Committee referred the draft regulations to the Postmaster-General's Department and the Public Service Board for comment. This brought some complaints from Public Service employees that the ABC regulations were more generous than their own.⁹⁹

Cleary was angry that 'outside' bodies had been consulted on a purely domestic ABC matter.¹ It is clear that both he and the Staff Association were anxious to reach agreement by now. In November 1944, for example, some reprimands relating to individual staff members' breaches of the 1939 Staff Rules were drafted but never sent.² Two months earlier, the Staff Association had added a new objective in its constitution: 'To foster the highest ethical and professional standards in the radio field generally and in the service of the Commission in particular',³ an equally conciliatory gesture.

In December 1944, both the Staff Association and the Senior Officers' Association expressed their agreement with the latest set of draft regulations compiled by the Commission. There was one qualification: the Staff Association wanted guarantees that, in the event of disagreement over an appointment or other matters, the case would be referred to an independent tribunal for arbitration. Bennett said this issue was of 'major importance'.⁴

The Standing Committee again called the parties together in February 1945 to discuss the independent tribunal. In its report, issued in April, it recommended an internal ABC committee to handle appointments, supporting the Staff Association's suggestion for an independent tribunal only in respect of promotions. Even this was unacceptable to the Commission which wanted no outside body with jurisdiction over ABC internal disputes.⁵ In June, the Staff Association responded with a motion of no confidence in the Commission.⁶

This new dispute, together with further problems over the position of journalists, delayed the introduction of the staff regulations for another two years. However, by 1945, agreement had been reached on most vital points. The latest draft of the regulations included provisions for prescribed salary ranges, annual increments, cost-of-living adjustments, entrance examinations for appointment to the clerical staff, the advertising of vacancies, three weeks' leave entitlement, and staff representation on both the appointments and appeals advisory committees.⁷ The Staff Association had shown itself a capable spokesman for its members, thus ensuring it of continued support into the post-war period. It had also revealed its mode of operation: there was never a hint of strike action.

By the closing months of 1944, Cleary's own position was becoming increasingly frustrating. He was tired of continuing interference from ministers, from Curtin, and from the Parliamentary Standing Committee on Broadcasting. In November, the vice-chairman, Foley, died of a heart attack, leaving Cleary to shoulder even heavier responsibility. But undoubtedly the main irritant was Moses.

Tensions between Cleary and Moses had been mounting since the late 1930s. There was a temporary lull from 1940 to 1942, while Moses was away with the Forces, but conflict resumed following his return to the ABC in March 1943. Cleary was not happy about the manner of Moses' return. On 22 January, Curtin had telephoned him, indicating that he thought it was time Moses came back, and that General Blamey was prepared to release him. Cleary resented Curtin's presuming to make decisions for the ABC, and persuaded him to defer action until the Commission had been consulted. After discussion, the Commission sent a telegram to Curtin: 'Understanding that the Army was releasing Lt. Col. Moses, the Commission would be ready to take him back as soon as he was released and fit to resume his duties'. Upon his arrival, Moses almost immediately informed Cleary that Curtin had given him the government's full support to do something about ABC programmes. As Curtin had not mentioned programme standards when urging Moses' return, Cleary saw the prime minister's actions as amounting to a motion of no confidence in the Commission.[8]

Early in 1945, Cleary received some further disturbing information about Moses from M. F. Dixon, after the former had departed for London to attend the Commonwealth Broadcasting Conference. To begin with, Dixon completely contradicted Moses' version, given to Cleary, of his reactions to a proposal to reorganize the News Department.[9] In addition, he quoted letters Moses had sent from Malaya, praising his work as news editor, urging him to continue his fight for an independent news service, and suggesting that the ABC might now possess one had there been 'a bit more guts behind it when we pressed for it'.[10] Dixon also confirmed Moses' private dealings with Curtin, and quoted the contents of a letter from the latter: 'I am not going to give you any directions, but I want you to report to me at the end of three months about any obstacles you meet in carrying out your plans'.[11]

Cleary was also upset to learn that Moses had told Bearup late in 1944: 'I want you to understand that I have the full confidence of the Government, of the Opposition, and of the Minister'.[12] By now, Cleary suspected that Moses, with Curtin's backing, was out to become both the chairman and the general manager of the ABC.[13] In a surprise move, on 19 February 1945, he sent a letter of resignation to take effect from 31 March.

When the resignation became public knowledge, the *Daily Mirror, Sun, Daily Telegraph,* and *Sydney Morning Herald,* among others, speculated that it was the result of interference from Senator Amour and the Standing Committee on Broadcasting.[14] The same theme was expounded in Parliament, but when H. L. Anthony mentioned Curtin's role in the return of Moses, Menzies issued a statement on the conflicting responsibilities of the general manager and chairman.[15]

G. C. Bolton suggested the following explanation for Cleary's resignation:

> The fact simply seems to be that Cleary could see no end to the time when he was at odds with either the parliamentary standing committee or Charles Moses, or both ... Cleary made up his mind that he was no longer the personality best able to further the interests of the A.B.C.; and, with characteristic honesty, at once withdrew from a scene where he could no longer be useful.[16]

Dixon, in his own record of events, interpreted the resignation slightly differently:

> I firmly believe that Cleary felt he had been 'let down' — had been misled and misinformed; and the blow to his pride induced him to submit his resignation as the best and quickest way of bringing matters to a head.[17]

Bolton's analysis is useful, though more emphasis should be placed on Moses' role. The first part of Dixon's interpretation is consistent with the evidence, but not so his suggestion that Cleary resigned to provoke an inquiry. Cleary's closing words in a letter to John Medley were: 'I have had enough experience to realise how my action will be misrepresented, and how tempted I will be to justify it. I can only hope that my resolution not to do so will remain as strong as it is at present.'[18] A second letter to Professor R. G. Cameron read: 'To tell the truth, now that I have decided to get out I am anxious to be quit of the whole thing and be free of the gossip and cross-firing and recriminations involved in any sort of wash-up'.[19]

Cleary never did disclose the reasons for his resignation, but there is good evidence of his motives in the letter he wrote to John Medley mentioned above. In it he said that he was resigning in view of Dixon's revelations about Moses, and that he intended to leave immediately to avoid working any longer with the man who had 'made life intolerable' for him.[20] In short, Cleary was fed up with Moses' attempts to undermine his authority.

There was an even more fundamental explanation for Cleary's action. The ABC organization in 1945 was a very different creature from that which Cleary knew and had helped to mould. While ABC programme philosophies remained basically intact, their manner of formulation and implementation was beginning to change. Cleary's personal style of control, particularly suited to the smaller ABC of the 1930s, was somewhat inappropriate for the now complex bureaucracy in which a shift of power from the Commission to the general manager and his staff was becoming daily more apparent. Part of the problem was that Cleary was not prepared to modify his style.

While demanding that management should not intrude into areas of policy, he had himself been guilty, from the beginning, of interfering in daily administration. His regular presence at Broadcast House encouraged this 'interference'. Even Herbert Brookes, one of Cleary's closest personal admirers, reflected: 'As a General Manager I have never met his equal; but the functions of the chairman of a Commission such as the ABC differ from those of a general manager who naturally is supreme in his own sphere.'[21] Cleary's system was built on loyalty to himself as chairman and on a commitment to the ABC as an institution. At a staff farewell, he indicated that this system no longer operated. The *Daily Mirror* reported: 'Because of certain happenings he could no longer rely on the loyalty of some people he had trusted and he felt it was time to get out.'[22] There was only a hint of optimism in a farewell note Cleary wrote for *Aerial* where he said of national broadcasting:

> I believed in its potentialities for enriching the life of the community, and I venture to hope that my faith has been borne out. . . . The important thing is never to lose sight of the goal and never to cease striving for it. Although my part in this crusade is now over, I hope the staff will strive to keep bright their vision of what national broadcasting might accomplish . . .[23]

Cleary's constant dream had been that of a committed staff, imbued with an institutional ethos, working towards a common goal. He could not generally sympathize with the new concerns of the staff, with their change in outlook, or at least with their apparent willingness publicly to articulate their disagreement with ABC policy and purpose.

Overall, the impact of the war on the ABC organization was considerable: new departments were added to the bureaucracy, a new Broadcasting Act had its effect, personnel increased and changed, and the organization lost its founding father. Cleary's departure, in addition to ending perhaps the most important phase in ABC history, highlighted the problem of control by general manager and a commission. Perhaps this was an insoluble problem, being too dependent on the personalities of particular incumbents, but it was one which interested Cleary's successor and which still troubles the ABC. Most importantly, the war witnessed a further advance towards public service unionism among ABC staff, with its implications for their relations with the Commission and for the future direction of ABC activities. For ABC employees, wartime provided an invaluable experience on which to build their ability to influence ABC programme philosophies as well as working conditions.

7
The Return to Peace

Just as the ABC alerted Australians to the outbreak of hostilities in September 1939, so one of its last 'acts of war' was to broadcast direct from Parliament House, Canberra, news of Germany's surrender on 5 May 1945. The announcement was followed by Chester Wilmot's description of the official surrender to General Montgomery, and speeches by Winston Churchill, Harry S. Truman, and the king. These broadcasts of triumph complemented the euphoric mood of crowds gathered in the highly decorated streets or attending one of the thanksgiving services. On 15 August, the scene was repeated when the new prime minister, Ben Chifley, broadcast the eagerly awaited news that the war with Japan was over.[1]

Chifley had succeeded Curtin as prime minister after the latter's death in office on 5 July. On 28 September 1946, he was reconfirmed as prime minister with majorities in both Houses at an election that saw the opposition parties, including the newly formed Liberal Party under Menzies, disunited. These political changes had important consequences for the ABC, but so, too, did the end of the war and the coincidental appointment of a new ABC chairman, R. J. F. Boyer.

The ABC of which Boyer became chairman was very different from that which Cleary had come to head in 1934. There were now twenty-nine ABC stations. Six years of war had revealed radio's full potential, and the 84 per cent of Australian homes which possessed radio sets in 1946 had high expectations of the post-war ABC.[2] Even before the war in the Pacific ended, the Commission began to think aloud about the place of national broadcasting in post-war Australia. It claimed that, despite the war, it had been able 'to preserve a continuity of ... main objectives which enables [the Commission] to enter the post-war period with undiminished impetus'.[3] In the broadest sense this was true, for the immediate post-war years, 1945—8, were marked by many continuities of ABC policy, programming, and style of operation; but they also witnessed some important changes to the national broadcasting service.

7 The Return to Peace

Determining the balance between changes and continuities was largely the responsibility of Boyer. His appointment as chairman took some months to be confirmed, owing to the mystery which surrounded Cleary's resignation. The press named W. A. Taylor, a vice-president of the Labor Party and member of the Commonwealth Bank Board, and T. S. Woodbridge, general manager of the APRA, as possible contenders, but from the government's point of view, Boyer was the only serious candidate.

Boyer had no special qualifications save for his experience on the Commission, but the chairmanship required breadth of vision and experience as much as anything, and these Boyer could supply amply. Born in August 1891 in Taree, New South Wales, he was educated at Newington College and at the University of Sydney where he obtained an MA in 1914. The son of a clergyman, his early ambition had been to enter the Methodist ministry, but after serving in the AIF as a lieutenant from 1915 to 1918 he returned to Australia and in 1920 acquired Durella, a pastoral lease in Queensland. He became president of various graziers' associations, and was the delegate of the Graziers' Federal Council of Australia at conferences in Sydney. In 1939 he was a Commonwealth delegate to the League of Nations Assembly, and in August 1940 he was appointed honorary director of the American division of the Department of Information.[4]

At the time of Cleary's resignation, Boyer was preparing to return from overseas. He first learnt of the crisis from Stanley Melbourne Bruce, Australian High Commissioner in London, who conveyed Curtin's offer of the chairmanship to him. Though delighted by the offer,[5] he responded cautiously, seeking further information about Cleary. When the government offered no clarification, he cabled Cleary himself, but received an equally vague reply: 'Actually intolerable climax to situation you and I discussed namely responsibility without secure foundations'.[6]

Meanwhile, John Medley spoke with Senator Don Cameron, the new postmaster-general, after which he cabled Boyer suggesting that it might embarrass the government if he delayed acceptance any longer. At this point, Boyer tentatively agreed to accept, pending a more detailed report on his return to Australia. He refused to commit himself further when pressed again as he passed through Washington. Back in Australia, he talked with Cleary. Both men agreed that the fundamental conditions of acceptance should be greater independence for the Commission and the removal of Moses. Boyer met with Medley and another commissioner, Edgar Dawes, on 5 and 6 April in Melbourne, where it was decided that unless the government offered a new deal on independence, all three would resign. On 12 April, Boyer saw Curtin and accepted the appointment on condition that Curtin published a statement guaranteeing two things: that the ministers' veto power over Commission expenditure would not be used as an excuse for interference, and that the government would in future deal directly with the Commission, not with the general manager or staff. It is interesting that Moses' removal was not mentioned.[7]

Curtin issued the requisite statement the same day, acknowledging that the purpose of the Broadcasting Act was 'to create a position of special independence of judgment and action for the national broadcasting instrumentality', and recognizing that responsibility for ABC operations rested solely with the commissioners, 'and not on either review by, or pressure from, any sources outside it, political or non-political'. The statement was drafted by Boyer, and approved by Dawes, Medley, and, of course, Curtin.[8] It was published in all metropolitan dailies, the *ABC Weekly*, and the *ABC Annual Report* for 1944/5. The ABC printed copies for distribution on every possible occasion.

On 5 May 1945, Cleary expressed the hope that Boyer's ideals would be shared and supported by governments and ABC staff. Despite the bitterness of his departure, he was pleased with his successor, knowing that his own ideals for the ABC and for Australia would find continuity, perhaps even fulfilment, under him. The two men, though from very different backgrounds, shared a common vision: the use of broadcasting to help build a tolerant, informed, critical, and cultured democracy in Australia. In this mission the ABC had for Boyer, as for Cleary, a distinctive role to play, its 'purposeful educative function' distinguishing it from commercial radio.[9]

Boyer's promotion was one of four changes to the Commission during the closing stages of the war. Edgar Dawes had become vice-chairman in December 1944, succeeding Foley who died of a heart attack. Ernestine Hill was replaced by Mrs Ivy Kent from Western Australia during the same month. Edgar Dawes, a fitter and turner by trade, was a former Labor member of the South Australian Parliament. He was former secretary of the South Australian Branch of the Australian Society of Engineers and of the Trades and Labor Council, former president of the South Australian Labor Party, and he had worked on various ABC advisory committees. Mrs Kent was a member of the ABC's Western Australian Advisory Committee. She was also a member of the Adult Education Board, vice-president of the Women Justices' Association, and a former president of Labour Women of Western Australia. To fill the

7 The Return to Peace

vacancy caused by Boyer's elevation to the chairmanship, the government appointed J. S. Hanlon, editor of the *Australian Worker* in Sydney.[10] Thus by the time Boyer became chairman, he and Medley were the only members of the Commission with non-Labor sympathies. Labor could be accused of stacking the Commission with its supporters, just as previous governments had done, yet Curtin made Boyer chairman, apparently without any questioning.

Relations between the Commission and its staff were still unsettled when Boyer assumed the chair. He aggravated the situation by opposing the demands for an independent appeals tribunal, thus making him head of the first Commission to suffer a vote of no confidence from its own staff. This vote was a sign that staff would no longer tolerate Commission indifference to their working conditions. Early in 1946, an editorial in *Aerial* foreshadowed a more militant outlook by the Staff Association as it entered the post-war period. It noted that war had given broadcasting a tremendous impetus, then asked: 'what have we, the people, for whom this highest skill is required, got out of it? Very little'.[11]

To assist the rehabilitation of officers returning from the war, the Commission placed Clewlow in charge of a staff training school which provided both refresher courses and, following representations from the Staff Association, induction courses for new staff.[12] Some employees, notably those working on shortwave transmissions, remained on semi-wartime activities for the time being. The Department of Information continued propaganda broadcasts to members of the Royal Navy still stationed in the Pacific region, hoping to persuade them to migrate to Australia, and entertainment was needed for Australian troops still camped throughout the Pacific awaiting demobilization.[13] However, the reabsorption of defence-leave staff and the gradual transfer of staff back to peacetime duties were minor problems compared with final promulgation of the staff regulations, still in the negotiating stages.

Notwithstanding differences over the independent appeals tribunal, both the Staff Association and the Senior Officers' Association approved the latest draft of the staff regulations produced early in 1945. The new delay was a result of the Parliamentary Standing Committee's decision to refer the regulations to the postmaster-general for comment.[14] In the meantime, neither the Staff Association nor the Senior Officers' Association was prepared to lose financially during the delay, and in November 1945 they served a log of claims relating to salaries and salary ranges to the Public Service arbitrator. In 1946, the Parliamentary Standing

Committee finally recommended that the government amend the Broadcasting Act to make Arbitration Court decisions binding on the ABC and to incorporate the most vital aspects of the staff regulations: the provision for appeal boards, stipulation of the grounds for promotion, dismissal, or retirement, and the Commission's powers to create, classify, or abolish positions. The Staff Regulations were gazetted on 27 February 1947. Although the regulations were not introduced fully until 1948, the appeal boards operated from the earlier date.[15]

Staff were pleased with the 'job regulation' gains they had made with the introduction of the Staff Regulations. The manner of recruitment was regularized: all positions were to be advertised, and there were to be entrance examinations for clerks, typists, machine operators, telephonists, and new cadets. There was machinery for appeal, including a Promotions Appeal Board and a Disciplinary Appeal Board with staff representation, and a formula for future cost-of-living adjustments was clearly spelled out.[16]

Much of the credit for the introduction of the Staff Regulations must go to the Staff Association, which was able to bargain effectively with the authority it gained during the war years. The Association maintained a strong membership figure into the postwar years, so that by 30 June 1948, 866 or 76.4 per cent of the total staff were members.[17] In March 1947, the first edition of *Radio-Active* appeared, an expanded and more sophisticated form of *Aerial*. Boyer gave the journal official blessing.[18] But the Association had no grounds for complacency. The level and range of ABC salaries had still to be argued out before the Public Service arbitrator.

While the general staff complained that their salaries had fallen behind Public Service and other levels because of the ABC's failure to pass on cost-of-living adjustments, Keith Barry, speaking for the senior officers, noted that some executives were on the same salaries as when first they joined the ABC thirteen years previously.[19] The arbitrator handed down his decision in March 1948, and granted sizeable salary increases. For example, an officer on £625 per annum had his salary increased to £813, representing a 25 per cent marginal increase plus a cost-of-living adjustment.[20]

Not all staff were happy with the determination. In particular there was dissatisfaction over the new relativities. The Staff Association held a special conference, as a result of which it decided to reopen the case.[21] After further hearings, the arbitrator varied the original determination in November, substituting a new salary scale of twenty-two grades in place of the previous eleven.[22] This change

7 The Return to Peace

satisfied most staff, but at least one group, the announcers, were quickly disillusioned by the Commission's cynical interpretation of the determination. Ellis Blain notes that not one announcer received a rise in pay, as the ABC merely transferred people to the new salary ranges at the same salary level as before.[23] That the announcers and other members of staff were dissatisfied with the result is possibly indicated by the temporary drop in Staff Association membership by 14 per cent over the ensuing twelve months, although this must be weighed against the numbers of staff who, satisfied with their new salaries, saw no further use for the Association.[24]

The cost of salaries heightened ABC concern about the size of its staff. During the 1946/7 financial year, £407 469 out of a budget of £1 132 284 went on salaries.[25] The belief that returning defence-leave staff would merely replace temporary officers recruited during the war proved to be ill-founded. From 1945 to 1948, the number of ABC staff grew by 157 positions.[26] This was possibly further evidence that many of the positions created during the wartime expansion were not adequately staffed at the time, but the increase may also have indicated a degree of bureaucratic inertia. A similar inability to retrench occurred one year later when, for administrative convenience, the New South Wales branch merged with Head Office.[27] Moses and the Commission again may have underestimated workloads, but the possibility that a large bureaucracy had begun to feed on itself should not be dismissed altogether.

The ABC remained a highly centralized bureaucracy. Heads of programme departments were now called 'directors', but Barry retained an overseer's role as controller of programmes and Holman continued to co-ordinate the work of the general staff as controller of administration. By June 1948, there were federal directors of music, drama, talks, variety, youth education, rural broadcasts, and features. Most of these departments were duplicated, on a much smaller scale, in the states. Of the total staff in 1948, 546 or nearly half worked in Sydney.[28]

Some of the ABC's state executives complained about the degree of centralization. They were acutely aware that most of the initiative in programme planning now lay with Head Office, and their presence at interstate programme controllers' conferences was not sufficient to satisfy their desire for more say in programme decisions. The Programme Development Fund was established in 1946 in answer to their complaints, ostensibly to enable them to exercise some discretion in initiating new programme ideas. But how serious was Head Office about delegating authority, however little? In March 1947, Moses threatened to abolish the Fund and 'return' all programme planning to Head Office because so few ideas were forthcoming from the state officers. The states responded by pointing out that the size of the Fund had precluded any significant experimentation.[29] It is easy to accuse Moses of cynicism, but he was not alone in wanting to maintain Head Office supremacy. At least one federal director, Clewlow, wanted even greater central control over programmes. Specifically, he wanted all drama scripts sent to his office for approval before broadcasting, to overcome what he saw as 'a lack of checking of scripts and attention to production details'.[30]

An important addition to the ABC central hierarchy which strengthened Head Office's position was the office of assistant general manager. Bearup assumed this title in March 1943 after Moses came back from the army, but at that stage it was merely a 'fill-in' position while the Commission finalized arrangements to put him in charge of an ABC office in New York. Curtin withheld permission to establish an American office on the grounds that it could prejudice Australia's relations with Britain where no similar office existed.[31] When, in November 1945, the ABC agreed to open a London office first, Bearup was sent to head it. R. C. McCall replaced him as assistant general manager, but left shortly afterwards to join the BBC. A. N. Finlay, the manager for Queensland, succeeded him in September 1946: it was from this time onwards that the position of assistant general manager became significant.

In promoting Finlay to the second most senior position, the ABC reaffirmed its policy on the type of person who could expect advancement within the organization. Like so many other senior officers, Finlay had a grammar-school background and a university education. He had distinguished himself at sport both within Australia and internationally, and during the war he had taken defence-leave from the ABC.[32] His appointment ensured that, at least in the upper echelons of the ABC, recruitment philosophies would continue, for in addition to the usual influence of a senior executive, the assistant general manager was chairman of the Appointments Advisory Committee.

Politicians readily cited the degree of centralization as the prime cause of the ABC's financial difficulties. At the beginning of 1946, the Commission forecast a deficit for 1945/6 of £25 000. To help the BBC meet the demands of the post-war period, the British government substantially increased the licence fee, but requests for similar action by the Chifley government proved fruitless.[33] Early in 1947, the ABC was forced to realize assets of about £25 000 and postponed plans to extend regional activities. Even these measures did

13 An ABC 'Listening Group'

14 Wilfrid Thomas (right) and Dick Bentley (left) in 'Out of the Bag', November 1940

15 Australian Broadcasting Commission Conference, early 1939. From left: Mrs E. M. R. Couchman, R. B. Orchard, C. J. A. Moses, W. J. Cleary, A. L. Holman, Col. L. R. Thomas, Herbert Brookes, J. W. Kitto.

16 Australian Broadcasting Commission Conference, 1943. Standing (from left): T. W. Bearup, R. J. F. Boyer, J. D. B. Medley, C. J. A. Moses. Seated (from left): P. G. J. Foley, Senator W. P. Ashley, W. J. Cleary, Ernestine Hill.

7 The Return to Peace

not reduce the possibility of a deficit for the 1946/7 financial year of nearly £60 000.³⁴ These figures, together with the fact that the ABC's budget now exceeded a million pounds, prompted politicians to ask why it was the ABC could not live within its means. Kim Beazley, Labor member for Fremantle, suggested that an official from Treasury might be appointed to the Commission.³⁵ This did not happen for the time being, but there was ready support for Calwell's suggestion that a committee of inquiry be appointed to examine the ABC's accounting and administrative procedures.³⁶

Calwell seems to have based his criticisms of top-heaviness on the simple equation of strong central control with bad management. Admittedly, Moses kept a 'tight rein on all matters from Head Office',³⁷ but this did not necessarily mean that the organization was inefficient. Nevertheless, Chifley granted Calwell's wish and in July 1947 appointed a committee to investigate this aspect of ABC affairs. A. A. Fitzgerald, an accountant and chairman of the Commonwealth Grants Commission, led the inquiry, assisted by E. G. Bonney, director-general of information, and W. T. Harris, a retired Treasury official.

The *Fitzgerald Report* went a long way towards silencing the critics. It approved the current form of organization as being the most appropriate for the ABC to meet its statutory obligations. Committee members found no evidence of over-staffing at Head Office, save for some doubts they expressed about the News Department, and they commented approvingly on the qualifications of all the senior officers. The single criticism of the administration was that the physical dispersal of staff in eight buildings in Sydney, four in Melbourne, three in Brisbane, and so forth, operated against maximum efficiency. But the Committee also recognized that the ABC's building programme had been obstructed continually by governments, and that little could be done until the official restrictions on building construction were removed. The ABC's accounting and financial procedures were found to be 'well designed' and 'effectively carried out'.³⁸

The wider public were more interested in the programmes they received in their homes than in the internal dynamics of the ABC bureaucracy. More light entertainment was the most noticeable addition to ABC programmes in the last two years of the war, but the Commission did not really attempt to define the place of this type of programme in its overall programme philosophy.

For much of 1945, light entertainment was the top item on the Federal Programme Committee's agenda. Audience surveys revealed a 'very small' audience for the ABC 'State' programme (comprising mostly locally produced material), compared with the national relays featured on the 'Alternative' programme. The reasons offered for this were the lack of 'star' attractions or big names on the State programme, the small publicity given to State programmes even in the *ABC Weekly*, the more frequent use of the ABC's better orchestras and bands on the Alternative programme, and the very designations 'State' and 'Alternative' to describe the two ABC networks. In addition, some of the transmission facilities for State programmes were not good: even station 2BL could not be heard in all parts of Sydney.[39]

In August 1945, the Programme Committee discussed the proposal, around since the early days of broadcasting, that one network in each city should be devoted exclusively to light entertainment. For the ABC, this was a revolutionary idea. As the Programme Committee observed: 'it would call for an almost complete reversal of policy; the dispensing of many house combinations [orchestras and the like] in order to get the money to enter this field, . . . [and] vastly improved technical facilities for the carrying of such relays.'[40] Yet when the proposal was put to the Commission in October the decision to introduce such an arrangement was unanimous.[41] This meant that from 1 September 1946, listeners in the main centres of Australia could for the first time choose between two quite different types of ABC programmes. The 'National' network was to carry the more serious programmes: the 'Country Hour', the 'Children's Session', serious talk programmes like 'Listening Groups' and 'Nation's Forum of the Air', weather reports and other service broadcasts, and large amounts of classical music. On the other network, now to be termed the 'Interstate' programme, listeners could hear lighter music, variety programmes, and the more popular talk sessions like 'Guest of Honour' and 'Science in the News'. The Interstate network would also carry symphonic music, but mainly the more well-known compositions, and it would still be markedly different from the commercial stations.[42]

This was one of the most significant programme policy decisions since the ABC's inception, and yet one which, at the Commission level, caused no heated debate. It is difficult to conceive of this change occurring with Cleary in the chair. Perhaps Boyer wished to silence critics who believed all ABC programmes were dull; perhaps, too, he wished to have an immediate, observable impact on programmes. In some respects, the new arrangement was a brilliant solution to the eternal problem of satisfying conflicting tastes. Yet it

7 The Return to Peace

would be wrong to suggest that the Commission had given up its cultural mission or that it had abdicated the primary role in policy formulation. Much of the impetus for the change had come from Moses and the programme controllers, probably much more than would have been tolerated in Cleary's time, but Boyer made it clear that there were definite limits to management's freedom of action when fundamental ABC philosophies were at stake. Soon after the Commission agreed to the dual programme policy, the Programme Committee urged the appointment of more 'popular announcers', the replacement of serious Sunday programmes with a 'Swing Session', and so on,[43] only to be reminded by Boyer that the new concessions to light entertainment were not to prejudice the ABC's more serious objectives. He said that in pursuing a 'mass audience', the ABC 'should be particularly careful' not to 'woo it with unworthy material', and that the ABC's claim to support 'must always be qualitative rather than quantitative achievement'.[44]

That quality music remained a high ABC priority is indicated by the maintenance of all the ABC's orchestras, dance bands, military bands, choral groups, and miscellaneous instrumental combinations. Australians' fondness for concert-going during the war, fed by the presence of many high-living American servicemen, led to a continuing thirst for public concerts when the war ended. By 1948, 29 159 people subscribed to ABC concerts, more than eight times the number in 1937.[45] The war also boosted the Australian content of concerts, partly through patriotic fervour, but mainly because of the difficulties of importing celebrity artists. According to the provisions of the 1942 Act, 2½ per cent of all music broadcast (which included broadcasts of concerts) must be by Australian composers, but this figure was always exceeded during the war and by 1948 it had reached 3.44 per cent.[46]

The ABC's financial position made it necessary to find new ways of funding these extra-broadcasting items. During the 1946/7 year, £223 127 or nearly one-fifth of the budget was spent on maintaining the musical combinations. As well, £9078 went towards subsidizing concert losses.[47] Following overseas example, the ABC looked to various local government bodies for support. In New South Wales, Moses held preliminary discussions with the state government and the Sydney City Council in 1944, during which he proposed that the ABC could contribute £36 000 per annum, and the state government and City Council £20 000 and £10 000 respectively, to maintain the Sydney Symphony Orchestra at from seventy-two to eighty-two permanent players. Agreement was reached in 1946, and Eugene Goossens became the first resident conductor.[48] During the same year, a similar agreement was concluded with the Queensland state government and the Brisbane City Council for a permanent orchestra of fifty-five players. Tasmania followed suit in February 1948.[49]

These orchestras, as well as orchestras in the other Australian states, still continue, a testimony to the success with which the ABC handled the musical education of Australia, or at least of a certain group of Australians. There were still many people in 1948 who regarded classical music as dull, but at least more Australians than ever before had been exposed to a new form of music. At the same time, the ABC continued to encourage Australian musical talent. Composers' competitions continued, and in 1947 the ABC held its first radio eisteddfod with prizes totalling £2500. The precedent this set for public support of the arts was taken up with varying enthusiasm by Australian governments in later years.

TABLE 7.1

Analysis of Programmes Broadcast by the ABC during the year ended 30 June 1948

Type of Programme	Percentage of Programme Time
Music	31.03
Variety	18.58
Drama	4.81
Children's sessions	3.01
Youth education	4.34
Talks	8.38
Religious	3.08
News	10.53
Sport	7.82
Features	0.13
Rural	2.17
General announcements	6.12

In terms of crude programme percentages, there appeared to be a major shift after 1946 from the ABC's traditional allocation of over 50 per cent of air time to music. Table 7.1 gives the percentage of programme time devoted to each type of broadcast for the year ended 30 June 1948.[50] 'Variety', however, is something of a misnomer: 11.47 per cent of 'Variety' programmes was dance music, hitherto included in the music category. The slight drop in music's share of air time was absorbed by slight increases in rural and educational broadcasts, and in sport which merely returned to its pre-war figure. A new category, 'Features' (documentaries), was

7 The Return to Peace 153

consistent with Boyer's wish to maintain the ABC's seriousness of purpose.

Overall percentages notwithstanding, the programme composition of the 'Interstate' network was quite different from anything pre-1946. It included large numbers of variety programmes: 'Once Upon a Tune', 'The Wilfrid Thomas Show', 'ABC Hit Parade', 'The Village Glee Club', 'Bob Dyer's Dude Ranch', the extremely popular Tommy Handley's BBC 'Itma' series, and others. Listeners also heard performances by Stanley Holloway, Rex Ramer, Tessie O'Shea, and other overseas stars, and frequent use was made of the ABC dance bands in Melbourne and Sydney.[51] The highlights of two typical days' programmes on station 3AR are given below:

Thursday, 2 September 1948

10.15 a.m.	Short Story
11.45	Rhythm Pianist
7.15 p.m.	Graeme Bell and his Jazz Band
8.30	Stand Easy (BBC)
9.15	Across the Styx (Third prize in ABC Feature competition)
10.30	Jim Gussey's Dance Band

Tuesday, 14 September 1948

11.30 a.m.	For Schools
6.40 p.m.	Enter Jimmy Strange
7.15	Itma (BBC)
8.00	ABC National Eisteddfod
9.15	Talking of Tight Ropes
10.25	Tuesday Story

In contrast, the 'National' network programmes were reminiscent of many earlier programme schedules. For example, station 3LO's programme for Tuesday 14 September 1948 included 'Gems from Great Composers', 'The Mitcham Choral Society', 'The BBC Symphony Orchestra', a play, a performance by the Melbourne Symphony Orchestra, plus the daily devotional broadcast and other 'service' sessions.

Rural broadcasting grew at a moderate but steady rate after the creation of a Rural Broadcasts Department in 1945. The main responsibility of its director, John Douglass, was to produce the 'Country Hour'. Boyer fully supported the continuation of *The Lawsons* segment which he believed was 'distinctly in the atmosphere of National radio'.[52] Perhaps, too, it was distinctly to the liking of one with a pastoralist background. Yet the serial retained the interest of city listeners all over Australia. In February 1947, sustained listener interest resulted in the publication of *The Lawsons* in comic-strip form in the *ABC Weekly*, but the final proof of the serial's popularity was its longevity and the undiminishing stock of listeners' letters that continued to the end. The man on the land could certainly identify with *The Lawsons*, but he more especially valued the weather and market reports, the items of rural news, and the agricultural talks which featured in the 'Country Hour'. Over the fifteen-month period to September 1947, there were more than 10 000 requests for transcripts of agricultural talks.[53]

When Douglass reviewed his department's first six years in February 1952, he expressed disappointment with the progress achieved, 'compared with what had been discussed with and promised by senior officers at the inception'. He accused the Commission of having frustrated the development of regional rural programmes.[54] But this was a little unfair to the Commission. His department was granted funds to conduct an annual Junior Farmer competition, but more importantly in 1947 state rural broadcast officers, hitherto classified as 'contract artists', were made full-time staff and were given secretarial assistance. In March 1948, there were more programme staff engaged in rural broadcasting than there were in sporting broadcasts, and only a few less than there were in variety.[55] Given the ABC's dual problems of tight finance and increasing demands for new types of programmes, rural broadcasting fared quite well.

Although sporting programmes increased their percentage of air time in line with the general increase in sporting activity after the return of peace, the status of sport within ABC programming philosophy remained uncertain. A Sporting Department was formed in 1945, but unlike other programme departments it did not have a director, merely a federal supervisor. There were as few as twelve staff in the department, and Tasmania did not even have a sporting broadcasts officer, the necessary duties being performed by a member of the state Publicity Department.[56]

Moses always wanted more sport on ABC radio, but he met resistance from his programme executives. When he requested an alteration in the programme layout to accommodate the 1947−8 cricket season, the response was hostile: John Douglass protested that similar alterations during the last season had caused a large drop in listeners to the 'Country Hour', and that to shift agricultural talks on to 1 p.m. would render them inaccessible to the farmers for whom they were intended; Clewlow refused to contemplate any change in

7 The Return to Peace

the 'Children's Hour' time-slot, arguing that last time it had led to a drop in listeners' letters from a weekly average of 1200 to a figure of 500.⁵⁷ There was also resistance at the Commission level. Early in 1948, Moses was unable to persuade the commissioners to appoint a director of sport. Boyer and Dawes especially believed there was already too much sport on the ABC.⁵⁸ In later years, ABC television became famous for its coverage of international sporting events and came to compete strongly with the commercial stations in this area. This was only possible after major changes in ABC programme policy and when the ABC became 'ratings' conscious; for the time being, sporting programmes remained a point of disjunction in programme policy.

Educational broadcasting was an area of programme expansion. There were school broadcasts in all states from 1936, and by 1941, 14 per cent of Australian schools were 'listening-in'.⁵⁹ The ABC was advised by a School Broadcasts Advisory Committee in each state and a Federal Educational Broadcasts Committee. Contributions by these bodies were not equal in value: it was once said of the Victorian committee that 'Most of the members have little or no contact with broadcasts for schools, and only one is noticeable for enthusiasm and ideas'. Yet it was believed they saved school broadcasts from 'the narrowness and pedantry of the teaching profession'.⁶⁰ Apart from the committees, the success or otherwise of the broadcasts depended on the co-operation of state authorities. In Britain, most local authorities met the whole or part of the cost of installing and maintaining radio sets in schools; in Australia, the only state to contribute any of the cost was South Australia. In Western Australia, there were radios in most schools, but for a time some teachers refused to turn them on.⁶¹

Despite these problems, the ABC remained keen to continue school broadcasts. Boyer took a special interest in them and helped to bring about the holding of a 'Radio in Education' conference in Canberra in 1946. Part of his opening address said:

> Precisely because Radio is a home instrument, it becomes thereby a permanent educative factor in the modern citizen's life almost literally from the cradle to the grave. Our infant Australian makes friends with the family listening set in the kindergarten session. ... Then our youthful citizen graduates into the children's and youth's sessions. ... In between the inevitable thriller serial, Bob Hope and Bing Crosby, he is introduced to a whole panoply of influences, musical and rational. He eavesdrops on his father listening-in to a political forum. He meets the great figures of the world. He is on nodding terms with Wickham Steed and Walter

Lippmann—or nearer to home he has come under the spell of Professor Dakin's fascinating science or Walter Murdoch's whimsical wisdom. Perhaps, too, he has peeped behind the curtain of orchestral mysteries.[62]

These words reflected Boyer's total commitment to radio as an instrument of mass education. By 1948, 4687 or almost 45 per cent of Australian schools were registered listeners to ABC school programmes: 1569 in New South Wales, 1401 in Victoria, 355 in Queensland, 687 in South Australia, 438 in Western Australia, and 237 in Tasmania. South Australia had the highest percentage of registered schools: 73 per cent.[63]

The question of ABC news programmes was finally settled in the post-war period. Labor had always favoured an independent news service and probably needed little of the lobbying done by Dixon during the war years.[64] Cleary, Moses, and Dixon had been in basic agreement about what the ABC wanted, both as regards news-gathering facilities and the content of bulletins, but Boyer was confronted with the issue at a time of financial crisis for the ABC. For this reason, he, Medley, and Dawes were more inclined to negotiate a further agreement with the newspapers for the time being. J. S. Hanlon favoured independence, but he was not prepared to oppose Boyer publicly.[65] Chifley therefore faced a dilemma: how to persuade the ABC to establish its own independent news service without appearing to dictate terms in breach of Curtin's guarantees of April 1945. When Boyer, Medley, and Dawes pressed their views on him, he temporarily avoided confrontation by referring the issue to the Standing Committee on Broadcasting.

At the hearing, Boyer argued that an independent news service would cost the ABC as much as £155 000 per annum, as against an estimated £20 000 per annum for a new agreement with the press. Added to this last figure would be the cost of a few additional staff.[66] Moses was fairly noncommittal in his evidence, but Dixon spoke enthusiastically about independence.[67] Rupert Henderson, representing the Australian Newspaper Proprietors' Association, claimed to the surprise of many present that it was a matter of 'supreme indifference' to his organization which option the ABC chose.[68]

The Standing Committee divided on party lines in giving its recommendations: the Labor majority recommended the establishment of an independent news service; the Liberal and Country party members urged the conclusion of a further newspaper agreement.[69]

Chifley accepted the majority recommendation and an amendment to the Broadcasting Act compelling the ABC to establish an independent news service was introduced on 31 July 1946, at the end

7 The Return to Peace

of the parliamentary session and just before the federal elections. Opposition senators, devoid of any reasonable arguments against the Bill, attacked its timing. Senator G. McLeay remarked: 'It is obvious that the proposal to set up an independent news-gathering organization is a political stunt, the object of which is to facilitate the dissemination of propaganda on behalf of the Labour party at the forth-coming general elections.'[70] In the House of Representatives, J. P. Abbott suggested that, following from the Bill, a future postmaster-general might cut out all news services until only Tass remained.[71] The majority report of the Standing Committee had argued that the main issue was to obtain news 'untainted by private interests',[72] not cost, and Labor members kept reiterating this point during the debate. L. Haylen, for example, said that 'If an independent news service will bring freshness, warmth and clean reporting into the air and into the 3 000 000 homes throughout Australia in which radio receivers are installed its cost will be fully justified.'[73] Eventually, the amendment passed without alteration, and the ABC's independent news service officially commenced at 7 p.m. on 1 June 1947.

As with entertainment the ABC had succeeded in claiming new territory, in effect extending its organizational boundaries into a hitherto highly guarded monopoly area. Unlike the earlier victory, this one had been achieved in spite of Commission attitudes and with the active support of the government. In a sense, therefore, the ABC sacrificed some of its autonomy in the process. Boyer was concerned about this encroachment on the ABC's freedom of action and at one stage considered resigning if Chifley did not approve his plan to renegotiate an agreement with the press.[74] He had not resigned, mainly because it would have achieved nothing: it is highly unlikely that Chifley would have backed down, and even if he had, Boyer would have been left with a divided Commission and resentment from within the ABC News Department. Yet in another sense there was very little sacrifice of autonomy. Boyer rejected an independent news service only on the grounds of cost, not as a matter of principle. Chifley certainly influenced the timing, but in the long term the ABC would probably have created an independent news service anyway.

The ABC had even less say in the introduction of broadcasts of Commonwealth Parliament debates in 1946. New Zealand had broadcast Parliament since 1936, but the Lyons government declined to introduce similar broadcasts in Australia in accord with its belief that nothing should be broadcast which encouraged public debate or political controversy.[75] The issue was revived in September 1945, when the Parliamentary Standing Committee on Broadcasting claimed that broadcasts of Parliament would 'raise the standard of debates, enhance the prestige of Parliament, and contribute to a better informed judgment throughout the community on matters affecting the common good and the public interest, nationally and internationally'. They would also help to overcome the problem of distance which prevented most Australians from attending Parliamentary sessions.[76] Although a subcommittee of Cabinet comprising Don Cameron, Ashley, Calwell, Beasley, and N. J. O. Makin endorsed these sentiments, Chifley deferred action, perhaps because of his personal misgivings about the value of broadcasting debates in full.[77]

While the government procrastinated, Boyer attempted to take the initiative by suggesting that the ABC could broadcast a half-hour review of the day's parliamentary proceedings between 10.30 and 11 p.m. The Labor Caucus rejected the proposal.[78] Chifley now bowed to the wishes of the party majority and a Parliamentary Proceedings Broadcasting Bill was introduced on 19 June 1946. Parliament House was wired for live broadcasts at a cost of more than £5000, and the first official broadcast took place on 10 July.[79] The *Sydney Morning Herald* criticized members for 'choosing' to debate a particularly boring Bill, the Overseas Telecommunications Bill. It also commented on a high-pitched whistle at the beginning of the broadcast during prayers: the result of W. M. Hughes adjusting his private listening device![80]

Some politicians tried to apply traditional ABC standards of 'balance' by demanding right-of-reply facilities whenever they were attacked in the House. Realizing this would create an impossible situation, Boyer warned that unless the requests ceased the ABC might find it necessary to eliminate parliamentary broadcasts altogether.[81]

The public displayed no enthusiasm for the broadcasts. When they were first suggested in 1936, many listeners expressed doubts about the usefulness of the sessions, and one cartoonist volunteered the opinion that listeners would prefer to hear the yapping of dogs.[82] The first broadcasts in 1946 merely confirmed these earlier predictions. One listener suggested 'someone should enlighten interjectors that their pearls of wit are unintelligible over the air and come through as boorish and uncouth grunts and shouts'. Another asked whether the ABC was still considering the pleasure of its audience.[83] A survey in July showed, perhaps predictably, that there was an 'above average' interest in 'Upper Class' homes, a 'well above average' interest in 'Middle Class' homes, and a 'below average' interest in 'Industrial Class' homes.[84] But no matter what results the survey had produced, it was unlikely that the politicians, having won their piece of the airwaves, would ever agree to relinquish it.

7 The Return to Peace

Throughout these programme developments the Commission never lost sight of its basic commitment to lead public taste. Programmes on the Interstate network were bound to attract new listeners, but the ABC had higher hopes than a mass audience. In Boyer's own words: 'We hope to recruit, through the Interstate Programme, audiences to listen to our National Programme'.[85] The attitude of the Commission, in contrast to some senior officers, remained generally one of indifference to listeners' opinions, although Boyer's commission, like its predecessors, wished to maintain an image of community consciousness. Boyer eagerly accepted public speaking engagements and personally answered mail addressed to the chairman, all good public relations. However, formal listener research was still at a token level, consisting of reports from 'Official Listeners' or the occasional questionnaire.[86] With radio now a firmly established medium and with the ABC's own position, by most predictions, assured, Boyer's commission could afford to be more culturally arrogant. That the ABC was more self-confident by now is suggested by Boyer's remarks to the Federal Programme Committee in June 1947: '[the ABC] has to work out its own standards, for which no other broadcasting organization overseas can serve as a complete precent [sic] or guide. We must adventure according to our own peculiar circumstances.'[87] Here we see the ABC going a step further than rejection of listener demands: the earlier reverence for the BBC is virtually cast aside. This was a far cry from Charles Lloyd Jones' promise in 1932 to 'walk in the footsteps of the BBC and fall in behind Britain'. Of course, the ABC still depended on large amounts of BBC material: BBC transcriptions, for example, took up approximately 38 per cent of variety programme time from June 1946 to June 1947.[88] And Boyer certainly retained a high personal regard for the BBC. But there was now an acknowledgement that both organizations operated in quite different milieux, and that the assumptions of the BBC controllers were not necessarily nor always appropriate for the ABC.

There were other areas of programming besides news and parliamentary broadcasts in which the ABC continued to experience political interference in the post-war period. The controversy surrounding Dr Norman Haire's broadcast on birth control during the war was but a portent of the battle over sex education broadcasts from 1944 to 1946. In April 1944, W. J. McKell, the premier of New South Wales, asked Curtin to refer the question of sex broadcasts to the Parliamentary Standing Committee on Broadcasting after the Australian Federation of Commercial Broadcasting Stations refused to co-operate in a campaign against venereal disease run by the state

Health Department. The Federation considered the talks were unsuitable for broadcasting. The ABC had no such qualms: it had already broadcast some talks on VD and more were contemplated.[89] However, the issue was now out of ABC hands.

The Standing Committee's report, published in March 1946, reveals much about contemporary attitudes to sexual relations. At least three of the signatories were Roman Catholic: S. K. Amour, W. G. Bryson, and C. Chambers. The religious leanings of two committee members, G. J. Bowden and H. Hays, are unclear, but they were both farmers who could be expected to have fairly conservative views. J. Francis was a Methodist, R. H. Nash and D. O. Watkins both Church of England, and J. A. Guy a prominent Presbyterian lay preacher and a supporter of the temperance movement.[90] The first part of the report justified their refusal to hear testimony from anybody not committed to Christian values of morality, in the process praising the public-spiritedness of one witness for denouncing a lecturer who admitted having 'no moral objection to abortion or masturbation'. It was then argued that since Australia was a Christian country, it would be a 'corruption of its ideals' to permit broadcasts which undermined Christian sexual standards. The Committee recalled the words of King George V, that 'the greatness of the nation rests on the sweet, clean life of the family', and it recommended that non-Christians should be denied facilities to broadcast sex talks. One argument the Committee considered worth quoting was that broadcasts on VD could damage Australia's image abroad by creating the impression that the disease was widespread.[91] Acting on these findings, the postmaster-general banned all broadcasts of matter relating to sex and VD.

Mrs Ruth Tyson, a listener from Tasmania, would no doubt have applauded the Standing Committee's recommendations. In August 1945, she wrote to the postmaster-general and thanked him for penalizing people who broadcast 'objectionable matter'. While admitting that she normally did not listen to such broadcasts, she confessed to sitting through an entire production of *The Perfect Marriage*, judging it to be 'the filthiest, most suggestive, and the most immoral thing that I have ever listened to', and added: 'What is to become of our young people, most of them without any religious training. ... The whole thing was sickening'.[92] To be fair, Mrs Tyson was not criticizing a sex education broadcast, but her comments reflected a singular lack of tolerance of any reference to sex on radio. However, it is questionable whether her views or those of the Standing Committee reflected majority opinion. The ABC's National Talks Advisory Committee condemned the postmaster-

7 The Return to Peace

general's ban.⁹³ But it is even more significant that, in giving evidence to the Standing Committee, the Rev. J. J. Booth (Anglican Archbishop of Melbourne), Dr C. H. Dickson of the BMA, Ivy Brookes (president of the National Council of Women), Mrs H. C. Marfell of the Country Women's Association, Miss Alice Bentham of the YWCA, the Rev. G. A. Judkins (representing the Council of Churches), and others all said that they had no objection whatever to sex education broadcasts.⁹⁴

Political broadcasts continued to draw criticisms from sections of the community, although direct government interference was, as G. C. Bolton points out, generally less than in preceding years.⁹⁵ The end of the war reduced the justification for censorship in the interests of national security, but the ABC was also fortunate to have a sympathetic prime minister who was less inclined to interfere with political broadcasts than some of his predecessors. Chifley did not have the close personal interest in the ABC that Curtin had. He listened to it mainly for news sessions or a bit of light dinner music.⁹⁶ Moses testified to Chifley's good record in a letter in 1949:

> I feel I must write to let you know how much I have appreciated the scrupulously fair and objective attitude you have always maintained towards the ABC. Never at any time have I been aware of the faintest suggestion of pressure from you when controversial issues were occupying our news sessions . . .⁹⁷

Initially cautious at the end of the war, the ABC had instructed McCall, then assistant general manager, to censor any political items from news bulletins, but this arrangement was discontinued shortly afterwards because of the administrative problems it caused and the heavy criticisms it received in Parliament.⁹⁸ In June 1946, a more flexible definition of 'balance' in programming was adopted so that in future controversial political material could be broadcast during news or other sessions without an immediate counter, provided that 'over a reasonable period' care was taken to present alternative views.⁹⁹

An indication that the Commission was willing to tolerate a similarly wide spectrum of political views within its own organization is a resolution it passed in 1946 stating that no directive would be issued on whether staff should participate in political activity.¹ In theory, this resolution meant ABC employees were free to join any political organization, the Communist Party included; in practice, it would have been a brave employee who did so. Community attitudes were as strong a deterrent to such action as any possible executive disfavour within the ABC. 'Respectable'

Australians at this time feared communism. Menzies had tried to ban the communist movement during his brief prime-ministership, and there is no doubt that large numbers of Australians supported him. Although Communist Party membership in Australia declined between 1945 and 1948, communist influence grew, especially among the leaderships of trade unions. This fed the belief that the ABC, as a public institution, should do what it could to silence communist spokesmen by denying them access to broadcasting facilities. B. A. Santamaria and the Catholic Social Studies Movement, an organization formed in the closing years of the war to prevent the possibility of a communist revolution in Australia, reinforced this belief through their propagandist activities.[2]

It was in this context that Professor F. A. Bland objected to an ABC news broadcast in December 1945, which reported statements by striking steelworkers at BHP. Bland alleged that the strikers were communists who had no right to be heard on the ABC. Boyer defended the broadcast, arguing that so long as the communist movement remained legal the ABC was obliged to report its activities impartially.[3] Some of the ABC news editors were not so broadminded: they asked for the authority to eliminate communist material from news bulletins. To Boyer's credit, he remained firm and insisted that while the communists were legal the ABC could not ignore them.[4]

Boyer's experiences in Germany from 1935 to 1939 had taught him the dangers of a broadcasting system which tolerated no dissentient opinion. He was determined, to the extent that he could influence events, that a similar system should not develop in Australia.[5] But the most noticeable thing about the December 1945 controversy was the lack of government intervention, a sign that the ABC really was being given a freer hand in political broadcasts than hitherto.

The Liberal-Country Party opposition experienced difficulty in citing examples of blatant political direction to the ABC in the late 1940s. On one occasion, trying to promote the idea of the ABC as a Labor propaganda station, the Liberals attacked a series of broadcasts by Dr H. C. Coombs, the director-general of post-war reconstruction. Far from propagandizing for the Labor Party, Coombs was conducting an innocuous but very useful public service by replying on air to letters from ex-servicemen about their repatriation rights, offering advice on the appropriate authorities to approach for benefits.[6]

Political interference was more evident in relation to overseas shortwave broadcasting, or Radio Australia as the overseas service

7 The Return to Peace

was now commonly called. The ABC still helped to produce overseas transmissions, but control remained, since 1944, under the Department of Information. Both the BBC and the CBC controlled the shortwave services in their countries; the ABC considered it invidious that it did not.

The main obstacle was A. A. Calwell, minister for information since 1943 and as well minister for immigration since November 1946. Calwell had urged the nationalization of broadcasting services in 1942, and he continued to believe in strong ministerial control. Boyer's repeated requests during 1945 for the return of Radio Australia were met by Calwell's assertions that the time was ripe for greater ministerial control 'in order to obviate the possibility of damage to Australia's prestige and interests abroad'.[7] It is therefore not surprising that in Parliament there were allegations that the 'Voice of Australia' was becoming daily more like the 'Voice of Calwell'.[8]

A number of incidents from 1945 to 1947 provided the government with convenient excuses for refusing to relinquish control of Radio Australia. In November 1945, Geoffrey Sawer broadcast a series of talks on the Indonesian crisis of 17 August, when Indonesian nationalists led by Sukarno and Hatta declared independence from Dutch rule. Sawer accused the Western powers of adopting hypocritical attitudes in the dispute. The Chifley government privately sympathized with the Indonesian nationalists, but was bound by diplomatic etiquette to support the Dutch. Chifley denounced the broadcast and denied that it in any way represented Australian government policy. As a result of this incident, all future shortwave broadcasts dealing with foreign policy were to be vetted by the Department of External Affairs.[9]

A second incident brought the ABC into direct conflict with Calwell. As minister for immigration, Calwell was determined that no one, including the ABC, should endanger his plans to bring out some 70 000 migrants each year. He fought hard to keep the Department of Information from being disbanded so that he could use its facilities to promote the immigration programme, and he was equally concerned that the press should provide fair coverage.[10] A problem arose when, before the commencement of the main immigration programme, he offered to accommodate 2000 of the 200 000 displaced Jews in Germany and Austria. The *Bulletin* and *Smith's Weekly* criticized the intake on the grounds that the refugees were receiving preferential treatment over potential British migrants. Calwell was furious, but could do nothing: the emergency powers he had once used during the war to suspend a number of newspapers for opposing his censorship regulations were no longer available.[11] However, he did consider he was in a position to tell the ABC what to do. On 20 September 1946, he protested to Boyer over a broadcast which satirized the Jewish refugees, claiming that it was 'calculated to inflame the passions of racial bigots and to discredit a phase of Government policy which is of the highest national importance'.[12] This incident strengthened his resolve to scrutinize ABC operations, and to keep overseas broadcasting, that area of operations currently under his control, out of ABC hands.

A further clash with Calwell occurred in May 1947, after both the ABC and the commercial stations approached the government to amend the Copyright Act. Calwell claimed that the ABC had agreed to collaborate with the Lang Labor group (which owned some commercial stations) in return for their moving a motion to transfer Radio Australia back to the ABC.[13] There is no evidence of this. The ABC recorded its disgust at Calwell's allegations, and the incident helped neither the ABC's continuing fight with the Australasian Performing Rights Association nor the dispute with Calwell himself.[14]

The Sawer controversy exposed the conflicts still existing over responsibility for Radio Australia broadcasts. Together with Calwell's obvious annoyance with the ABC, it delayed the transfer of Radio Australia back to the ABC until the end of the decade.

Politicians who still had complaints about the ABC could voice them during debate on the new broadcasting Bill introduced in 1948.

M. F. Dixon believes that Chifley was about to nationalize all broadcasting services just before introducing this Bill.[15] Boyer probably would not have opposed nationalization, for he once admitted to a member of the Standing Committee on Broadcasting that he favoured a monopoly public broadcasting service, and that he believed the effect of commercial stations in Australia had been 'little short of disastrous'.[16] Chifley certainly was not averse to the idea of nationalization of industries and services. In July 1947, his government nationalized Qantas. It also nationalized overseas telecommunications. In October 1947, it attempted to nationalize the banks, but this measure produced a very fierce reaction which possibly influenced Chifley's decision not to attempt nationalization of the broadcasting system at this stage. This move no doubt disappointed those within his party who supported the statement on nationalization signed by the three Labor members of the Gibson Committee. Nevertheless, it was the recommendations of the

7 The Return to Peace

Fitzgerald Committee which prevailed and which were incorporated into the new Act.

Don Cameron outlined details of the legislation on 27 October 1948. Membership of the Commission was to be increased to seven to 'strengthen' the ABC. One of the new members would come from Treasury, the other from the Postmaster-General's Department. The Treasury representative could advise on the ABC's financial problems, but he was no doubt to perform a watchdog function also. Control of the ABC's technical services remained with the postmaster-general, against ABC wishes, but the representative from his department would advise the Commission in this area. Most importantly, the Bill changed the method of funding the ABC. In future, all ABC income would come from consolidated revenue. Funding would be triennial, with the ABC having to submit budget estimates to Treasury just like any government department. An additional feature of the Bill was the establishment of the Australian Broadcasting Control Board. Consisting of three members, its job would be to co-ordinate national and commercial programmes, to monitor technical and programme standards, and to advise the postmaster-general on the allocation of commercial broadcasting licences.[17]

Before the Bill's introduction, Chifley denied that the proposed Broadcasting Control Board was a 'socialistic' enterprise, but the *Sydney Morning Herald* said the new Bill demonstrated the government's desire to dictate to the ABC.[18] Inside Parliament, the opposition's criticisms were extraordinary. A. W. Fadden labelled the Bill 'one of the most subtle and dangerous pieces of legislation' introduced in recent times. He claimed that it went very close to nationalization.[19] Senator Annabelle Rankin read into the Bill a 'sinister and abhorrent determination to dragoon all broadcasting to a pre-determined government pattern', and saw it as a move towards a totalitarian state.[20]

In the event, the Control Board gradually absorbed the functions of the Standing Committee on Broadcasting and proved to be a far less interfering body. The Bill actually foreshadowed the eclipse of the Standing Committee by removing the compulsion on the minister to refer matters to it. Indeed, the Committee had long ceased to be regarded as a worthwhile body. The Country Party boycotted it and the Liberal Party condemned it.[21] Some politicians called for its abolition, some for its reform, and at one stage Earle Page moved, albeit without success, for the disallowance of the running expenses of the Committee.[22] The 1948 Act left the Standing

Committee intact, but the Chifley government referred no more items to it, and the subsequent Menzies government appointed no one to it. It was formally disbanded in 1950. For all practical purposes it was superseded by the Broadcasting Control Board which, despite the initial objections, continued until 1976.

The opposition did have cause for complaint against one new clause which extended the ban on dramatized political broadcasts to any issue not more than five years old. Hitherto, the ban applied only during election campaigns. The government was apparently embarrassed by a recent series of dramatizations by one 'John Henry Austral', the stage name of a journalist who had once been a press secretary for the Labor Party. John Henry Austral had left Labor to work for the Liberal Party. He constructed a series of political plays for commercial radio, which contained impersonations of the prime minister, the speaker, the minister for labour and national service, and others.[23] Some Labor men feared that the public would mistake the plays for the real thing, but banning was a questionable solution. Kim Beazley was one of the younger members of the party who tried to thwart this attempt at 'political suppression'. At a Caucus meeting on 7 October 1948, he urged a more thorough examination of the proposed legislation but to no avail.[24] The opposition could hardly have let the clause pass undebated. 'Destroy the "John Henry Austral" series', declared E. J. Harrison, 'and more will be destroyed than a mere series of broadcasts that criticize the activities of a government in power. A principle that distinguishes a democracy from a dictatorship will be destroyed'.[25]

Many people may have believed Harrison, and many more the *Daily Telegraph* which said the Bill had a 'Goebbels Touch'.[26] It could be argued, on the other hand, that Chifley's further amendment clarifying the ABC's powers over political and controversial broadcasts bolstered the ABC's position.[27] But did it? In many ways, the independence manifested in this amendment and earlier in Curtin's declaration of 1945 was a mere paper assurance. The government's record from 1945 to 1948 held out bleak prospects for greater ABC freedom of action. The autonomy the ABC temporarily gained in political broadcasts it forfeited in financial control. A guaranteed share of the listener's licence fee had provided some semblance of independent income: now the ABC was totally dependent on government generosity. For technical services, it continued to rely on a government department. Radio Australia remained, for the time being, outside its jurisdiction. The ABC's power over its workforce was circumscribed by the introduction of

7 The Return to Peace

statutory Staff Regulations and the need to abide by the decisions of the Arbitration Court. The Commission had been overridden on the question of news services and on the nature of parliamentary broadcasts. And now the placement of two public servants on the Commission increased the avenues for government supervision and direction. In fact, there were few matters of significance on which the ABC could act without government approval; this had always been the case and would continue to be so.

Conclusion

During the 1930s and 1940s, the ABC commissioners were members of a cultural elite who believed that through radio they could enrich Australia's cultural life. They hoped that by creating an Australian BBC they could achieve a result similar to that of Reith and his successors: as they saw it, a more tolerant, informed, and 'cultured' society. However, by the end of the 1940s, they had been forced to modify their conception of what was appropriate broadcasting material for the ABC.

In some respects, the ABC commissioners set themselves an impossible task. They wanted to improve the cultural standards of the community, but the conservative, Old World values they espoused courted resistance from a community more interested in entertainment for its own sake. They wished to present an image of community consciousness, but were constantly subject to accusations of catering only to the wishes of a privileged, educated minority and of employing only people with the right background who shared the ABC's approach and 'ideology'. They wanted to raise political debate in Australia to new levels, but they were forced to bend to the wishes of governments all too eager either to stifle mention of political topics, or, from the late 1930s on, to use broadcasting as a means of influencing voters. In general, they had constantly to compromise their idealism for more pragmatic interpretations of policy to ensure the ABC's continuance in an unsympathetic political and social climate.

Though leaders in the communications field, they revealed themselves unable to communicate with the very people they wished to reach. From their own experiences, they wrongly assumed that once exposed to new cultural forms the bulk of the population would be enticed away from the popular fare of the commercial stations. In the event, many people not only ignored ABC programmes, since they were considered 'highbrow' and dull, but also became hostile towards the ABC. Their hostility was reinforced by their having to pay a licence fee to finance an organization whose aims they either resented or failed to understand.

Conclusion

A similar lack of communication was evident in the Commission's relations with its staff, especially those in the lower echelons of the organization. The success of the ABC's cultural mission depended to some extent on staff co-operation. Many staff members undoubtedly shared the commissioners' goals, but at the same time the ABC was for them, above all, a livelihood. Thus as the organization grew and pressures of work increased it was working conditions, not the higher purposes of the ABC, which increasingly occupied their minds. The formation of the Staff Association and the Senior Officers' Association in the late 1930s forced the Commission to face the problems inevitably attendant on an expanding bureaucracy. Thereafter a new formality entered into relations between the Commission and its staff, culminating in the introduction of the statutory Staff Regulations in 1948. The development of careerism was an inescapable consequence of the ABC's desire to extend its boundaries and take on new functions, but it was an aspect of institutional growth which received slow recognition and not altogether sympathetic action from the Commission. The commissioners' backgrounds may have affected their views; but much of their inertia stemmed from the depth of their conviction about the rightness of the ABC's purpose and their corresponding inability to sympathize with the more immediate bread-and-butter preoccupations of their employees.

A further problem for the Commission was that as the growing ABC organization developed a momentum of its own, not only staffing but programme policies were called into question. The introduction of the light entertainment network in 1946 was as much the result of pressures from within the organization as of a profound change in outlook on the part of the Commission. G. R. Curnow sees this tendency already present in the ABC of the 1930s, arguing that for the period up to 1942 virtually every programme decision was based upon the recommendations of the general manager and his staff rather than the Commission.[1] To accept this view is to understate the importance of Cleary in these years. Cleary was a forceful, full-time chairman who nursed his general manager through the vital years during which the basic organizational structure and fundamental programme philosophies of the ABC were established. Moses was certainly an enthusiastic, capable chief executive, but he was firmly under Cleary's direction at this time. There is no evidence that Cleary had lost any of the initiative until 1943 at least, when Curtin brought Moses back from the army. He determined policy, albeit in conjunction with Moses, the senior officers, and the Programme Committee, and he evolved a very personal, highly centralized administrative structure which ensured the implementation of all important policy directives. Indeed, just as one can speak of a 'Reithian ethos' for the BBC during the 1930s, so one can see the ABC of the 1930s and early 1940s as pervaded by Cleary's ideas. Yet in the end it was this strong centralized control which produced, perhaps ironically, a strong unionist feeling among the staff, and which was used by Moses to extend his own influence on staffing and on programming.

The ABC commissioners worked on the rather naive assumption that their organization would perform only those functions they intended for it, underestimating the distortions which not only internal but external pressures could produce. Cleary, for example, intended through the promotion of talk sessions to stimulate community discussion on controversial issues. While there can be no doubt that the ABC was a 'major reforming influence' in this area,[2] the very pursuit of the policy attracted government attention, resulting in heavy external and internal censorship. Only safe topics were broadcast, and the ABC, rather than perform the stimulatory role envisaged for it, became a political tool in the hands of a conservative government, helping to perpetuate community apathy on political topics. When war broke out, politicians reversed this trend and used the ABC to stir up wartime fervour, a development which was also in conflict with the commissioners' original intentions to encourage rational and critical thinking. Nevertheless, the commissioners responded to the pressures of the time and accepted that new functions, such as the dissemination of propaganda, were appropriate for the ABC in the circumstances. Thus originally unforeseen functions adopted by the ABC to a very large extent reflected changes in the political and social milieu. The ABC never operated in a vacuum: despite the commissioners' reiterated desire to remake Australian society, they were never really free to do so.

Nevertheless, the ABC was not without substantial achievements. Though it is not possible to estimate precisely the ABC's influence on the Australian people between 1932 and 1948, since no satisfactory means of measurement exist, there can be no doubt that it became Australia's best-known cultural institution and that it affected the lives of millions. It had pegged an indisputable claim to a piece of the entertainment and media world. Even the older established interests with whom it continued to compete, such as the APRA and sporting authorities, recognized this. Almost everyone had a view of the ABC. It came to symbolize many different things: to some, authority, veracity, impartiality; to others, moral laxity,

Conclusion

dullness, pretentiousness, or worse. That such a spectrum of attributions was possible indicates that the ABC was a many-faceted organization, not the faceless monolith of popular mythology.

In general terms, ABC initiatives may have rigidified the divisions between the cultural elite and the bulk of the population, yet, by 1948, less wealthy, less well-educated Australians could find common ground with their cultural 'superiors'. This was true especially of musical appreciation. Before 1932, only a privileged few Australians had experienced a live symphony concert, watched a performance by an artist of international distinction, or heard recordings of classical music. Now, at least in theory, the opportunity to enjoy these different cultural forms was not the preserve of any one group in the community.

The ABC's model of 'high culture' and the extent to which it was revered, despised, or emulated, may well be a measure of ABC influence. Standards both of performance and of appreciation were set by the ABC, which many people, including those involved in the other media (even in commercial radio) began to observe as the desired levels in a cultured society. Even those people who rejected or belittled the ABC's conception of 'high culture' by their own actions admitted of its existence and of its recognition within the community.

More important perhaps, through its national network, the ABC helped to bridge the huge distances which separated Australians. Addressing the Fitzgerald Committee in 1947, Boyer spoke of the ABC's responsibility 'to develop through radio a sense of national unity and to aid in the breaking down of excessive parochialism'.[3] It is undeniable that, in some degree, the ABC had helped to combat the 'tyranny of distance' by bringing Australians into contact with each other and with other parts of the world. Admittedly, this achievement can be seen as a function of the introduction of radio generally, but the ABC played a central part through the development of regional broadcasting centres and through its many national and international relays.

The ABC stands out as a major qualification to the popular view of the 1930s in Australia as one of the 'mean' decades during which intolerance, apathy, and economic insecurity allegedly combined to prevent the flowering of ideas or other cultural achievements. It was during these years that the ABC was playing a highly innovatory role in music, literature, drama, and the arts generally. This is true also of the war years and beyond. While the importance of radio should not be exaggerated, there can be no doubt that Australian cultural life received a much-needed stimulus from the ABC. It, much more so than the commercial stations or other sections of the media, patronized the arts, providing both a means of employment for many creative people and an opportunity for the community to appreciate their talent.

The commissioners' hopes for the ABC were understandable in view of the expectations that accompanied the introduction of radio technology in Australia. Radio was a new thing, a technological miracle with, so it was believed, unlimited potential for producing far-reaching social changes. Although many of these expectations were dashed, radio did cut deeply into many people's thinking, affecting their attitudes and their way of life. There were new rituals of performance and of listening. In politics, for example, radio was partly responsible for new modes of electioneering: members of Parliament had now to worry much more about public images. As one contemporary put it: 'broadcasting has largely taken the place of the platform speaker and the public meeting in influencing the public'.[4] People listened either collectively or individually to broadcasts of plays, educational debates, talks, concerts, international sporting events, and so forth, all signalling a communications revolution in which the ABC was an essential ingredient.

The ABC today is a large bureaucracy of more than 6000 people. It is still a highly centralized organization, though nowadays there is less likelihood that a directive issued at the top will find accurate translation at the lower levels. Control continues to be by a commission and a separate executive, with the latter now much more influential in policy formulation. Some of the old problems persist. The latest annual report notes that 'The rising cost of rights to provide coverage of major sporting events . . . continues to concern the Commission'.[5] There is also comment on the budgetary problems, as the ABC continues to be at the mercy of government appropriations. ABC staff maintain their campaigns for a greater say in their own affairs. The battle for a staff commissioner was won, only to be negated by the actions of a new government and the acquiescence of a new Commission. The staff now strike to make their dissatisfaction known, with resultant black-outs on both radio and television. Calls for greater independence for the ABC are still in the air, and politicians of both parties continue to pay lip-service to this widespread demand. Yet the ABC continues to do well what it has always done best. During the 1977/8 year, attendances at ABC concerts numbered 970 665, and a recent survey showed that ABC news bulletins more than hold their own against alternative sources of news.[6] The ideas of cultural uplift are gone, but ABC commitments to the maintenance of standards remain firm, on radio

Conclusion

if not on television. ABC English, ABC drama, ABC musical productions, and ABC modes of presentation generally continue to be the standard by which many other performances are judged.

The ABC of the 1930s and 1940s derived much of its glamour from the awe the new radio technology inspired in Australians, and much of its drive and purpose from the fact that its commissioners firmly believed that the ABC could help produce a better-educated, more culturally aware population. While today the same glamour is not apparent, the policies and practices of the ABC still bear a very close resemblance to those of its early years. Cleary and Boyer and their fellow commissioners not only set a pattern for programming and staffing which has survived for almost fifty years, but devised an administrative style that, from time to time, has enabled the ABC to withstand severe political and social pressures.

Appendix 1

Australian Broadcasting Commission Programme Analysis, 1939–45

Type of Programme	Percentage of Programme Time for Year Ended 30 June						
	1939	1940	1941	1942	1943	1944	1945
Music	60.08	54.07	50.30	52.21	53.36	57.62	54.97
News							
Bulletins	4.99	9.49	12.68	12.49	13.19	10.15	10.92
Commentaries	1.93	2.66	2.92	2.77	2.40	1.69	2.48
Total	6.92	12.15	15.60	15.26	15.59	11.84	13.40
Sport	7.28	7.61	5.19	3.31	1.80	2.00	2.44
Religion	3.12	3.36	3.17	3.38	3.29	2.55	2.57
Plays	3.53	3.73	3.06	2.84	3.32	3.46	3.35
Serials	1.76	1.51	0.69	1.02	1.04	1.38	1.73
Talks							
General	2.31	1.16	0.87	0.57	0.75	0.86	2.79
Special subjects	10.29	10.17	10.95	11.68	11.05	10.79	12.33
Total	12.60	11.33	11.82	12.25	11.80	11.65	15.12
Other	4.71	6.24	10.57	9.63	9.80	9.20	6.42

Because the ABC changed the headings under which programmes were classified from time to time, these figures should be treated with some caution, although they can be taken as accurate indicators of trends.

Figures from ABC Annual Reports, 1939–45.

Appendix 2

Australian Broadcasting Commission Organization, 1932 and 1948

ABC ORGANIZATION, 1932

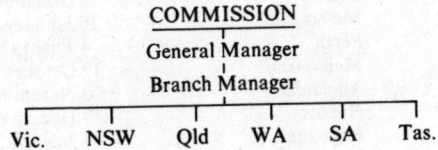

ABC ORGANIZATION, 1948

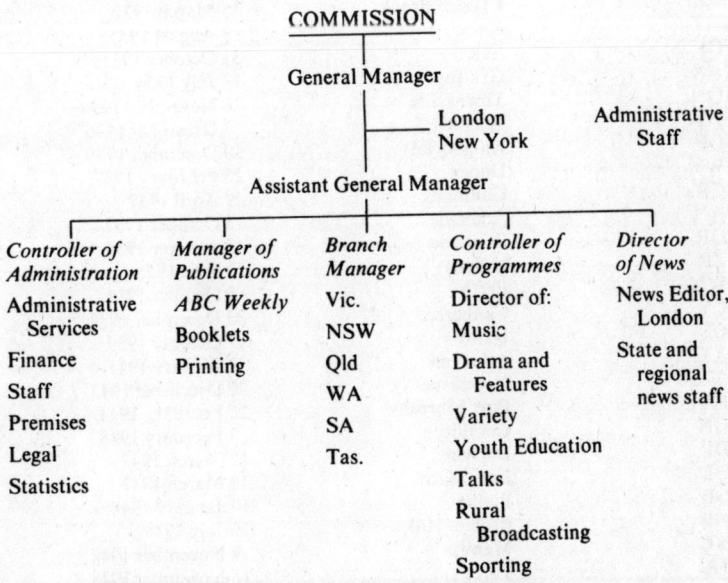

Appendix 3

Australian Broadcasting Commission Stations, 1932—48

CALL SIGN	LOCATION	DATE COMMENCED
2BL	Sydney	13 November 1923
2FC	Sydney	5 December 1923
3AR	Melbourne	26 January 1924
6WF	Perth	4 June 1924
3LO	Melbourne	13 October 1924
5CL	Adelaide	20 November 1924
7ZL	Hobart	17 December 1924
4QG	Brisbane	27 July 1925
2NC	Newcastle	19 December 1930
4RK	Rockhampton	29 July 1931
2CO	Corowa	16 December 1931
5CK	Crystal Brook	15 March 1932
7NT	Kelso	3 August 1935
3GI	Sale	31 October 1935
2NR	Grafton	17 July 1936
4QN	Townsville	26 November 1936
6WA	Wagin	7 December 1936
6GF	Kalgoorlie	10 December 1936
3WV	Dooen	25 February 1937
2CR	Cumnock	29 April 1937
5AN	Adelaide	15 October 1937
4QR	Brisbane	7 January 1938
7ZR	Hobart	22 June 1938
6WN	Perth	5 October 1938
2CY	Canberra	23 December 1938
4QS	Dalby	17 October 1939
4AT	Atherton	27 January 1941
2NA	Newcastle	20 December 1943
9PA	Port Moresby	26 February 1944
6GN	Geraldton	3 February 1945
5DR	Darwin	12 March 1947
4QL	Longreach	19 March 1947
4QB	Pialba	14 January 1948
2NB	Broken Hill	29 July 1948
2NU	Manilla	9 November 1948
2TR	Taree	15 November 1948
5AL	Alice Springs	30 November 1948

Notes

Introduction

[1] See, for example, the very substantial thesis by N. Petersen, 'Policy Formation in the ABC News Service, 1942-1961' (MA Thesis, University of Sydney, 1977), and M. F. Dixon's *Inside the ABC: a Piece of Australian History* (Melbourne, 1975).
[2] A. Briggs, *The Birth of Broadcasting* (London, 1961), p. 4.
[3] See, for example, L. Rees, *The Making of Australian Drama* (Sydney, 1973), which has excellent sections on ABC radio plays.
[4] R. Rivett, *Australian Citizen: Herbert Brookes 1867-1963* (Melbourne, 1965), ch. 13.
[5] G. C. Bolton, *Dick Boyer: An Australian Humanist* (Canberra, 1967).
[6] J. Rydon, 'The Australian Broadcasting Commission, 1932-1942: the Study of a Public Corporation', *Public Administration*, XI, n.s. (1952), 12-25; ditto '1942-48', 190-205.
[7] E. Blain, *Life with Aunty: Forty Years with the ABC* (Sydney, 1978).
[8] G. R. Curnow, 'The History of the Development of Wireless Telegraphy and Broadcasting in Australia to 1942, with especial reference to the Australian Broadcasting Commission: A Political and Administrative Study' (MA Hons Thesis, University of Sydney, 1961).
[9] J. A. La Nauze, *Walter Murdoch: A Biographical Memoir* (Melbourne, 1977), p. 111.

1 Great Expectations

[1] Figures from *ABC: First Annual Report* and *Official Year Book of the Commonwealth of Australia*, 1932, p. 272; 1933, pp. 197, 214. See general comments on the Depression in J. Robertson, '1930-39' in F. K. Crowley (ed.), *A New History of Australia* (Melbourne, 1974), pp. 419-44, R. Ward, *Australia* (Sydney, 1965), pp. 190-1, and G. C. Bolton, *A Fine Country to Starve In* (Perth, 1972), *passim*.
[2] Prices based on sample advertisements in radio journals. The 'weighted average nominal weekly adult male wage' in July 1932 was £4 5s. 8d.; see *Commonwealth Year Book*, 1933, p. 716.
[3] Quoted in P. Geeves, 'The Golden Jubilee of Australian Broadcasting', *Newsletter of the Royal Australian Historical Society*, April 1973, p. 3, and by the same author, 'Australia's Radio Pioneers — 3', *Electronics* (Australia), July 1974, p. 37.
[4] C. Porter, 'Broadcasting in Queensland', *Journal of the Royal Historical Society of Queensland*, VI, no.4 (1961-2), 752.
[5] The breakdown of subscription charges was 2SB, 10s.; 2FC and 3AR, £3 3s.; and 6WF, £4 4s.

6. *Report of the Joint Parliamentary Committee on Wireless Broadcasting* (hereinafter cited as the *Gibson Report*), March 1942, p. 8. A copy of the report is printed in *CPP*, vol. II (1940-3).
7. Figure from *ABC First Annual Report*, p. 7. For the inquiry's findings, see *Report of the Royal Commission on Wireless, CPP*, vol. IV (1926-7).
8. Some information about the Company is contained in P. Game, *The Music Sellers* (Melbourne, 1976), p. 239. See also *Australian Broadcasting Company Year Book, 1930* (Sydney, 1931), especially pp. 22-3 where comment is made about the difficulties of operation.
9. See T. W. Bearup's evidence to the Gibson Committee, *Minutes of Evidence*, p. 505. Biographical details of Brown are given in *Who's Who in Australia*, 1935, p. 89. See also an obituary in *Canberra Times*, 6 June 1967.
10. *SMH*, 15 March 1932.
11. W. Macmahon Ball, *Press, Radio and World Affairs: Australia's Outlook* (Melbourne, 1938), pp. 145-6.
12. Reported in *Argus*, 21 January 1932.
13. *SMH*, 21 January 1932.
14. *SMH*, 17 February 1932.
15. Some of these questions were raised in articles in the *SMH*, 22 October 1932. On 11 March 1935, it devoted an editorial to the problem of noise.
16. Quoted in *Daily Telegraph*, 28 January 1933.
17. Noted in *SMH*, 21 September 1932.
18. Quoted in P. Game, *The Music Sellers*, p. 241. One Sydney firm's sheet-music sales fell from 1 009 950 in 1927 to 275 000 in 1932—see other figures in *Report of the Royal Commission on Performing Rights*, 1933, p. 21.
19. See comments in *SMH*, 7 and 18 October 1932.
20. P. Game, *The Music Sellers*, pp. 240-1.
21. *Daily Telegraph*, 29 September 1932.
22. *Wireless Weekly*, 2 January 1931, reported the increase.
23. See, for example, an article in *Radio Business*, 14 January 1937, which argues that radio is responsible for increasing attendances.
24. *Argus*, 18 January 1932.
25. Noted in *SMH*, 8 January 1932.
26. Quoted in F. K. Crowley (ed.), *Modern Australia in Documents*, vol. I: *1901-1939* (Melbourne, 1973), pp. 379-80.
27. Quoted in M. Goot, 'Radio Lang' in H. Radi and P. Spearritt (eds), *Jack Lang* (Sydney, 1977), p. 119.
28. Quoted in *ibid.*, p. 131.
29. *Ibid.*, pp. 132-3.
30. See *CPD*, vol. 129, 2 May 1931, pp. 2408ff, and vol. 131, 6 August 1931, p. 5084, and see G. A. Roberts, 'Business Interests and the Formation of the ABC', *Politics*, VII, no. 2 (November 1972), 149.
31. Quote taken from speech by A. E. Green, former Labor postmaster-general, *CPD*, vol. 133, 10 March 1932, p. 955. Note his further comments that eventually the commercial stations will have to be controlled, that ultimately 'Nothing short of a complete national scheme will do', in *ibid.*, p. 957.
32. See chapter four.
33. *CPD*, vol. 133, 9 March 1932, p. 845.
34. See, for example, *Argus*, 10 March 1932.
35. Reported in *CPD*, vol. 133, 3 May 1932, p. 277.
36. *Ibid.*, 28 April 1932, p. 90.
37. *Ibid.*, 10 March 1932, p. 959.

Notes (Chapter 1) 179

[38] *SMH*, 15 March 1932. See also *Wireless Weekly*, 21 November 1930 and 2 January 1931.
[39] See announcement in *Argus*, 15 March 1932.
[40] *CPD*, vol. 133, 10 March 1932, p. 959.
[41] *CPD*, vol. 134, 28 April 1932, p. 121.
[42] *CPD*, vol. 133, 9 March 1932, p. 847.
[43] *CPD*, vol. 134, 5 May 1932, p. 372.
[44] Clauses 21 (1) and 21 (2c) of Act no. 14 of 1932.
[45] See Minutes of Special Meeting, 15 March 1932 in P. Weller (ed.), *Caucus Minutes*, vol. 3, p. 47. The reasons for the Labor Party's attitude are not clear. It may have been trying to curb the power of the press and the commercial stations. See, for example, N. J. O. Makin's comments in *CPD*, vol. 134, 3 May 1932, p. 265.
[46] Quoted in *Argus*, 10 March 1932.
[47] G. A. Roberts, 'Business Interests and the Formation of the ABC', p. 151.
[48] Details in *CPD*, vol. 134, 3 May 1932, pp. 258-62.
[49] See further discussion of this issue in G. A. Roberts, 'Business Interests and the Formation of the ABC', pp. 149-54.
[50] The Senate amendment was discussed in the House of Representatives on 13 May; see *CPD*, vol. 134, 13 May 1932, pp. 764-5.
[51] T. Burns, *The BBC: Public Institution and Private World* (London, 1977), p. 7; Asa Briggs, *The Birth of Broadcasting* (London, 1961), p. 402.
[52] Radio manufacturing had only flourished in Australia since 1930 when protective tariffs on radio components were lifted. See some comments on the industry in D. P. Mellor, *The Role of Science and Industry* (Canberra, 1958), p. 482.
[53] See provisions of Act no. 14 of 1932 in *Commonwealth Statutes*, 1932, pp. 43-53.
[54] *Argus*, 18 January 1932; *SMH*, 5 March 1932.
[55] *SMH*, 5 March 1932.
[56] Figure given in *SMH*, 15 February 1932; and see Paterson to Brookes, 13 January 1932, Brookes Papers, National Library of Australia, MS 1924, Series 1.
[57] *Argus*, 21 May 1932.
[58] For biographical details of Jones see *Rydges' Business Journal*, III (February 1930), 112-14, and articles in *Signature*, I, no. 3 (November-December 1968), 10-13, *Daily Telegraph*, 13 July 1958, *Argus* and *SMH*, 24 May 1932, and *Who's Who in Australia*, 1935, p. 260.
[59] See Message no. 46 (1932), Brookes Papers, Series 26; and see diary entries for 14 and 30 March 1932, Brookes Papers, Series 2.
[60] Senator W. Massey-Greene to Brookes, 23 May 1932, Brookes Papers, Series 26.
[61] Brookes' biography has been written by his nephew; see R. Rivett, *Australian Citizen: Herbert Brookes 1867-1963* (Melbourne, 1965).
[62] Brief details of Wallace's life are given in *SMH*, 24 May 1932. See also *Who's Who in Australia*, 1935, p. 472.
[63] There is a short biography of Mrs Couchman in the *Royal Commonwealth Society Journal*, no. 316 (July 1969), p. 16. See also *SMH*, 24 May 1932; H. M. Burton, 'The Burlesque of Broadcasting', *Australian Rhodes Review*, no. 4 (1939), p. 86; and *Who's Who in Australia*, 1974, p. 249.
[64] Biographical details of Orchard are given in *SMH*, 24 May 1932 and in *Daily Sun*, 3 May 1937. See also *Who's Who in Australia*, 1935, p. 364. See Beasley's attack on his appointment in *CPD*, vol. 135, 15 September 1932, p. 560.
[65] See, for example, *CPD*, vol. 134, 24 May 1932, p. 1253, and vol. 135, 16 September 1932, p. 568.
[66] See some of Beasley's attacks in *CPD*, vol. 135, 15 September 1932, p. 560, and the

government's response in *CPD*, vol. 136, 27-28 October 1932, p. 1735.
[67] Quoted in *SMH*, 5 May 1933.
[68] *ABC: First Annual Report*, p. 29.
[69] This matter is discussed briefly in F. Moorhouse, 'The ABC's Search for Identity', *Current Affairs Bulletin*, vol. 46, no. 10 (October 1970), p. 149.
[70] Details from *Argus* and *SMH*, 2 July 1932.
[71] Quoted in *Argus*, 28 May 1932.
[72] The statute was finally ratified by the Curtin Labor government in 1942.
[73] J. Robertson, '1930-39', p. 434.

2 Problems and Personalities, 1932—4

[1] Some of these details are outlined in *ABC: First Annual Report*, pp. 3-4, 27.
[2] *Ibid.*, p. 19.
[3] Kirke to Williams, 15 November 1932, GM's Correspondence with Manager for WA File (July—December 1932), ABCA.
[4] *ABC: First Annual Report*, p. 28. See comments on the different quality of state programmes in Report by H. P. Williams to the Commission (1932), in private notebook held by Miss Pat Kelly, ABCA.
[5] See, for example, *Truth*, 24 April 1934, and *Daily Telegraph*, 21 April 1934.
[6] *SMH*, 20 March 1934.
[7] Details in Commission Minutes, 27 May 1932.
[8] A fairly comprehensive survey of Bearup's career up to 1932 is contained in his application for the position of general manager—see GM Applications Files (1932, 1933), ABCA. See also 'Notes on history of general managers', Cleary Papers, MS 5632, File no. 2. He used the word 'edutainment' in an interview with me in Adelaide on 31 January 1978.
[9] For further biographical details see *Radio Trade Annual of Australia* (1935), p. 25, and *Broadcast Year Book and Radio Listener's Annual of Australia* (hereinafter *Broadcast Year Book*) (Sydney, 1934), p. 60.
[10] Details in *Broadcast Year Book*, 1934, p. 64.
[11] E. Blain, *Life with Aunty*, p. 129. Other details about Kirke may be found in *Radio Trade Annual of Australia*, 1935, p. 25.
[12] Details in *Radio Trade Annual of Australia*, 1934, p. 23.
[13] See *ibid.*, 1935, p. 25.
[14] Commission Minutes, 10 August and 18 September 1933.
[15] See reminiscences recorded in *Radio Active* (July 1972) p. 4.
[16] Biographical details of Williams may be found in *SMH* and *Labor Daily*, 6 March 1933.
[17] Brookes Diary, 4 August 1932. (Diaries for most of the years Brookes was vice-chairman are contained in the Brookes Papers, MS 1924, Series 2). See also Cabinet Minute, CRS A2694, vol. 3, Agenda no. 259, 4 August 1932.
[18] *CPD*, vol. 135, 15 September 1932, p. 561; vol. 136, 27-28 October 1932, p. 1717.
[19] *Sunday Sun and Guardian*, 12 March 1933.
[20] See remarks in Brookes Diary, 17 and 22 March 1933, and see Heinze to Brookes, 13 March 1933, Brookes Papers, Series 26.
[21] Quoted in *Labor Daily*, 1 April 1933. Biographical details of Conder may be found in *Who's Who in Australia* (1935), p. 126; Transcript of Interview with Major Conder by John Cribbin, 1974, ABCA; GM Applications Files (1932, 1933), ABCA; *Herald*, 9 August 1922; *SMH*, 1 April 1933; and *Sun*, 31 March 1933. There is also a small uncatalogued collection of Conder's personal papers in the National Library of Australia.
[22] *Daily Telegraph*, 3 April 1933.

Notes (Chapter 2) 181

[23] *Sports and Radio* (Brisbane), 8 April 1933 and Transcript of Interview with Major Conder by John Cribbin, 1974, pp. 18-20, ABCA.
[24] See, for example, comments in *CPD*, vol. 144, 14 July 1934, pp. 158-9. G. R. Curnow, 'The History of the Development of Wireless Telegraphy and Broadcasting...', p. 293.
[25] Commission Minutes, 27 February 1934; Horner in evidence to the Gibson Committee in 1942, see Gibson Committee, *Minutes of Evidence*, p. 504. Some impressions of staff conditions can be gained from various memoranda and notes in SP 655/1, Box 1, File no. 14.19/E/1, AA. For an example of personal connections influencing appointments, see Jones to Conder, 13 March 1934, GM's Correspondence File (January—July 1934), ABCA.
[26] Transcript of Interview with Major Conder, 1974, pp. 16-17, ABCA.
[27] See Staff Lists and Staff and Establishment Files, ABCA.
[28] G. R. Curnow, 'The History of the Development of Wireless Telegraphy and Broadcasting...', p. 292; *CPD*, vol. 144, 4 July 1934, p. 159.
[29] E. Blain, *Life with Aunty*, p. 20.
[30] Memorandum from Conder to the manager for Victoria, 28 December 1934, held by the ABC Archivist.
[31] *CPD*, vol. 151, 8 October 1936, p. 874. Conder apparently had trouble persuading some commissioners that Lewis was a suitable replacement: see Conder to Brookes, 16 January 1934, Brookes Papers, Series 26.
[32] Figures in Lewis to Conder, September 1933, SP 306/1, Box 2, File no. 9.23/B/1, AA; G. E. Caiden, *Career Service: An Introduction to the History of Personnel Administration in the Commonwealth Public Service of Australia 1901-1961* (Melbourne, 1965), p. 231.
[33] See Horner to Conder and Hosking to Conder, 17 July 1934, SP 306/1, Box 2, File no. 9.23/B/1, AA.
[34] See comments in E. Blain, *Life with Aunty*, p. 113.
[35] For more details about these radio personalities, see *Australian Radio News*, 5 November 1932, *Broadcast Year Book*, 1934, pp. 59-63, and *Radio Pictorial of Australia*, 1 April 1936, pp. 12-14.
[36] Ellis Blain described the loneliness thus: 'I remember, in Hobart, coming up to the fifth floor in the bronze-sprayed lift cage one morning early and being overcome by a feeling of loneliness such as I have seldom experienced in my whole life. During the six-hour solo stint, talking to a microphone or an equally moribund technician through the glass, I felt totally cut off from all human contact': *Life with Aunty*, p. 115.
[37] *Radio Pictorial of Australia*, 1 May 1936, pp. 20-1.
[38] The ABC continued to attract many applicants for announcing positions throughout the 1930s; see Gibson Committee, *Minutes of Evidence*, p. 228.
[39] Kirke to the general manager, 18 November 1933, GM's Correspondence with Manager for W.A. File (January—December 1933), ABCA.
[40] Commission Minutes, 6 June 1932.
[41] Details of this broadcast are given *Sun*, 27 December 1932, and *Labor Daily* 26 December 1932. The headlines concentrated on the technological achievement the broadcast represented.
[42] Programme for Monday, 5 June 1933.
[43] Incomplete collections of most of these publications are held in the Mitchell Library, the State Library of New South Wales, and the State Library of Victoria. The National Library holds some issues.
[44] The Commission Minutes and attachments are presently held by the ABCA, but are in the process of being transferred to the Australian Archives.
[45] Commission Minutes, 24 June 1932 and 27 February 1934.

Notes (Chapter 2)

[46] Commission Minutes, 23 June 1932.
[47] Brookes Diaries, various years, Brookes Papers, Series 2. See also discussion in R. Rivett, *Australian Citizen*, p. 179.
[48] Brookes Diary, 17, 23 and 24 June 1932, 7, 8, 26 and 27 July 1932, and 20 November 1933.
[49] Jones to Brookes, 19 September 1932, Brookes File, ABCA.
[50] Comment of Mrs Wilga Wind (*née* Armstrong), former ABC employee, during an interview with me in Melbourne on 7 February 1978.
[51] Brookes to Brown, 11 August 1933, Brookes Papers, Series 26.
[52] See, for example, Jones to Brookes, 20 December 1932, Brookes Papers, Series 26.
[53] Brookes Diary, 30 June 1932. See also Commission Minutes, 6 June 1932.
[54] Jones to Brookes, 19 September 1932, Brookes File, ABCA.
[55] *Ibid.*
[56] Brookes Diary, 15 February 1933. A later entry on 27 February said that Conder should become more conscious of the Commission.
[57] *CPD*, vol. 144, 4 July 1934, p. 160. See Conder's justification of one lot of expenditure in a letter to Brookes, 17 April 1934, Brookes File, ABCA.
[58] Brookes Diary, 27-29 March 1934; Commission Minutes, 29 March 1934.
[59] See miscellaneous entries, especially for 1932 and 1933.
[60] This point is made in a footnote in G. R. Curnow, 'The History of the Development of Wireless Telegraphy and Broadcasting . . .', p. 289, and rests on the oral evidence of a later ABC chairman, William James Cleary.
[61] *ABC: First Annual Report*, p. 10.
[62] *Ibid.*, p. 8.
[63] See Bearup's comments in Gibson Committee, *Minutes of Evidence*, p. 507.
[64] For some years, radio had been a common fall-back for artists unable to secure regular theatre work—see comments on the early days at 2FC in the *Overseas Telecommunications Veterans' Association Newsletter* (October, 1976), p. 20.
[65] Commission Minutes, 6 June 1932.
[66] *ABC: First Annual Report*, p. 10.
[67] See comments on the history of community singing concerts in *Labor Daily*, 25 September 1937.
[68] The full programme is printed in *Wireless Weekly*, 11 August 1933.
[69] For a fuller list of operas broadcast, see *ABC: First Annual Report*, pp. 12-16.
[70] See *SMH*, 2 and 18 June 1934; *Argus*, 31 May 1934; *Daily Telegraph*, 8 June 1934; and *ABC: Second Annual Report*, pp. 10-11.
[71] Quoted in *Sunday Sun and Guardian*, 18 December 1932.
[72] *SMH*, 24 February 1933; *ABC: First Annual Report*, p. 17. The entries included 295 from New South Wales, 265 from Victoria, 77 from Queensland, 73 from South Australia, 60 from Western Australia, and 31 from Tasmania—breakdown given in *SMH*, 20 July 1933.
[73] *ABC: First Annual Report*, p. 16.
[74] For some comments about Heinze' appointment, see Brookes Diary, 25 April 1934, and *Smith's Weekly*, 9 August 1934.
[75] *Report of the Royal Commission on Performing Rights*, 1933, p. 23.
[76] *ABC: Fourth Annual Report*, p. 13.
[77] *Report of the Royal Commission on Performing Rights*, 1933, pp. 36-7; *Broadcast Year Book*, 1934, pp. 91-3.
[78] Reported in *Sun*, 13 October 1932.
[79] *Report of the Royal Commission on Performing Rights*, 1933, p. 24.
[80] Some discussion of the copyright issue is contained in the Gibson Report, pp. 70-1, and in the *Minutes of Evidence* p. 203.

Notes (Chapter 2)

[81] *ABC: First Annual Report*, p. 10.
[82] E. Blain, *Life with Aunty*, p. 38.
[83] Commission Minutes, 27 May 1932.
[84] *Wireless Weekly*, 11 August 1933.
[85] *Daily Telegraph*, 10 May 1933; *Labor Daily*, 10 May 1933.
[86] *Daily Telegraph*, 11 May 1933.
[87] See M. F. Dixon, *Inside the ABC*. There is also a short piece by P. Mitchell, 'Development of the Australian Broadcasting Commission's News Service, 1932-42' (BA Hons thesis, University of Sydney, 1974), and the thesis by Neville Petersen, 'Policy Formation in the ABC News Service, 1942-1961', *passim*.
[88] N. Petersen, 'Policy Formation in the ABC News Service, 1942-1961', p. 37.
[89] Details of the agreements can be found in M. F. Dixon, *Inside the ABC*, pp. 9, 21-22; *Gibson Report*, pp. 19-20; and Commission Minutes, 30 September 1932.
[90] Ellis Blain recalls that this procedure could have unfortunate consequences: 'The custom was for several copies of the morning paper to be delivered direct to the studio . . . The announcer on duty would pick up one of these as soon as he arrived . . . One morning, the day after a holiday, the cleaners had not been in to collect the unopened copies left over from the day before. The announcer arrived, out of breath and short of time, picked up the nearest paper, made his selection and read it. It wasn't until the technician buzzed him on the intercom that the poor fellow realized he had brought the citizens of Hobart a colourful account of the previous day's happenings.': *Life with Aunty*, p.16.
[91] Commission Minutes, 7 June 1932.
[92] See Jones' comments in a letter to Brookes, 29 October 1932, GM's Correspondence File (June 1932–December 1933), ABCA.
[93] Some of the early plans regarding educational broadcasting advisory committees are discussed in Commission Minutes, 24 June and 8 November 1932.
[94] A survey of the growth of children's programmes is contained in L. Gash, 'The History of the Australian Broadcasting Commission's Children's Session, *c*. 1929-1945' (BA Hons dissertation, Monash University, 1975).
[95] Some details of Murdoch's early experiments are contained in ABC Staff and Organization File, Victorian Branch (1932-4), ABCA.
[96] The term is noted in *ibid*.
[97] Quoted in L. Gash, 'The History of the Australian Broadcasting Commission's Children's Session, *c*. 1929-1945', p. 23.
[98] There is an excellent account of Murdoch's contribution as a broadcaster in J. A. La Nauze's *Walter Murdoch*, chapter 8.
[99] An extensive list of guest speakers during the first year of operations is given in *ABC: First Annual Report*, pp. 10-12.
[1] *SMH*, 17 May 1933.
[2] *Ibid*.
[3] Conder to the chairman, 21 September 1933, GM's Correspondence File (June 1932–December 1933), ABCA.
[4] Phrase used in *ABC: First Annual Report*, p. 5.
[5] A breakdown of the percentage of programme time allocated to each is given in *ibid*., p. 10.
[6] See list in *Broadcast Year Book*, 1934, p. 86.
[7] *ABC: First Annual Report*, p. 17.
[8] *Ibid*., p. 7; *Report of the Royal Commission on Performing Rights*, 1933, p. 20; *Broadcast Year Book*, 1934, p. 14.
[9] For example, *Daily Telegraph*, 26 August 1936, gave a figure of 18 per cent.
[10] *ABC: First Annual Report*, p. 5.

11. Figures in *ibid.*, p. 9, and in *ABC: Second Annual Report*, p. 13.
12. *Labor Daily*, 21 August 1933. See also information summary of Listeners' Letters in MP 237/7, Box 2, AA.
13. The results published in the *Daily Telegraph* on 5 April 1933 showed listeners' preferences as: radio plays (730), dance music (541), musical comedy (532), grand opera (464), brass bands (256), orchestral concerts (211), vaudeville (201), symphonic concerts (167), community singing (110), and revues (93).
14. *Daily Telegraph*, 12 June 1933.
15. See comments in Brookes Diary, 31 May 1934, and Jones' letter of resignation to the governor-general, Isaac Isaacs, 6 June 1934, CRS A461, Bundle 540, File no. Z422/1/6, pt 1, AA.
16. *SMH*, 27 June 1934.
17. *Sun*, 7 June 1933, noted that Wallace offered no radical suggestions to the Commission and Brookes recorded in his diary on 9 June 1933 that Wallace's statements on his trip were 'not informative'.
18. R. Rivett, *Australian Citizen*, pp. 175-6.
19. Cabinet Minute, CRS A2694, vol. 10, Agenda no. 864, 25 October 1933.
20. A. Etzioni discusses the general problem of defining organizational goals in *Modern Organisations* (New Jersey, 1964), pp. 10ff. See also J. D. Thompson and W. J. McEwen, 'Organisational goals and environment: goal setting as an interaction process', in G. Salaman and K. Thompson (eds), *People and Organisations* (London, 1973), pp. 155-67.
21. Williams to Kirke, 25 July 1932, GM's Correspondence with Manager for W.A. File (July-December 1932), and Jones to Williams, 14 November 1932, GM's Correspondence File (June 1932-December 1933), ABCA.
22. This is mentioned in Kirke to Williams, 17 October 1932, GM's Correspondence with Manager for W.A. File (July-December 1932), ABCA. Kirke also notes that the bonus never eventuated.

3 Cleary and the ABC

1. G. C. Bolton, *Dick Boyer: An Australian Humanist* (Canberra, 1967), p. 101.
2. See Cleary's draft essay on a boy named Johny in file marked 'Photos, News, Cuttings, Accounts—Bushwalking', Cleary Papers, MS 5539, National Library.
3. There are some brief details of Cleary's career at Tooth's in *Brewer and Bottlers' Gazette*, 15 July 1920, pp. 27-8, and *Smith's Weekly*, 14 April 1928. Most of the biographical details which follow are contained in the Cleary Papers, MS 5539, National Library.
4. *Sunday Sun*, 7 August 1932.
5. Newsletter no. 103 of the Department of Supply and Development, 29 July 1949, Box marked 'Bushwalking, Personal Papers, Misc.', Cleary Papers, MS 5539.
6. See, for example, Jensen to Cleary, 29 December 1936, Cleary Papers, MS 5539, in which he says that the standards of the commercial stations should not be 'worked down to' by the ABC.
7. Cleary to Jensen, 21 November 1929, Cleary Papers, MS 5539.
8. Cleary's salary at Tooth's in 1929 was estimated to be £7000. The government allegedly offered an equivalent amount, but Cleary is said to have insisted that £5000 was the maximum he could accept for performing a public service. His daughter claims that when he surrendered part of his salary, the example was not followed nor appreciated by many colleagues who resented the pressure it placed on them to do likewise (interview with Mrs Pauline Watson in Sydney in October

1977). See other comments on Cleary's drop in salary in *Sunday Sun and Guardian*, 18 December 1932.
9. Unlabelled press cutting in Cleary Press Cutting Book, Bundle of documents labelled 'Early Records', ABCA. Other businessmen certainly gave up private positions for public office, but this usually involved a rise in salary. See, for example, the story of Sir Herbert Gepp in C. D. Kemp, *Big Businessmen: Four Biographical Essays* (Melbourne, 1964), pp. 31-2—the size of Gepp's salary on assuming public office occasioned much public comment.
10. Cleary to Jenkins, 21 November 1929, Cleary Papers, MS 5539.
11. Jensen to Cleary, 12 November 1929, *ibid*.
12. Cleary intimated the reason for his resignation in a letter to Stevens, 16 December 1932, *ibid*. Other details of Cleary's time in the railways may be found in *ibid*., Box marked 'Railways'; see also *Sunday Sun and Guardian*, 18 December 1932; *SMH*, 28 February 1945; and bundle of Cleary's 'Early Records', ABCA.
13. *SMH*, 27 February 1945 noted this offer.
14. Phrase from article in *Smith's Weekly*, 3 August 1938.
15. Noted in Brookes Diary, 9 June 1934. Mention of some division of opinions between the Victorian and New South Wales members of Cabinet can be found in Brookes Diary, 27 and 28 June 1934. See also *Argus*, 28 June 1934.
16. Note dated 4 July 1934 (9 a.m.), File marked 'Notes on the ABC', Brookes Papers, Series 26; Brookes Diary, 3 and 4 July 1934; and see R. Rivett, *Australian Citizen*, p. 177. Mrs Couchman's remarks are in a letter to Brookes, 31 July 1934, Brookes Papers, Series 26.
17. *SMH*, 7 July 1934.
18. T. Dunbabin to Cleary, 4 July 1934, Cleary Papers, MS 5539.
19. *Smith's Weekly*, 20 July 1934.
20. See a large selection of letters of congratulations in the Cleary Papers, MS 5539.
21. *Wireless Weekly*, 3 August 1934; Cleary to Brookes, 3 June 1936, Brookes Papers, Series 26.
22. See his comments in a letter to Brookes, 30 August 1934, Brookes File, ABCA. There is brief mention of 'canned culture' in C. M. H. Clark, *A Short History of Australia*, (Sydney, 1969), pp. 230-1.
23. Gibson Committee, *Minutes of Evidence*, p. 243.
24. Address delivered by Cleary from Adelaide at the opening of station 5AN, 15 October 1937, Cleary Papers, MS 5539.
25. Gibson Committee, *Minutes of Evidence*, p. 241.
26. Chairman's New Year's Eve Address, 1935, Cleary Papers, MS 5539.
27. For Brookes' views, see Rivett, *Australian Citizen*, p. 192. The *Daily Sun*, 21 May 1938, reports Kitto's remarks about taste, and *Smith's Weekly*, 27 February 1935, outlines all the commissioners' views.
28. Quoted in F. K. Crowley (ed.), *Modern Australia in Documents*, vol. 1: *1901-1939*, p. 557.
29. Ingamells hoped to build a completely local culture from the bottom up, but his emphasis on Aboriginal imagery failed to gain acceptance within the community; see I. Turner, *The Australian Dream* (Melbourne, 1968), pp. 299-300, and G. Serle, *From Deserts the Prophets Come* (Melbourne, 1973), pp. 132, 143.
30. See Conder to Brookes, 15 and 20 November 1934, Brookes File, ABCA, and see Transcript of Interview with Major Conder by John Cribbin, 1974, ABCA.
31. Term used in Cleary to Brookes, 30 August 1934, Brookes File, ABCA.
32. *Ibid*.
33. The Commission Minutes for 24 June 1935 give no detail. Brookes' diary entry for 12 March 1935 noted that Conder's position was 'critical', but most of the details

are contained in the following correspondence: chief auditor to the secretary of the ABC, 25 February 1935; Holman to the chairman, 12 March 1935; Holman to 'A.S.', 30 March 1935; memorandum compiled by Holman, 2 April 1935; and Holman to the chairman, 17 December 1935, held by Miss Kelly, ABCA.

[34] Brookes Diary, 24 March 1935.
[35] Commission Minutes, 25 June 1935.
[36] Brookes Diary, 25 June 1935.
[37] Brookes Diary, 29 June 1935.
[38] *Labor Daily*, 27 June 1935.
[39] *Truth*, 30 June 1935.
[40] See speculation in *Argus*, 1 and 5 July 1935, and Cleary's reply on the latter date. Bearup probably was seriously considered, for in 1936 he was sent around the world (as a consolation prize?) for the ABC.
[41] Brookes Diary, 23 August 1935.
[42] Cleary to Brookes, 30 August 1934, Brookes File, ABCA; Gibson Committee, *Minutes of Evidence*, p. 227.
[43] *CPD*, vol. 147, 27 September 1935, p. 312, 2 October 1935, p. 390 and 16 October 1935, p. 735; *Argus*, 25 October 1935.
[44] Brookes Diary, 26 October 1935.
[45] Commission Minutes, 30 October 1935; Brookes Diary 30 October 1935.
[46] Some details of these broadcasts are given in *Pix*, 20 July 1938, but a much fuller and interesting description is in E. Blain's *Life with Aunty*, pp. 39-40.
[47] Biographical details of Moses may be found in *Radio Pictorial of Australia*, 1 December 1935; *Argus*, 5 November 1935; *Who's Who in Australia*, 1977, p. 800; and in a paper outlining Moses' history in the Cleary Papers, MS 5632, File 2.
[48] Moses to Cleary, 29 June 1935, Cleary Papers, MS 5632, File 2.
[49] *CPD*, vol. 148, 13 November 1935, p. 1486.
[50] This story was told in *ABC Weekly*, vol. 7, no. 45 (10 November 1945), p. 4, and was confirmed by Cleary's daughter (Pauline Watson) at an interview with me in Sydney in October 1977.
[51] See some discussion of the decision to centralize the administration in the Parliamentary Standing Committee on Broadcasting's *Tenth Report*, p. 4. See also *ABC: Fourth Annual Report*, p. 23.
[52] See Staff and Establishment Files, ABCA. For brief biographies of the controllers, see *Radio-Active*, (February 1949), p. 7, for Clewlow; (March 1949), p. 8, for Barry; (July 1949), p. 11, for James; (July 1949), p. 5, for Molesworth; and (August 1950), p. 17, for Bronner.
[53] See Staff and Establishment Files, ABCA.
[54] See Appendix 3.
[55] See *ABC: Eighth Annual Report, passim,* and *ABC: Seventeenth Annual Report,* p. 29.
[56] This crossing of responsibilities is discussed in G. R. Curnow, 'The History of the Development of Wireless Telegraphy and Broadcasting in Australia . . .', pp. 305, 323. See also Horner's comments in Gibson Committee, *Minutes of Evidence,* p. 504.
[57] *Daily Telegraph*, 18 May 1933.
[58] Point raised at interview with T. W. Bearup in Canberra, 21 November 1977.
[59] Memorandum from Cleary to Lyons, 24 October 1938, Cleary Papers, MS 5632, File 2.
[60] Gibson Committee, *Minutes of Evidence*, p. 611.
[61] *Teleradio*, 20 August 1938; *SMH*, 11 August 1938; and memorandum from Kirke to all staff, n.d. but *c*. mid-1938, in Cleary Papers, MS 5632, File 2.

Notes (Chapter 3)

[62] Details in Cleary to Brookes, 15 November 1938, Cleary Papers, MS 5632, File 2.
[63] This actually occurred: see Commission Minutes, 3-4 April 1940.
[64] See comments in, for example, E. Blain, *Life with Aunty*, p. 130.
[65] Interview with Cleary in *Sunday Sun and Guardian* (date unknown) in Cleary press-cutting book in 'Early Records', ABCA.
[66] Dixon speaks of Cleary's 'coldness and reserve towards the staff as a whole' in *Inside the ABC*, p. 12.
[67] See, for example, comments in *CPD*, vol. 158, 30 November 1938, p. 2277.
[68] *CPD*, vol. 157, 26 September 1938, p. 165, and 28 September 1938, p. 288.
[69] Gibson Committee, *Minutes of Evidence*, p. 227.
[70] *Ibid.*
[71] *Ibid.*, p. 228.
[72] See reports in *Daily Telegraph* and *SMH*, 5 November 1935.
[73] A. Briggs, *The Golden Age of Wireless* (London, 1965), p. 414. This process closely parallels Etzioni's more general observations about organizations with 'culture goals': see A. Etzioni, *A Comparative Analysis of Complex Organizations* (New York, 1965), pp. 82-3.
[74] See 'Comparisons between the Public Service and the ABC in respect of salaries', in SP 289/1. Box 2-3, File marked 'Comparisons of ABC with the Public Service, Commonwealth Bank and National Airlines', AA.
[75] Details in J. Deans to the general manager, 10 January 1940, and Holman to the general manager, 19 June 1940, SP 655/1, Box 1, File no. 14.19/E/1, AA.
[76] E. Blain, *Life with Aunty*, p. 116.
[77] Details in Horner to the general manager, 2 September 1937, SP 655/1, Box 1, File No. 14.19/E/1, AA.
[78] Federal Programme Committee Minutes, 7-8 April 1938.
[79] See Commission Minutes, 18-20 March 1936, 9-10 February, and 16-17 March 1937.
[80] There is a copy of the document headed 'Chairman's Advice to Mr Charlton, 1936' in the ABCA. See the requirement of Head Office approval stipulated in Moses to the managers for New South Wales and Victoria, 13 February 1937, SP 655/1, Box 1, File no. 14.19/E/1, AA.
[81] Kirke to Cleary, 10 September 1935, and Cleary to Kirke, 11 October 1935, SP 613/1, Box 4, File no. 15.15/C/7, AA.
[82] A. Briggs, *The Golden Age of Wireless*, p. 414.
[83] *Ibid.*, pp. 418-19.
[84] See full Sidney Webb quotation in E. J. Hobsbawn, *Labouring Men: Studies in the History of Labour* (London, 1968), p. 267.
[85] See, for example, Moses refuse a bonus in Moses to Cleary, 6 June 1938, Cleary Papers, MS 5632, File 2.
[86] Memorandum from Horner to the general manager, 24 April 1937, SP 306/1, Bundle 3, File no. A41, pt 2, AA.
[87] See 'An Appeal to All Members', August 1938, SP 724/1, Box 7, File no. 5/1/1; Sheehan to the chairman, 21 December 1938, SP 289/1, Box 3, ABC Staff Association General Claims and Correspondence File, 1938-46, AA; and ABC Staff Association Minutes, 29 November 1938.
[88] M. Skill to Moses, 28 February 1938, SP 289/1, Box 3, ABC Staff Association General Claims and Correspondence File, 1938-46; and Alexander to the general manager, 8 June 1938, SP 724/1, Box 7, File no. 5/1/1, AA. The minutes of meetings of the Association, though incomplete, give some finer detail of this earlier period. They are housed in the Staff Association's office in St Leonard's, Sydney.

Notes (Chapter 3)

[89] Holman to the general manager, 27 October 1938, SP 724/1, Box 7, File no. 5/1/1, AA. A brief history of the Association is given in *Radio-Active* (September 1948), pp. 13-14.
[90] Commission Minutes, 30 November–1 December 1938. Moses was acting partly on the Public Service Inspector's opinion that to agree to the request might prove an embarrassment at some future time—see J. A. Y. Denniston to the general manager, 24 November 1938, SP 289/1, Box 2-3, ABC Staff Association General Claims and Correspondence File, 1938-46, AA. The request was eventually granted; see Commission Minutes, 1-2 November 1939.
[91] A copy of the Staff Rules is held by the ABC Archivist.
[92] See complaints in Alexander to Sheehan, 22 May 1939, and hand-written notes on typescript copy of the Staff Rules, both in Correspondence File on ABC Staff Regulations, ABC Staff Association Archives. See also Gibson Committee, *Minutes of Evidence*, p. 440.
[93] Alexander to Cleary, 4 January 1940, SP 289/1, Box 2-3, ABC Staff Association General Claims and Correspondence File, 1938-46, AA.
[94] Mentioned in *ibid*. See also Alexander to Moses, 14 September 1939, *ibid*.
[95] Gibson Committee, *Minutes of Evidence*, p. 440.
[96] Point mentioned by Cleary, see Gibson Committee, *Minutes of Evidence*, p. 96. See also *Smith's Weekly*, 2 January 1943.
[97] Molesworth to the general manager, 31 October 1939; Barry and Molesworth to Moses, 29 December 1939. See also document marked 'Reasons which prompted Senior Officers to form an Association and seek to register it', SP 289/1, Box 3, File no. 15.12/C/4-5, AA.
[98] Molesworth was actually asked to attend the Commission meeting on 31 January 1940 to explain the senior officers' actions. It was then that the document outlining their motives was drawn up. A copy of the Constitution and Rules of the Senior Officers' Association is contained in SP 289/1, Box 3, File no. 15.12/C/4-5, AA.
[99] This definition of 'job regulation' comes from M. Mann, *Consciousness and Action among the Western Working Class* (Melbourne, 1973), pp. 20-1.
[1] Submission to Cabinet by A. G. Cameron, 14 March 1939, CRS A461, Bundle 540, File no. V422/1/6, AA.
[2] Cleary to Brookes, 30 August 1934, Brookes File, ABCA.
[3] Unfortunately, not all the minutes of the Federal Programme Committee meetings survive. Those that do are housed in the ABC Archives, beginning 31 August 1936.
[4] Federal Programme Committee Minutes, 6-7 September 1937.
[5] *Ibid.*, 4-5 March 1937.
[6] *Ibid.*, 1 September 1936, 26-27 November 1937, and 9-10 May 1938; Gibson Committee, *Minutes of Evidence*, p. 506.
[7] *ABC: Seventh Annual Report*, p. 46.
[8] *Ibid.* p. 12.
[9] The best surveys of technical developments are contained in the *Radio Trade Annual of Australia*, 1934, pp. 17-18; 1935, pp. 16, 18; 1936, pp. 17-18, 86-9; 1937, pp. 11, 12 and 14; 1938, pp. 11-13, 139-40.
[10] Commission Minutes, 8 June 1934; Federal Programme Committee Minutes, 1 September and 21-22 October 1936. See also B. Tildesley's comments in 'The Cinema and Broadcasting in Australia: Reports Presented to the Pan-Pacific Conference of Women, 1934', *Australian Quarterly*, no. 24 (December 1934), p. 135.
[11] See Cleary's complaints in Commission Minutes, 16-17 December 1936.
[12] Details of sporting broadcasts may be found in *ABC: Fourth Annual Report*, p. 26; *ABC: Sixth Annual Report*, pp. 37-9; *ABC: Seventh Annual Report*, pp. 37-9; and *Radio Pictorial of Australia*, 1 September 1936, p. 47.

Notes (Chapter 3)

[13] L. Gash, 'The History of the Australian Broadcasting Commission's Children's Session, c. 1929-45', p. 43; Federal Programme Committee Minutes, 11-12 September 1936 and 9-10 May 1938.
[14] Memorandum from Moses to the federal controller of productions, 8 August 1938, and Clewlow to the general manager, 12 September 1938, SP 617/1, Box 2, National Children's Session File, 1938-9, AA.
[15] See comments in Brookes to Cleary, 22 May 1939, Brookes Papers, Series 26.
[16] *Smith's Weekly*, 16 November 1935; N. Petersen, 'Policy Formation in the ABC News Service, 1942-1961', pp. 38-44.
[17] G. R. Curnow 'The History of the Development of Wireless Telegraphy and Broadcasting in Australia . . .', p. 350.
[18] N. Petersen, 'Policy Formation in the ABC News Service, 1942-1961', p. 49, demonstrates this clearly.
[19] Federal Programme Committee Minutes, 11-13 August 1938.
[20] H. J. Stephens to Dixon, 16 June 1937, SP 286/2, Box 1, GM's File, January–June 1937, AA.
[21] Commission Minutes, 22 August 1935.
[22] *ABC: Third Annual Report*, p. 10.
[23] A list of the artists brought out each year is contained in the ABC's annual report.
[24] *CPD*, vol. 156, 3 June 1938, p. 1850; vol. 158, 1 December 1938, p. 2671.
[25] Paper marked 'Answers to Questions submitted by H. B. to B. H.', Brookes Papers, Series 26. Similar assurances of employment of Australian artists before overseas performers were sought in Parliament: see *CPD*, vol. 151, 8 October 1936, p. 843. The musician, Alfred Hill, complained in the *Sunday Sun and Guardian*, 26 May 1935. See also letter from G. de Cairos-Rego, secretary of the Music Council of Australia, to Cleary, 7 February 1938, SP 617/1, Box 1, Departmental Organization File, 1937-8, I, AA.
[26] Moses to the director-general of Posts and Telegraphs, 3 August 1937, CRS A461, Bundle 539, File no. D422/1/6, pt 1, AA; *ABC: Fifth Annual Report*, p.13.
[27] E. J. Tait to Cleary, 20 July 1934, MP 544/2, File no. BA/7/4, AA.
[28] *ABC: Fifth Annual Report*, pp. 26-7; *ABC: Sixth Annual Report*, p. 25; Commission Minutes, 26-27 February 1936.
[29] Commission Minutes, 26-27 February 1936; Gibson Committee, *Minutes of Evidence*, p. 395; and F. Tait to Moses, 28 March 1936, MP 544/2, File no. BA/7/4, AA.
[30] See reports in *Daily Telegraph*, 25 July, 10 and 18 August 1936; Commission Minutes, 17 August 1936; and see *Radio Retailer*, 14 May 1937.
[31] See Cleary to the director-general of Posts and Telegraphs, 3 March 1936, CRS A461, Bundle 540, File no. T422/1/6, AA.
[32] Cleary to Brookes, 14 February 1938, Cleary Papers, MS 5539.
[33] Cleary to McLachlan, 11 June 1938, MP 544/2, File no. BA/7/4; McLachlan to Cleary, 6 July 1938, CRS A461, Bundle 540, File no. T422/1/6, AA.
[34] McLachlan to Cleary, 6 July 1938, CRS A461, Bundle 540, File no. T422/1/6, AA.
[35] Noted in Cleary to Lyons, 14 September 1938, *ibid*.
[36] Gibson Committee, *Minutes of Evidence*, p. 395; G. R. Curnow, 'The History of the Development of Wireless Telegraphy and Broadcasting . . .', p. 310.
[37] *Gibson Report*, p. 47; R. Covell, *Australia's Music*, pp. 112-14; *ABC: Fifth Annual Report*, pp. 16-17.
[38] *Sunday Sun and Guardian*, 30 June 1935; H. Bainton, *Remembered on Waking* (Sydney, 1960), pp. 68-9.
[39] See, for example, Cleary's reply to requests from Western Australia's Professor A. D. Ross, 24 August 1935, SP 613/1, Box 4, File no. 15.15/C/7, AA.
[40] *Daily Sun*, 22 March 1937.

41 See Cleary's comments in paper headed 'Chairman's Remarks to the Orchestra, 21 October 1935', Cleary Papers, MS 5539; R. Covell, *Australia's Music*, p. 111; G. Serle, *From Deserts the Prophets Come*, p. 157; and A. Briggs, *The Golden Age of Wireless*, pp. 315-16.
42 Figure from *ABC: Seventh Annual Report*, p. 11. Other details from various annual reports, 1934-9, and from a private notebook held by the ABC archivist.
43 Gibson Committee, *Minutes of Evidence*, pp. 13-14.
44 *Ibid.*, p. 244; 'Australian Broadcasting Commission: Statement of Subscribers to Orchestral Concerts' attached to talk entitled 'Why National Broadcasting?' in Cleary Papers, MS 5539; and *The Sydney Symphony Orchestra* (Publicity pamphlet, ABC reference library), p. 7.
45 See Gibson Committee, *Minutes of Evidence*, p. 244.
46 Heinze to Conder, 1 March 1935, Heinze File, ABCA.
47 For example, the *Home*, 1 October 1936, gives photographs of a garden party held for Malcolm Sargent—the men are in top hats, the women in expensive dresses, and the guest list includes senior diplomats.
48 Some of these questions were discussed in the *Sunday Sun and Guardian*, 4 June 1939.
49 See comments in the *Australian Women's Weekly*, 29 November 1938, and the Gibson Committee, *Minutes of Evidence*, p. 243.
50 L. Rees, *The Making of Australian Drama* (Sydney, 1973), p. 154.
51 Figure from paper headed 'Australian Drama Week—Talk by W. J. Cleary, 18 April 1937', Cleary Papers, MS 5539.
52 Quoted in E. Blain, *Life with Aunty*, p. 50.
53 Noted in 'Australian Drama Week—Talk by W. J. Cleary, 18 April 1937', Cleary Papers, MS 5539; Afford to Moses, 11 May 1936, SP 617/1, Box 6, Max Afford File, AA; *Radio Pictorial of Australia*, 1 August 1935, p. 25.
54 Details in *Radio Pictorial of Australia*, 1 December 1935, pp. 10-11.
55 See article on Cecil in *Radio Pictorial of Australia*, 1 January 1936, pp. 2-3; and see L. Rees, *The Making of Australian Drama*.
56 Figures in memorandum from Clewlow to the general manager, 7 February 1938, SP 617/1, Departmental Organization File, 1937-8, I, AA, and in Gibson Committee, *Minutes of Evidence*, p. 415.
57 Figure from Gibson Committee, *Minutes of Evidence*, p. 415.
58 Quoted in *Radio Pictorial of Australia*, 1 January 1936, p. 2.
59 Extract from 'Chairman's advice to Mr Charlton, 1936', ABCA.
60 See Barry's discussion of serials in memorandum to the general manager, 29 September 1937, SP 617/1, Box 1, Department Organization File, 1937-8, II, AA.
61 See his comments in *Daily Telegraph*, 27 August 1936.
62 Some samples of these attempts at audience research can be found in, for example, Report of the Voluntary Listeners' Panel, June—August 1938, SP 767/3, Item no. FPR/1-10/1-1, and Report on Special Enquiry into Sporting Programmes, SP 767/3, Item no. FPR/1-12/1-1, AA.
63 Complaints in *Australian Women's Weekly*, 15 November 1934. See the range of viewpoints in Listeners' Letters Summaries, MP 284/1, Boxes 1 and 2, and MP 237/7, Box 2, AA.
64 W. Macmahon Ball, *Press, Radio and World Affairs*, p. 133. See further discussion on average listeners and 'highbrows' and 'lowbrows' in *SMH*, 24 June, 7 July 1937; *Sunday Sun and Guardian*, 16 April 1933; and *ABC: Fifth Annual Report*, p. 13.
65 See, for example, Cleary's comments in *Hotel Australia Spring Book*, 1937, p. 27, and in *Daily Telegraph*, 23 July 1934.

66 These attitudes were often reflected in newspapers like *Truth* which insisted radio was for relaxation, and that 'One does not sit down to listen "in cold blood"'—*Truth*, 30 October 1932.
67 E. Blain, *Life with Aunty*, pp. 32-3. See an acknowledgement that the ABC's light entertainment productions were lacking in Federal Programme Committee Minutes, 15-16 January 1937. This matter is discussed more fully in chapter seven.
68 Memorandum from Moses to the manager for New South Wales, 23 March 1937, Light Entertainment Department File, I, (1937-47), R17, Box 70, ABCA.
69 Letter in *Australian Women's Weekly*, 8 February 1934.
70 *Labor Daily*, 21 October 1935.
71 Details in *Radio Pictorial of Australia*, 1 May 1937, p. 9, and in *Daily Telegraph*, 1, 5, and 6 July and 28 August 1937.
72 See p. 42.
73 Gibson Committee, *Minutes of Evidence*, p. 650.
74 A. Briggs, *The Golden Age of Wireless*, p. 7.
75 T. Burns, *The BBC: Public Institution and Private World* (London, 1977), pp. 42-3.
76 See the commercial stations discussed in G. R. Curnow, 'The History of the Development of Wireless Telegraphy and Broadcasting . . .', pp. 396, 402-5, and 416; *Bulletin*, 17 October 1934; *CPD*, vol. 148, 3 December 1935, pp. 2365-7; *Broadcasting Business*, 8 April 1937; and *Labor Daily* 19 and 26 March, 2 April 1937.
77 I. K. Mackay, *Broadcasting in Australia* (Melbourne, 1957), p. 114.
78 Curnow mentions a similar point, only conversely; see G. R. Curnow, 'The History of the Development of Wireless Telegraphy and Broadcasting . . .', p.405.

4   The Politics of Broadcasting

1 Chairman's New Year's Eve Broadcast, 31 December 1938, Cleary Papers, MS 5539.
2 J. A. La Nauze gives an excellent account of Murdoch as a broadcaster in his *Walter Murdoch*, pp. 108-13.
3 The problem of dullness is mentioned in, for example, National Talks Advisory Committee Minutes, 29-30 October 1937, MP 237/1, Box 68, File no. TKS/14, AA. See also W. Macmahon Ball, *Press, Radio and World Affairs*, p. 132.
4 Discussed in B. Tildesley, 'Broadcast Programmes', *Australian Quarterly*, VIII, no. 31 (September 1936), 66.
5 Mrs Freer was an Englishwoman who was barred from entering Australia on the extraordinary ground that she might commit adultery and hence break up an Australian marriage. Huge protests eventually forced the government to let her land in July 1937. See Commission Minutes, 7-8 July 1937.
6 Barry told Clewlow that there was no need to tell children about international politics, and he particularly criticized references to Roosevelt, Mussolini, Hitler and Franco in the *Mike* segment of the programme—see memorandum from Barry to the federal controller of productions, 2 May 1939, SP 617/1, Box 2, National Children's Session File, 1938-9, AA.
7 See Molesworth's comments in *Labor Daily*, 5 May 1938.
8 E. Blain, *Life with Aunty*, p. 73.
9 Figures in *CPD*, vol. 149, 23 September 1936, pp. 440, 443.
10 See, for example, Statement by Chairman re the Prime Minister, 19 August 1937, Cleary Papers, MS 5539.

[11] On 17 March 1932, the then minister for trade and customs, Henry Gullett, even introduced an amendment aimed at boosting the autonomy of the ABC and reducing the opportunities for ministerial interference—see *CPD*, vol. 133, 17 March 1932, p. 1257. See also comments in H. M. Burton, 'The Burlesque of Broadcasting', *Australian Rhodes Review*, no. 4 (1939), p. 84.

[12] *CPD*, vol. 151, 1 October 1936, p. 753. See discussion of the general issue of ministerial direction in G. Nettheim, 'Public Broadcasting and Government', *Australian Quarterly*, XXXV, no. 1 (March 1963), 36-42. There is also a thesis by W. H. N. Hull, 'A Comparative Study of the Problems of Ministerial Responsibility in Australian and Canadian Broadcasting' (Ph.D. Thesis, Duke University, 1959), which discusses the technicalities of ministerial powers, but unfortunately gives very little detail of actual cases in Australia. See also C. Stokes, 'The Politics of Radio', in R. Lucy (ed.), *The Pieces of Politics* (Melbourne, 1975), pp. 296-312.

[13] See, for example, *Truth*, 17 March 1934 and 24 April 1938.

[14] Details in *ABC: Sixth Annual Report*, pp. 46-7, and in *Gibson Report*, pp. 16-17.

[15] See, for example, *Daily Telegraph*, 21 April 1934; *Truth*, 24 April 1938; *CPD*, vol. 152, 11 November 1936, p. 1701, 2 December 1936, p. 2677, and vol. 153, 22 June 1937, p. 203.

[16] Gibson Committee, *Minutes of Evidence*, p. 221, and *Gibson Report*, p. 15.

[17] G. R. Curnow, 'The History of the Development of Wireless Telegraphy and Broadcasting . . .', p. 390.

[18] Discussed in J. Rydon, 'The Australian Broadcasting Commission, 1932-1942: the Study of a Public Corporation', *Public Administration*, XI, n.s. (1952), 23.

[19] Cleary to Brookes, 15 November 1938, Brookes Papers, Series 26.

[20] Quoted in M. F. Dixon, *Inside the ABC*, p. 133.

[21] Cleary to Brookes, 15 November 1938, Brookes Papers, Series 26.

[22] Cleary to Harrison, 2 December 1939, and see earlier comments in Brookes to Cleary, 22 May 1939, *ibid.*

[23] A new broadcasting Act was not passed until 1942, under the Curtin Labor government. See speculation in, for example, *SMH*, 11 December 1937; *Daily Telegraph*, 7 October 1938; and *Truth*, 10 April 1938.

[24] *CPD*, vol. 157, 26 September 1938, p. 166. For Cabinet discussion on Cleary's salary, see Cabinet Minutes and Submissions, CRS A2694, Agenda no. 1747, vol. 15, pt 2, 23 May 1936; vol. 16, pt 1, 23 September 1936; and vol. 16, pt 2, 24 November 1936.

[25] Noted in *Labor Daily*, 20 September 1938.

[26] See his remarks in *SMH*, 19 August 1937.

[27] Cabinet Minutes and Submissions, CRS A2694, Agenda no. 456, vol. 18, pt 5, 11 October 1938.

[28] See Cleary's arguments in Cleary to Lyons, 24 October 1938, Brookes Papers, Series 26.

[29] Cleary noted as early as September 1938 that the European situation was dwarfing all other Cabinet issues — see Cleary to Brookes, 21 September 1938, Cleary Papers, MS 5539.

[30] Cleary to Harrison, 2 December 1939, Brookes to McLachlan, 16 April 1937, and Brookes to Harrison, 6 June 1939, Brookes Papers, Series 26.

[31] Cleary to Harrison, 2 December 1939, *ibid.*

[32] Report of visit to the postmaster-general by Cleary, Brookes, the other commissioners and the general manager on 18 June 1936, contained in Commission Minutes, 17-18 June 1936.

[33] Paper headed 'Chairman's Interview with the Postmaster-General, 28 November 1938', Cleary Papers, MS 5539.

Notes (Chapter 4)

34 See Well's comments in *Daily News*, 28 January 1939, and *Daily Telegraph*, 27 January 1939. There are some general details and figures concerning censorship of the printed media in P. Coleman, *Obscenity, Blasphemy and Sedition: 100 Years of Censorship in Australia* (Sydney, 1974), pp. 13, 82.
35 P. Coleman, *Obscenity, Blasphemy, and Sedition*, p.13.
36 *Ibid.*, pp. 110-11.
37 Details in memorandum from Cleary to commissioners, 28 November 1938, Cleary Papers, MS 5632, File 2.
38 See allegation in memorandum from Cleary to commissioners and Moses, 10 October 1938, WP.
39 W. Macmahon Ball, *Press, Radio and World Affairs*, p. 145.
40 See comments in McLachlan to Page, 1 July 1937, CRS A461, Bundle 539, File no. D422/1/6, pt 1, AA.
41 See comments in *Daily Telegraph*, 10 August 1937.
42 *SMH*, 18 August 1937; *Daily Telegraph*, 19 August 1937.
43 *Gibson Report*, p. 12. See also Commission Minutes, 1932-48, *passim*, and see comments in, for example, J. A. McCallum to Cleary, 19 May 1958, Cleary Papers, MS 5632, in which Cleary is given credit for his 'complete objectivity' while ABC chairman.
44 Reported in *Daily Telegraph*, 18 September 1936.
45 Commission Minutes, 7-8 July 1937.
46 See also comments in *Daily Telegraph*, 8 July 1938, under the heading 'A.B.C. Discreet with Hitler'.
47 For some further details of the Foster controversy, see *Labor Daily*, 6 and 10 May 1938; *Daily Telegraph*, 7 and 9 May 1938; *SMH*, 5 and 7 May 1938; *Smith's Weekly*, 11 May 1938; *CPD*, vol. 155, 11 May 1938, p. 1019; and Cleary to Brookes, 11 May 1938, Brookes Papers, Series 26. Egon Kisch was a communist sympathizer who was refused permission to land in Australia to address anti-fascist rallies—see a brief summary of the case in J. Robertson, '1930-39', pp. 447-8.
48 Biographical details of 'The Watchman' may be found in *Who's Who in Australia*, XIth edition, 1941, p. 462; *Smith's Weekly*, 27 March 1940; *ABC Weekly*, vol. 2, no. 33 (17 August 1940), p. 6; Mann to Bearup, 17 October 1940, WP. The Watchman Papers (ABCA) are contained in five files headed: Listeners' Letters Pro The Watchman, 1938-40; Listeners' Letters Anti The Watchman, 1938-40; Listeners' Letters complaints to the PMG; Libel Case; and Overseas Visit.
49 The ABC Archives possess 196 of 'The Watchman's' scripts. Another 151 (some duplicate) scripts are held in the Victorian Branch of the Australian Archives, MP 298/4, Box 10.
50 E. M. Andrews, *Isolationism and Appeasement in Australia: Reactions to the European Crises, 1935-1939* (Canberra, 1970), p. 197.
51 E. F. Halkyard to Cleary, 11 November 1938, WP.
52 Recorded in Federal Programme Committee Minutes, 14-16 September 1936.
53 See comments in *ABC Weekly*, vol. 2, no. 33 (17 August 1940), p. 6. See also note compiled by M. F. Dixon, 1 September 1936, entitled 'Complaint re "Spectators" Commentaries', SP 286/2, Box 1, General Manager's File (August–December) 1936), AA, and E. Andrews, *Isolationism and Appeasement*, p. 21.
54 Quotes taken respectively from G. H. Nielsen to Moses, 13 February 1940 and W. G. Bondfield to Cleary, 11 November 1938, WP.
55 W. Macmahon Ball, *Press, Radio and World Affairs*, p. 130.
56 The volume of letters is discussed in a memorandum from Cleary to Harrison, 25 November 1939, WP. See also figures from *Monthly Information Summary*, ABC Public Relations Department, 1 July 1939, WP, which show that in the period from

April 1938 to June 1939, 867 letters were received by the Victorian branch, 83 were of New South Wales origin, and 16 were from short-wave listeners. See also Quarterly Summary of Listeners' Letters and Telephone Calls, 26 June–24 September 1938, MP 284/1, Box 1, File no. S/1/2, AA.

[57] In Parliament, one member even asked whether 'The Watchman' spoke on behalf of the government—see *CPD*, vol. 163, 24 May 1940, p. 1258.

[58] See comments in memoranda from Barry to Moses, 20 October 1938, SP 341/1A, Box 1, File no. 1, and from Mrs Moore to Horner, 21 May 1937, SP 286/6, Box 2, File marked 'The Watchman', AA. See also memorandum from McCall to the federal controller of talks, 13 July 1938, WP.

[59] J. C. Smith to Cleary, 24 February 1940, WP.

[60] Memorandum from Horner to Dixon, 17 March 1937, WP. This point was also made by Sir Charles Moses in an interview with me in Sydney, 3 August 1976. See also J. A. La Nauze's comments in his *Walter Murdoch*, p. 110, where he says of 'The Watchman': 'I still recall with distaste his throbbing tones'.

[61] See this matter discussed in memorandum from Cleary to the postmaster-general, 5 June 1939, WP.

[62] See his statements in 'At Home and Abroad', 12 August 1937, and Moses' instructions on this point in memorandum to the manager for Victoria, 15 September 1937, WP.

[63] 'At Home and Abroad', 4 March 1940. See complaints in E. F. Trist to Hon. J. A. Beasley, 4 March 1940, WP. See other remarks on the by-election in 'News Behind the News', 7 May 1940.

[64] See, for example, 'At Home and Abroad', 26 March 1940.

[65] 'At Home and Abroad', 6 and 14 February 1940.

[66] By May 1938, only six other countries out of twenty-nine original signatories had ratified the agreement. A copy of the agreement and related correspondence is contained in MP 544/1, Box 3, AA.

[67] See J. Malone to Moses, 17 September 1937, SP 286/2, Box 1, General Manager's File, July–December 1937, AA.

[68] See brief details in J. Robertson, '1930-39', pp. 452-3.

[69] 'At Home and Abroad', 17 May 1937.

[70] *Ibid.*, 26 May 1937.

[71] Extract from 'At Home and Abroad', quoted in letter from T. W. White to McLachlan, 23 July 1937, WP.

[72] 'At Home and Abroad', 4 July 1937.

[73] See T. S. Nettlefold to the postmaster-general, 5 July 1939, and J. Hume-Cook to the postmaster-general, 25 October 1939, WP.

[74] Memorandum from Cleary to Harrison, 14 August 1939, WP.

[75] P. Coleman, *Obscenity, Blasphemy and Sedition*, p. 83.

[76] T. W. White to McLachlan, 23 July 1937; memorandum from Moses to all commissioners, *c.* July 1937, WP. See also Commission Minutes, 2-3 September 1937.

[77] Memorandum from Moses to the manager for Victoria, 5 August 1937, WP.

[78] Story reported in *Radio Retailer*, 21 January 1938. See memorandum from R. Himmer to Moses, 2 February 1938, WP, in which he states that he is unaware of any such censorship having been exercised.

[79] For example, see the postmaster-general's statements in *SMH*, 7 May 1938.

[80] Moses mentions this in memorandum to Dixon, 14 February 1939, SP 286/6, Box 2, 'The Watchman' File, AA.

[81] See the exchange of viewpoints in J. Malone to Moses, 3 June 1937, M. Haley to the officer in charge, 4QG, 12 January 1939, N. Vowles to Cameron, 22 December

Notes (Chapter 4)

1938, and accompanying memorandum from McCall to Moses, 23 January 1939, and Moses to Haley, 22 February 1939, WP. See also memorandum from Moses to Dixon, 14 February 1939, SP 286/6, Box 2, 'The Watchman' File, AA.

[82] Memorandum from Moses to Dixon, 14 February 1939, SP 286/6, Box, 'The Watchman' File.

[83] E. Andrews, *Isolationism and Appeasement*, p. 145.

[84] 'At Home and Abroad', 22 August 1939. See his earlier predictions in 'News Behind the News', 24 October 1938.

[85] *Age*, 5 and 8 October 1938.

[86] *Bulletin*, 19 October 1938.

[87] Memorandum on 'The Watchman and the Crisis' compiled by the Melbourne Office of the ABC, WP.

[88] Extract from 'At Home and Abroad' in letter from Moses to director-general of the PMG's Department, 11 March 1938, SP 286/6, Box 2, File marked 'The Watchman', AA. For a complaint of 'Eden propaganda', see Ella M. Gruin to the minister for defence, 26 and 28 February 1938, WP. See also Dixon's memorandum to Moses, 5 March 1938, WP.

[89] D. Watson, 'Anti-Communism in the Thirties', *Arena*, no. 37 (1975), p. 49.

[90] Mann to Moses, 14 April 1938, WP.

[91] Cleary to Brookes, 29 November 1937, WP.

[92] Memorandum from Barry to Moses, 5 October 1938, WP. The resolution is contained in the National Talks Advisory Committee Minutes, 31 January–1 February 1939, SP 613/1, Box 6, File no. 2/4/2, pt 1, AA.

[93] The secretary nevertheless recommended that the Commonwealth Investigation Branch should make a record of talks given by broadcasters 'known to be provocative in their language'—see memorandum from W. R. Hodgson, secretary of the Department of External Affairs to the secretary of the Prime Minister's Department, 18 October 1938, CRS A461, Bundle 541, File no. AA 422/1/6, AA.

[94] Lyons to the postmaster-general, 24 October 1938, *ibid*.

[95] 'At Home and Abroad', 21 September 1939. The content of the telephone conversation is reported in a memorandum from Cleary to all commissioners and the general manager, 21 September 1939, WP. See also Commission Minutes, 4-5 October 1939, and memorandum from Cleary to Harrison, 21 September 1939, SP 286/2, Box 2, General Manager's File (July–December 1939), AA. Cleary also related this story in evidence to the Parliamentary Standing Committee on Broadcasting—see *Summary of Evidence*, 1943, p. 74.

[96] Mentioned in memorandum from McCall to Moses, 25 September 1939, WP.

[97] Mann to Moses, 29 September 1939, WP.

[98] Memorandum from Cleary to all commissioners and the general manager, 10 October 1939, WP. See also Cleary to A. L. Tipping, 8 September 1939, WP.

[99] Moses to Mann, 11 October 1939, WP.

[1] W. Macmahon Ball to the manager for Victoria, 16 October 1939, WP.

[2] See questions in *CPD*, vol. 159, 18 May 1939, p. 563, and vol. 162, 16 November 1939, p. 1233. See also Commission Minutes, 30 November–1 December 1938.

[3] See Bearup's memorandum to all commissioners, 25 August 1940, Bearup to Mann, 15 October 1940, and Mann to Bearup, 17 October 1940, WP.

[4] Memorandum from C. Charlton to Bearup, 20 June 1941, WP.

[5] See, for example, the satisfaction expressed at being relieved of the responsibility of further defending or scrutinizing 'The Watchman' in a letter from one commissioner, namely, 'unless our Commentators are prepared to carry out the policy of the Commission and exclude their personal opinions on the matter of politics, there is no other course open to us but to withhold their reappointment. The fact that he has

resigned from our service solves the rather difficult position'—S. J. McGibbon to Bearup, 21 October 1940, WP.
⁶ This concept is discussed briefly in relation to the ABC in G. R. Curnow, 'The History of the Development of Wireless Telegraphy and Broadcasting . . .', pp. 429-33; also in G. Nettheim, 'Public Broadcasting and Government', *Australian Quarterly* (March 1963), p. 41; and in H. Wolfsohn, 'The Ideology Makers', in H. Mayer (ed.), *Australian Politics: A Reader* (Melbourne, 1966), pp. 79-80; and see, for example, 'News Behind the News', 7 May 1940, in which 'The Watchman' condemns extremist ideas.

5 Wartime Programming

¹ Figures calculated from *Commonwealth Year Book*, 1939, p. 392, Gibson Committee, *Minutes of Evidence*, p. 46, and *ABC: Seventeenth Annual Report*, p. 29.
² Memorandum from Moses to federal controllers and all states, 9 April 1940, SP 286/2, Box 1, General Manager's File (January–December 1940), AA.
³ Decisions noted in Commission Minutes, 27-28 May 1940.
⁴ Reported in M. F. Dixon, *Inside the ABC*, p.35.
⁵ Memorandum from Dixon to the acting general manager, 21 January 1942, SP 286/2, Box 3, Programme Policy File, AA.
⁶ See predictions in memorandum from Barry to Moses, 1 September 1939, SP 341/1A, Box 1, General Programme Policy File no. 1 (1936-42), AA.
⁷ Bearup to Calwell, 28 November 1942, Chairman's Copies File, ABCA.
⁸ Details in P. Hasluck, *The Government and the People, 1939-1941* (Canberra, 1952), pp. 201-3.
⁹ Figures in *ABC: Tenth Annual Report*, p. 4, and *ABC: Twelfth Annual Report*, p. 17.
¹⁰ See discussion in P. Hasluck, *The Government and the People 1939-1941*, pp. 383-5. Quote from p. 385.
¹¹ *Ibid.*, p. 389.
¹² For details of campaigns conducted by the DOI, see SP 109/11, Box 81, unmarked file, AA, and *ABC Weekly*, vol. 3, no. 43 (25 October 1941), p. 6.
¹³ See details in memoranda from Bearup to the manager for Victoria, 7 June 1940, MP 237/1, Box 73, File no. WAR/3; from Ball to the director-general of information, 1 August 1940, SP 109/11, Box 81, File no. 31/8/2, pt 1; from P. Hemery to the manager for Victoria, 13 May 1941, and from Molesworth to the manager for Victoria, 29 July 1941, MP 237/1, Box 73, File no. WAR/2, AA. See also the *Broadcaster* (WA), 23 June 1943.
¹⁴ See McCauley to Ogilvy, 27 May 1942, and McCauley to George Edward Players Pty Ltd, 30 March 1942, ABC and Broadcasting File, SP 109/6, Bundle 4, Box 70, AA.
¹⁵ See Welch to the acting manager for Victoria, 26 June 1942, and Thomas to Welch, 2 July 1942, MP 237/1, Box 68, File no. TKS/19, AA.
¹⁶ *Daily Telegraph*, 18 February 1942.
¹⁷ G. Long, *The Six Years War: A Concise History of Australia in the 1939-45 War* (Canberra, 1973), p. 180.
¹⁸ Script no. 11 of 'The Jap as he really is', 6 April 1942, SP 300/1, Box 7, AA.
¹⁹ Script no. 2 of 'The Jap as he really is', 25 March 1942, *ibid*.
²⁰ Script no. 3 of 'The Jap as he really is', 26 March 1942, *ibid*.
²¹ *ABC: Tenth Annual Report*, p. 5. William Macmahon Ball said that he personally complained about these early broadcasts until they were stopped—interview with me in Melbourne, 9 February 1978.

Notes (Chapter 5)   197

[22] Quoted in Molesworth to the acting general manager, 12 October 1942, Trade Union Talks File (1941-4), R17/19, Box 3, ABCA.
[23] Bearup to the secretary of the Department of Information, 12 October 1942, and Hawes to Bearup, 13 October 1942 and 1 February 1943, *ibid.*
[24] J. V. Stout to McCauley, 23 June 1944, SP 109/6, Bundle 2, Box 68, ACTU Broadcasts File, AA.
[25] Lord Mayor of Melbourne to the general manager, 21 April 1942, MP 237/1, Box 9, File no. CEL/18, AA.
[26] Memorandum from Barry to the acting general manager, 8 May 1942, *ibid.*
[27] Figures given in memorandum from R. Himmer to the Federal Concerts Department, 11 January 1945, *ibid.*
[28] *ABC: Tenth Annual Report*, p. 8. See further details in 'Appeals for Patriotic Funds', 24 October 1939, SP 341/1A, Box 1, General Programme Policy File no. 1 (1936–December 1942); memorandum from Bearup to all states, 12 May 1941, MP 237/1, Box 73, File no. WAR/3; and memorandum from Moses to all states, 24 October 1939, MP 237/1, Box 9, File no. CEL/16, AA.
[29] Commission Minutes, 27-28 May 1940 and 1-2 October 1941.
[30] Story reported in *Commercial Broadcaster*, 12 January 1940.
[31] *SMH*, 30 May 1941.
[32] *ABC Weekly*, vol. 3, no. 25 (21 June 1941), p. 5.
[33] Bearup to Ball, 9 December 1941, MP 272/3, Bundle 1, File no. A2/II. See sample broadcasts of 'Wives Calling Husbands' in MP 237/1, Box 67, File no. STW/1, AA.
[34] Some details are contained in ABC Staff and Organization File, Victorian Branch, 1932-4, ABCA; and see memorandum from Clewlow to the general manager, 25 November 1938, SP 617/1, Box 2, National Children's Session File, 1938-9, AA.
[35] Details in L. Gash, 'The History of the Australian Broadcasting Commission's Children's Session, c. 1929-45', pp. 57-61.
[36] Details from *ABC Weekly*, vol. 3, no. 44 (1 November 1941), p. 10; Commission Minutes, 1-2 October 1941.
[37] Figure in *ABC: Fourteenth Annual Report*, p. 13.
[38] Memorandum from Bearup to all commissioners, 29 June 1940, SP 289/1, Box 2-3, AA.
[39] Brief profiles of some of these women are given in *ABC Weekly*, vol. 4, no. 18 (2 May 1942), p. 17.
[40] See memorandum from Moses to the manager for Victoria, 22 January 1940, MP 237/1, Box 73, File no. WAR/3, AA; and see Commission Minutes, 8-9 January 1940.
[41] Some biographical details are contained in the *ABC Weekly*, vol. 2, no. 37 (14 September 1940), p. 18; Moses to Cleary, 28 October 1942, Cleary Papers, MS 5632, File 2; and memorandum from Ball to the minister for information, 1 February 1941, MP 272/3, Bundle 1, File no. A2/II, AA.
[42] Commission Minutes, 23-24 January 1941.
[43] *Smith's Weekly*, 13 September 1941.
[44] See pamphlet entitled *Talks for Listening Groups: Co-operation or Conflict*, MP 298/4, Box 1, Discussion Groups Broadcasts File, AA.
[45] Commission Minutes, 19 July 1935, and see main details in memorandum from J. C. Rookwood Proud to the manager for Victoria, 15 June 1939, MP 237/1, Box 68, File no. TKS/19, and National Talks Advisory Committee Minutes, 3-4 February 1938, SP 613/1, Box 6, File no. 2/4/1, I, AA.
[46] Memorandum from Proud to the manager for Victoria, 23 June 1939, MP 237/1, Box 68, File no. TKS/19, AA.
[47] Report on Discussion Groups, 27 July 1939, *ibid.*

Notes (Chapter 5)

[48] See Cleary's comments in an address entitled 'Why National Broadcasting?' delivered at a Legacy Club luncheon on 8 August 1940—copy in the Cleary Papers, MS 5539.

[49] See MP 298/4, Box 1, AA, for some typical Listening Group broadcasts.

[50] National Talks Advisory Committee Minutes, 17-19 August 1943, File no. 2/4/1, I and 22-24 August 1944, File no. 2/4/1, II, both in SP 613/1, Box 6, AA.

[51] Figures in National Talks Advisory Committee Minutes, 13-14 August 1940, SP 613/1, Box 6, File no. 2/4/1, I, AA. There were 94 manual workers to 1 librarian, 5 university lecturers and 4 journalists.

[52] See such complaints in the general manager to Foley, Medley and Mrs Hill, 5 May 1943, Foley File, ABCA, and in report of Cleary's interview with Curtin in Commission Minutes, 21-23 June 1943.

[53] Federal Publicity Handout, April 1941, Dick Bentley Press Cuttings File (1938-68), SP 1011/2, Box 37, AA.

[54] See biographical details of Bentley in *ibid*.

[55] See report of Curtin's conversation with Moses after his return from active duty, namely, 'I have brought you back because I have had complaints about the Commission's programmes. General Blamey tells me that the troops don't listen to them. I expect you to put this right', contained in Cleary's statement to Commission Meeting, 8-9 March 1945, Cleary Papers, MS 5539.

[56] Minutes of the Interstate Programme Controllers' Conference, 8-9 July 1942 (part of the Federal Programme Committee Minutes). See also memoranda from Barry to Bearup, 8 and 27 June 1943, Light Entertainment Department File, I (1937-47), R17, Box 70, ABCA.

[57] Memorandum from Clewlow to the general manager, 24 December 1943, SP 617/1, Box 4, Light Entertainment File, 1936-44, AA.

[58] Commission Minutes, 15-18 March 1943; *SMH*, 23 June 1943.

[59] Minutes of the Interstate Programme Controllers' Conference, 6 September 1944.

[60] Clewlow to controller of programmes, 10 November 1942, and Bearup to the controller of programmes, 8 October 1942, SP 341/1A, Box 1, General Programme Policy File no. 1 (1936—December 1942), AA.

[61] James to the controller of programmes, 13 November 1942, *ibid*.

[62] See contents of a file marked 'Lawsons—Blue Hills Story', ABCA. The interviews are in *ABC Weekly*, vol. 7, no. 46 (17 November 1945), *passim*.

[63] There is a short biography of Gwen Meredith in *ABC Weekly*, vol. 8, no. 21 (8 June 1946), p. 4.

[64] Commission Minutes, 21-23 June 1943.

[65] L. Rees gives a brief but detailed discussion of these plays in his *The Making of Australian Drama*, pp. 161, 217, and 233.

[66] The percentage of broadcasting time occupied by plays was 3.53 per cent in 1939 and 3.35 per cent in 1945. Figures from *ABC: Seventh Annual Report*, p. 11, and *ABC: Thirteenth Annual Report*, p. 20.

[67] Details in memorandum from Dixon to the general manager, 18 December 1939, SP 286/2, Box 1, General Manager's File, (July—December 1939), AA.

[68] M. F. Dixon, *Inside the ABC*, p. 10.

[69] *Ibid.*, p. 35.

[70] Details of conference in *Gibson Report*, p. 22; *Commercial Broadcasting*, 28 September 1939; and M. F. Dixon, *Inside the ABC*, pp. 37-9.

[71] Discussed in M. F. Dixon, *Inside the ABC*, pp. 44-6.

[72] *Sun*, 16 February 1942.

[73] Biographical details in memorandum from Dixon to the general manager, 25 March 1939, SP 286/17, Bundle 32, Warren Denning File (1939-48), AA.

[74] Moses to Denning, n.d., *ibid*.

Notes (Chapter 5)

[75] Reported in *Daily News*, 21 September 1939.
[76] Figure given in memorandum from Dixon to general manager, 8 March 1940, SP 286/2, Box 1, General Manager's File (January–December 1940), AA.
[77] M. F. Dixon, *Inside the ABC*, pp. 63-4; G. C. Bolton, *Dick Boyer*, pp. 111-12.
[78] National Talks Advisory Committee Minutes, 28-29 January 1942, SP 613/1, Box 6, File no. 2/4/1, I, AA.
[79] Bearup's letter was quoted in *CPD*, vol. 170, 6 March 1942, p. 224.
[80] *Ibid.*, 25 February 1942, p. 67, and 5 March 1942, p. 202.
[81] Quoted in P. Hasluck, *The Government and the People, 1942-1945*, p. 750.
[82] Noted in memorandum to Calwell, 1 May 1945, Cabinet Minutes and Submissions, CRS A2700, vol. 15, Agenda no. 835 (1945), AA.
[83] Quoted in *SMH*, 4 May 1945.
[84] *SMH*, 2 May 1945.
[85] *Gibson Report*, p. 26; Commission Minutes, 15-16 February 1939.
[86] *Smith's Weekly*, 6 December 1939.
[87] Cabinet Minutes and Submissions, CRS A2694, vol. 19, pt II, Agenda no. 596, 15 March 1939; *Daily News*, 26 May 1939; G. R. Curnow, 'The History of the Development of Wireless Telegraphy and Broadcasting . . .', p. 370.
[88] *CPD*, vol. 159, 24 May 1939, p. 666.
[89] Letter quoted in *Gibson Report*, p. 27. See reference to continuing concern within Parliament in, for example, *Daily Telegraph*, 20 May 1939, and *SMH*, 19 May 1939.
[90] Point made in *Century*, 21 July 1939.
[91] For example, in the quarter ending November 1941, sales reached only 37 000 per week—*Gibson Report*, p. 27. See also McGibbon to Moses, 16 February 1940, McGibbon File, ABCA.
[92] Point raised, for example, by Senator E. B. Johnston in *CPD*, vol. 159, 18 May 1939, p. 501.
[93] The 'Gibson Committee' was the joint parliamentary committee on wireless broadcasting. Gibson estimated that advertising costs would have been twice the cost of publishing a journal: see *CPD*, vol. 170, 30 April 1942, p. 649, and *Gibson Report*, p. 29.
[94] *Gibson Report*, p. 28.
[95] M. F. Dixon, *Inside the ABC*, pp. 39-41; G. R. Curnow, 'The History of the Development of Wireless Telegraphy and Broadcasting . . .', p. 376.
[96] M. F. Dixon, *Inside the ABC*, p. 40.
[97] The decision to suspend is recorded in Cabinet Minutes and Submissions, CRS A2697, vol. 7, Agenda no. 599, 6 June 1941. See McLeay's submission recommending this dated 5 March 1941 in CRS A2697, vol. 6, Agenda no. 599, 12 March 1941; and see Bearup to McGibbon, 11 July 1941, McGibbon File, ABCA.
[98] As an historical source the *Weekly's* value is limited. Many of the letters to the editor were obviously written by ABC staff and therefore offer no gauge of public reaction. Very little space was devoted to internal ABC matters, though there was the occasional biography and certainly useful information about new programmes.
[99] Noted in Commission Minutes, 26-28 February 1941. See notes on radio censorship in memorandum from F. Strahan to the secretary of the Department of Defence, 1 September 1939, CRS A1608, Bundle 33, File no. D/21/1/2, AA. See also R. R. Walker, *The Magic Spark* (Melbourne, 1973), p. 41.
[1] See 'National Broadcasting in the Second World War—GM, 25/7/46', ABCA; memoranda from Barry to state managers and federal officers, 2 September 1939, SP 341/1A, Box 1, General Programme Policy File no. 1 (1936–December 1942); Ball to Mitchell, 13 August 1942, MP 272/1, Bundle 2, File no. 15/2; Molesworth to the manager for Victoria, 15 April 1941, MP 237/1, Box 73, File no. WAR/3;

Notes (Chapter 5)

SP 195/3, Unregistered File containing Broadcasting Censorship Orders, AA; and *Daily Telegraph*, 16 September 1939. Weather reports were later re-introduced.
[2] Commission Minutes, 26 May 1941.
[3] National Talks Advisory Committee Minutes, 29-30 January and 20-21 August 1941, and memorandum from Henderson to the federal controller of talks, 3 February 1942, in National Talks Advisory Committee Minutes Discussion File, SP 613/1, Box 6, File no. 2/4/5, I, AA.
[4] Memorandum from Henderson to the federal controller of talks, 3 February 1942, *ibid*.
[5] Memorandum from the Tasmanian Talks Advisory Committee to the chairman of the National Talks Advisory Committee, 28 January 1944, in National Talks Advisory Committee Minutes, 1-3 February 1944, and from Moses to all commissioners, 19 October 1944, *ibid*.
[6] Memorandum from Bearup to the manager for Victoria, 6 January 1941, MP 237/1, Box 73, File no. WAR/3, AA; Commission Minutes, 5-6 June 1940.
[7] *Century*, 23 February 1940.
[8] Broadcasting Censorship Order, 1 March 1940, SP 195/3, Unregistered File, AA.
[9] Cabinet Minutes and Submissions, CRS A2697, vol. 6, Agenda no. 603, 6 March 1941.
[10] *ABC: Tenth Annual Report*, p. 5.
[11] P. Hasluck, *The Government and the People, 1942-1945* (Canberra, 1970), p. 403.
[12] See censored script in SP 109/3, File no. 318.20, AA.
[13] Memorandum from Molesworth to the acting general manager, 11 March 1941, *ibid*.; *CPD*, vol. 166, 13 March 1941, pp. 43, 138.
[14] Rorke to chief publicity censor, 13 March 1941, SP 109/3, File no. 318.20, AA.
[15] Memorandum from Burns to acting chief publicity censor, 13 March 1941, *ibid*.
[16] Commission Minutes, 17-19 July 1940, and memorandum from Bearup to the manager for Victoria, 11 July 1940, MP 237/1, Box 73, File no. WAR/3, AA.
[17] Gibson Committee, *Minutes of Evidence*, p. 605.
[18] Curtin read out the extract in the House; see *CPD*, vol. 170, 6 March 1942, p. 252.
[19] See above, chapter four.
[20] See Labor politicians' complaints in, for example, *Labor Daily*, 4 July 1934, 19 September and 2 October 1936, and in *CPD*, vol. 151, 1 October 1936, p. 749; vol. 154, 8 September 1937, p. 664.
[21] Details in Commission Minutes, 9-12 February 1943, and in the *Second Report* of the Parliamentary Standing Committee on Broadcasting, p. 5.
[22] *Gibson Report*, pp. 23, 77.
[23] All these comments were reported in *Daily Telegraph*, 14 September 1941. For the actual letters, see file marked 'Objectionable Programme Matter: Correspondence with PMG, 1940-5', R17, Box 70, ABCA.
[24] Gibson Committee, *Minutes of Evidence*, p. 237.
[25] See Rev. W. N. Lock to the Joint Committee on Wireless Broadcasting, 10 July 1941, and memorandum from Bearup to the manager for Victoria, 24 October 1940, Merry Go Round File (October 1940–September 1941). See also memoranda from Clewlow to the general manager, 22 October 1940, and from Bearup to the acting general manager for Victoria, 25 March 1941, and a letter from Cleary to Mr Eva, 22 October 1940, Out of the Bag File (1940-2), R17, Box 70, ABCA.
[26] The details of the debate were summarized by Cleary in his submission to the Parliamentary Standing Committee on Broadcasting; see *Minutes of Evidence*, 8 February 1945, pp. 195-8.

Notes (Chapter 5)

[27] *Ibid.*; see also Moses to Strahan, 4 September 1944, CRS A461, Bundle 540, File no. W422/1/6, AA.
[28] Parliamentary Standing Committee on Broadcasting, *Minutes of Evidence*, 8 February 1945, p. 198.
[29] P. MacKinnon's letter to the *ABC Weekly*, vol. 6, no. 40 (30 September 1944), p. 8; Rev. W. Hobbin to the prime minister, 18 August 1944, CRS A461, Bundle 540, File no. W422/1/6, AA.
[30] Parliamentary Standing Committee on Broadcasting *Minutes of Evidence*, 8 February 1945, p. 198.
[31] Minutes of Managers' Meetings held in Sydney, 3-5 October 1944, SP 613/1, Box 8, File no. 3/1/4, pt 1, AA.
[32] *CPD*, vol. 179, 14 September 1944, p. 765.
[33] *Ibid.*, 20 September 1944, p. 1022.
[34] Comments respectively in *ibid.*; vol. 180, 27 September 1944, p. 1473; and vol. 179, 20 September 1944, p. 1031.
[35] Parliamentary Standing Committee on Broadcasting, *Minutes of Evidence*, 8 February 1945, p. 199.
[36] See comments in Bearup to McGibbon, 29 December 1941, McGibbon File, ABCA.
[37] *SMH*, 3 August 1936; Cleary to Brookes, 23 July 1936, Brookes Papers, Series 26. There are some statements concerning Sunday devotional services and the problems involved in MP 1170/3, File no. BR/6/1, pt I, AA.
[38] Details in Cleary to Moses, 11 November 1942, Cleary Papers, MS 5632, File 2. There is a very thick file of complaints on the Woodruff incident in MP 544/1, Box 3, AA.
[39] Cleary to Calwell, 23 October 1942, MP 1170/3, File no. BR/6/1, pt I, AA.
[40] See comments by Henderson, August 1943, in file marked 'Clerical Intonation', Religious Broadcasts File, ABCA.
[41] See 'Annual Report', 21 July 1944, in Advisory Committee Correspondence, Religious Broadcasts File ABCA.
[42] *Gibson Report*, p. 42.
[43] Details in Report on World Range Broadcasting compiled for Sir Henry Gullett by Ernest Fisk, 6 October 1939, MP 272/3, Bundle 1, File no. A2, I, AA.
[44] See Information Summary, June 1939, MP 237/7, Box 2, AA, and P. Hasluck, *The Government and the People, 1939-1941*, p. 202.
[45] Commission Minutes, 1-2 November 1939. See also Note on Shortwave Broadcasting Services for Overseas Propaganda compiled by E. J. Harrison, and submission for Cabinet by Sir Henry Gullett, 29 November 1939, both in MP 272/3, Bundle 1, File no. A2, I, AA.
[46] See document marked 'For Cabinet—Shortwave Broadcasting Service for Overseas Propaganda', *ibid.*
[47] Paper entitled 'The Short-wave Work of the Broadcasting Division of the DOI' by W. M. Ball, 10 December 1940, *ibid.*
[48] Quoted in *Daily Telegraph*, 21 December 1939.
[49] See details of the Australia Calling session in *ABC Weekly*, vol. 2, no. 40 (9 November 1940), p. 9.
[50] Overseas Short-Wave Broadcasts Report submitted to the general manager by Kirke, Molesworth and Smith, 24 January 1940, MP 272/5, General Correspondence File, AA.
[51] See Ball's memorandum to Foll, 1 February 1941, and his report, 'Shortwave Broadcasting and Organisation in Australia, 27 November 1941', MP 272/3,

Bundle 1, File no. A2, II, AA.
[52] Commission Minutes, 26-28 February 1941.
[53] Memorandum from 'E.S.' to Ball, 3 June 1941, MP 272/3, Bundle 1, File no. A2, II, and from Ball to the acting director of information, 4 June 1941, SP 195/1, Bundle 1, File no. 3/2/6A, AA.
[54] Noted in Commission Minutes, 21-26 August 1941.
[55] *Sunday Telegraph*, 1 March 1942; Commission Minutes, 28-30 January and 26-27 February 1942; M. F. Dixon, *Inside the ABC*, p. 64.
[56] M. F. Dixon, *Inside the ABC*, p. 65.
[57] Memorandum from Ball to the acting general manager, 20 July 1942, and the minutes of the first meeting of the Political Warfare Committee, 16 July 1942, both in MP 272/3, Bundle 2, File no. I/1. Sawer mentions his responsibilities in a letter to H. Eather, 4 December 1944, MP 272/5, Correspondence with Director-General File, AA. For clarification on the organization of the propaganda machinery, I am indebted to Mr John Hilvert whose MA Hons thesis, 'Expression and Suppression: the Department of Information, 1939-1945' is soon to be submitted at Macquarie University.
[58] Commission Minutes, 26-28 August 1942.
[59] Ball to Timperley, 2 September 1942, MP 272/3, Bundle 2, File no. I/1, AA.
[60] See comments in Sawer to Tom [Hoey], 17 May 1944, MP 272/1, Bundle 1, File no. 15/2, and Bonney to Sawer, 12 February 1945, MP 272/5, Correspondence with Director-General File. For further details of the changes in control, see 'Notes Concerning the Transfer of Shortwave Division from the DOI to the Commission', compiled by Ball, 24 August 1945, SP 613/1, Box 1, File no. 1/6/2, AA, and Commission Minutes, 5-10 May 1944.
[61] Noted in Commission Minutes, 1-2 July 1942.
[62] Memorandum from Ball to the state publicity censor, 10 February 1944, MP 272/1, Bundle 2, File no. 15/2. See comments on the difficulties of operation in Ball to the secretary of the Department of the Army, 13 August 1942, MP 272/1, Bundle 3, File no. 24/1, and in 'Notes on the ABC Overseas Shortwave Broadcasting Service in its relation to Political Warfare', compiled by Ball, 25 August 1942; and the Political Warfare Committee Minutes, 17-18 September 1942, MP 272/3, Bundle 2, File I/1, AA.
[63] Molesworth and Smith had recommended Offenburg's appointment in their Overseas Shortwave Broadcasts Report, 24 January 1940, MP 272/5, General Correspondence File. See other details in Ball to Dixon, 13 August 1940, and Dixon to Ball, 29 October 1940, SP 286/12, Box 1, William Macmahon Ball File (1938-43), AA, and *Home*, 1 June 1940.
[64] Memorandum from Ball to the director of the Department of Information, 26 February 1941, MP 272/3, Bundle 1, File no. A2, II, AA.
[65] Cabinet Minute, CRS A2697, vol. 6, Agenda no. 602, 7 April 1941. See also memorandum from Ball to the acting general manager, 14 July 1942, and one marked 'Shortwave Transmission Facilities' placed before the Political Warfare Committee, July 1942, MP 272/3, Bundle 2, File no. I/1, AA.
[66] For some debate on this question, see R. Bell, 'Censorship and War: Australia's Curious Experience 1939-1945', *Media Information Australia*, no. 6 (November 1977), pp. 2-3, and J. Hilvert, 'More on Australia's Curious War Censorship', *ibid.*, no. 7 (February 1978), p. 44. See also some press cuttings and letters in SP 195/2, File no. 331.33, AA.
[67] See memorandum from Nicholls to the acting manager for Victoria, 20 November 1941, MP 237/1, Box 67, File no. STW/1, AA; see also L. Ross, *John Curtin: a Biography* (Melbourne, 1977), p. 351, and P. Hasluck, *The Government and the People, 1942-1945*, p. 400.

Notes (Chapters 5–6)

⁶⁸ Supplementary Report on Censorship by M. F. Dixon for the acting general manager, 3 January 1941, SP 286/13, Box 1, Censorship File, AA.
⁶⁹ Memoranda from Ball to the chief publicity censor, 12 and 16 November 1942, MP 272/1, Bundle 2, File no. 15/1, AA. The same file contains examples of disputed scripts—see, for example, Hoey to the chief publicity censor, 28 October 1942.
⁷⁰ Memorandum from Sawer to the deputy director of the Department of Information, 24 June 1944, MP 272/3, Bundle 2, File no. I/1, AA; *ABC Weekly*, vol. 5, no. 8 (20 February 1943), p. 6.
⁷¹ See memorandum from Stokes to Ball, 26 October 1942, MP 272/3, Bundle 3, File no. I/5a. For a copy of the British and American 'Plan', see CRS A1608, Bundle 182, File no. E.57/1/1, pt 2, AA.
⁷² *Ibid.*; see also draft memorandum for officers engaged in writing news and commentaries for Transmission 3 (Japanese), drawn up by W. M. Ball, 16 January 1943, MP 272/3, Bundle 3, File no. I/5a, AA.
⁷³ These main themes are outlined in Paper 165 of the Political Warfare (Japan) Committee: Plan for Warfare Against Japan, CRS A1608, Bundle 182, File no. E.57/1/1, pt 2, AA.
⁷⁴ Ball to officer in charge, Political Warfare Division, Department of External Affairs, 12 March 1943, R17/19, Box 3, File marked 'Overseas Propaganda Dilemma 1942-3', ABCA.
⁷⁵ Ball to Sawer, n.d. (c. October 1942), MP 272/3, Bundle 3, File no. I/5a, AA.
⁷⁶ English script of talk to be broadcast in Japanese in Transmission 2, 26 October 1942, MP 272/1, Bundle 2, File no. 15/1, AA.
⁷⁷ Mentioned in memorandum from Stokes to Ball, 1 October 1943, MP 272/3, Bundle 3, File no. I/5a, AA.
⁷⁸ L. Meo, *Japan's Radio War on Australia 1941-1945* (Melbourne, 1968), p. 2.
⁷⁹ A. Briggs, *The War of Words* (London, 1970), p. 8.
⁸⁰ These facts were given by Ball to the Gibson Committee, see *Minutes of Evidence*, p. 88.
⁸¹ See comments re reception in reply to a question in Parliament, *CPD*, vol. 178, 31 March 1944, pp. 2540-1. See also memorandum from Stokes to Bonney, 17 August 1944, MP 272/3, Bundle 2, File no. I/2, AA.
⁸² See comments in memorandum dated 28 August 1945 in Cabinet Minutes and Submissions, CRS A2700, vol. 17, Agenda no. 897; and see memorandum from Stokes to Fanning and all members of the Allied Political Warfare Committee, 27 February 1945, MP 272/3, Bundle 2, File no. I/2, AA.
⁸³ Extract of letter from Masuda contained in memorandum from Sawer to Bonney, 17 September 1945, MP 272/5, Correspondence with Director-General File, AA.
⁸⁴ See figures in ABC Annual Reports, 1939-45.
⁸⁵ See Appendix 1.
⁸⁶ *Ibid.*
⁸⁷ Compiled from ABC *Annual Reports*, 1939-45.
⁸⁸ A. Marwick, *Britain in the Century of Total War* (London, 1968), p. 300.
⁸⁹ See Appendix 1.

6 The Other Side of War

¹ Cabinet Minutes and Submissions, CRS A2697, vol. 3, Agenda no. 264, 19 December 1939.
² R. Rivett, *Australian Citizen*, p. 174.
³ See diaries in Brookes Papers, Series 2.
⁴ See, for example, *Century*, 5 January 1940, and *Daily Telegraph*, 30 December 1939.

⁵ Cabinet Minutes and Submissions, CRS A2697, vol. 5, Agenda no. 493, 9 December 1940, and vol, 6, Agenda no. 587 (withdrawn). See also Cleary's comments in memorandum to McLeay, 4 June 1941, Chairman's Copies File, ABCA.
⁶ Cabinet Minutes and Submissions, CRS A2697, vol. 7, Agenda no. 684, 23-24 June 1941.
⁷ Some biographical details of members of the Gibson Committee may be found in *ABC Weekly*, vol. 3, no. 29 (19 July 1941), pp. 13-14. See comments on the commercial stations in Bearup to McGibbon, 11 July 1941, McGibbon File, ABCA.
⁸ McGibbon to Bearup, 8 October 1941, McGibbon File, ABCA.
⁹ Minutes of Meeting, 26 March 1941, in P. Weller (ed.), *Caucus Minutes*, vol. 3, p. 267.
¹⁰ See details in Bearup to McGibbon, 11 October 1941, McGibbon File, ABCA; M. F. Dixon, *Inside the ABC*, p. 50; Gibson Committee, Typescript of evidence taken in camera, 9 July 1941, pp. 7-8, ABC Federal Reference Library; and Commission Minutes, 21-26 August 1941.
¹¹ *Gibson Report*, p. 77.
¹² G. Sawer discusses the different attitudes to the Act in his *Australian Federal Politics and Law, 1929-1949* (Melbourne, 1963), p. 136.
¹³ *Gibson Report*, p. 5.
¹⁴ Act no. 33 of 1942.
¹⁵ Commission Minutes, 21-26 August 1941.
¹⁶ M. F. Dixon, *Inside the ABC*, p. 88.
¹⁷ Memorandum dated 5 July 1941, recording Cleary's interview with the postmaster-general, Cleary Papers, MS 5632, File 2.
¹⁸ Brief profiles of each of these appointees are contained in 'Statement by the Prime Minister, 10 June 1942', a copy of which is in the Cleary Papers, MS 5632.
¹⁹ Parliamentary Standing Committee on Broadcasting, *First Report*, p. 24.
²⁰ Noted in Commission Minutes, 13-16 October 1942.
²¹ Quoted in *Sun*, 8 February 1945.
²² Gibson Committee, *Minutes of Evidence*, p. 224, and Commission Minutes, 26-28 February 1941.
²³ Details in G. R. Curnow, 'The History of the Development of Wireless Telegraphy and Broadcasting ...', pp. 284-6; Gibson Committee, *Minutes of Evidence*, pp. 204, 219; and *Gibson Report*, p. 72.
²⁴ Calculated from figures in SP 655/1, Box 1, File no. 14.19/E/1, File marked 'Hours of Duty', AA.
²⁵ See Cleary to Ashley, 4 June 1943, SP 613/1, Box 13, File no. 4/1/1, AA, and ABC Annual Reports, 1940-42.
²⁶ Calculated from figures in ABC Annual Reports, 1933-46.
²⁷ Ashley to Moses, 15 June 1944, SP 613/1, Box 13, File no. 4/1/1, and Cabinet Minutes and Submissions, CRS A2700, vol. 11, Agenda no. 688 (1944), AA.
²⁸ Cabinet Minutes and Submissions, CRS A2700, vol. 11, Agenda no. 688A, memorandum dated 5 June 1945. See also Bearup to the acting director-general of Posts and Telegraphs, 1 May 1945, SP 613/1, Box 13, File no. 4/1/1, AA.
²⁹ *Gibson Report*, pp. 15-16, and *Minutes of Evidence*, p. 419; *Daily Sun*, 6 November 1940; *SMH*, 15 January 1941.
³⁰ Memorandum from Bearup to the federal controller of programmes, 18 March 1941, SP 341/1A, Box 1, General Programme Policy File (1936-42), no. 1, AA.
³¹ National Talks Advisory Committee Minutes, 19-20 August 1942, SP 613/1, Box 6, File no. 2/4/1, I, AA; *Gibson Report*, p. 18; memoranda from Molesworth to

Notes (Chapter 6)

the acting general manager, 24 September 1942 and from Bearup to Molesworth, 4 November 1942, SP 613/1, Box 6, File no. 2/4/5, I, AA.
[32] Noted in Commission Minutes, 21-23 June 1943.
[33] Memorandum from National Talks Advisory Committee to the Commission, n.d. (stamp indicates it was received at Central Files on 24 August 1943), SP 613/1, Box 6, File no. 2/4/5, I, AA.
[34] Ibid.
[35] Noted in National Talks Advisory Committee Minutes, 29-31 January 1946, SP 613/1, Box 6, File no. 2/4/1, II, AA.
[36] Details in Note headed 'Talks Programmes' addressed to the Commission from Moses, 30 November 1945, and memoranda from Molesworth to the general manager, 10 January 1946, and from Moses to the director of talks, 22 January 1946, SP 613/1, Box 6, File no. 2/4/5, II, AA.
[37] This administrative reorganization is described in the General Manager's Operational Instructions File, ABCA. See also Cleary's description in Parliamentary Standing Committee on Broadcasting, Typescript of Evidence, 7 February 1945, p. 2, ABC Federal Reference Library.
[38] Memorandum from Moses to all senior officers, 16 April 1943, entitled 'G. Manager's Operational Instruction no. 1: Administration—Divisional Re-Organisation', General Manager's Operational Instructions File, ABCA.
[39] See paper headed 'ABC Organisation, August 1944', ibid.
[40] Minutes of the Interstate Programme Controllers' Conference, 8-9 July 1942, ABCA.
[41] Memorandum from Moses to the federal controller of programmes, 16 November 1943, Light Entertainment Department File, I (1937-47), R17, Box 70, ABCA.
[42] Given in Parliamentary Standing Committee on Broadcasting, Seventh Report, p. 15.
[43] Record of Interview with ABC Staff Association, 30 September 1941, SP 289/1, Box 2-3, AA.
[44] E. Blain, Life with Aunty, p. 107.
[45] See, for example, Commission Minutes, 3 October 1935, and Federal Programme Committee Minutes, 4-5 March 1937.
[46] Gibson Report, p. 24.
[47] Parliamentary Standing Committee on Broadcasting, Typescript of Evidence, 7 February 1945, p. 7, ABC Federal Reference Library.
[48] Ibid., passim; see also Gibson Committee, Minutes of Evidence, p. 606.
[49] G. R. Curnow, 'The History of the Development of Wireless Telegraphy and Broadcasting ...', p. 344, and file marked 'Advisory Committees', prepared for Commission Meeting, 14-15 March 1963, ABCA. These committees are not to be confused with the advisory committees referred to in the 1942 Act. The latter were appointed by the postmaster-general, and comprised representatives of both national and commercial stations.
[50] Minutes of the Western Australian Advisory Committee, 24 September 1941, SP 613/1, Box 4, File no. 15.15/C/7, AA.
[51] Noted in memorandum for Barry to the federal superintendent, 1 September 1944, ibid., File no. 2/4/5, I.
[52] See note on 'National Talks Advisory Committee Minutes for August 1945' dated 17 September 1945, ibid., II, and McGibbon to Moses, 7 March 1940, McGibbon File, ABCA.
[53] Parliamentary Standing Committee on Broadcasting, Summary of Evidence, 15 November 1943, p. 70. See early discussion of listener research in memorandum from McCall to federal controllers et al., 11 January 1943, SP 341/1A, Box 5,

Listener Research File no. 1 (1937-43), and National Talks Advisory Committee Minutes, 2-4 February 1943, SP 613/1, Box 6, File no. 2/4/1, I, AA.

54 Memorandum from the federal superintendent to the acting general manager, 28 February 1945, SP 724/1, Box 52, File no. 24/1/1, AA.

55 See Staff and Establishment Files, ABCA.

56 ABC Staff Association Minutes, 25 June 1941; and see Alexander to the acting general manager, 26 June 1941, SP 289/1, Box 2-3, AA.

57 Commission Minutes, 17-19 July 1940.

58 Figure from *ABC: Twelth Annual Report*, p. 16. Commission Minutes, 1-2 October 1941, gives a sample list of employees who enlisted. Moses' photograph appeared on the cover of *ABC Weekly*, vol. 2, no. 33 (17 August 1940).

59 Noted in ABC Staff Association Minutes, 11 March 1942.

60 Parliamentary Standing Committee on Broadcasting, Typescript of Evidence, 7 February 1945, pp. 9-10, ABC Federal Reference Library.

61 Minutes of the Interstate Programme Controllers' Conference, 8-9 July 1942.

62 Commission Minutes, 4-5 October 1939.

63 *Ibid.*, 28-30 January 1940.

64 Parliamentary Standing Committee on Broadcasting, *Seventh Report*, p. 11.

65 Concannon to the chairman, 4 February 1942, SP 289/1, Box 2-3, AA.

66 Details from *Daily News*, 25 November 1939.

67 Commission Minutes, 28-30 January and 26-27 February 1942.

68 Details in *Daily Telegraph*, 30 December 1941 and 5 February 1942; Commission Minutes, 9-11 April 1942; and *ABC Weekly*, vol. 8, no. 15 (27 April 1946), p. 3.

69 *Aerial*, vol. 3, no. 3 (October–November 1944), in SP 724/1, Box 7, File no. 5/1/2, AA.

70 See 'Comparison between the Commonwealth Public Service and the ABC in respect of Salaries', SP 289/1, Box 2-3, AA.

71 Noted in Parliamentary Standing Committee on Broadcasting, *Seventh Report*, p. 9. See comparisons of ABC and Public Service typist salaries in Gibson Committee, *Minutes of Evidence*, p. 232.

72 For a comparison of salaries in 1945, see Parliamentary Standing Committee on Broadcasting, *Summary of Evidence* (1944-5), p. 206. See ABC Staff Association Minutes, 27 February 1941, where it records a decision to push the Commission on this issue. The Commission's otherwise reluctance to award automatic increases is stated clearly in a memorandum from Bearup to all states and federal officers, 1 August 1941, SP 306/1, Bundle 5, File no. A 92, AA.

73 Details in *Daily Telegraph*, 7 September 1944 and 23 January 1945.

74 *Sunday Sun and Guardian*, 18 February 1945.

75 Noted in Minutes of the Interstate Programme Controllers' Conference, 8-9 July 1942.

76 Gibson Committee, *Minutes of Evidence*, p. 234; ABC Staff Association Minutes, 14 December 1939 and 29 July 1942.

77 Gibson Committee, *Minutes of Evidence*, p. 440; ABC Staff Association Minutes, 24 September 1941; and G. Griffiths, acting president of the Staff Association, to Holman, 3 March 1944, SP 289/1, Box 203, AA.

78 Figures in Gibson Committee, *Minutes of Evidence* p. 439, and *Aerial*, vol. 3, no. 3 (October–November 1944), p. 2, SP 724/1, Box 7, File no. 5/1/2, AA.

79 Noted in Parliamentary Standing Committee on Broadcasting, *Seventh Report*, p. 13.

80 See comments by J. C. James on behalf of the AJA in Gibson Committee, *Minutes of Evidence*, p. 275.

81 Parliamentary Standing Committee on Broadcasting, *Seventh Report*, p. 6.

Notes (Chapter 6)

[82] See ABC Staff Association Minutes, 4 December 1940, 27 February and 24 September 1941.
[83] *Ibid.*, 10 and 16 July 1941.
[84] *Ibid.*, 27 August 1941, 29 April 1942, and 26 May and 5 August 1943.
[85] Details in *Radio-Active* (September 1948), p. 15.
[86] Commonwealth Bureau of Census and Statistics, *Labour Report*, no. 35 (1945 and 1946), p. 148.
[87] These are general impressions gained from a reading of for example, T. Sheridan, 'Labour v. Labor: the Victorian Metal Trades Dispute of 1946-47', in J. Iremonger, J. Merritt, and G. Osborne (eds), *Strikes* (Sydney, 1973), pp. 176-224, and R. Gollan, *Revolutionaries and Reformists: Communism and the Australian Labour Movement, 1920-1955* (Canberra, 1975), *passim*.
[88] Details in Cabinet Minutes and Submission, CRS A2697, vol. 3, Agenda no. 206, 1 November 1939; ABC Staff Association Minutes, 24 September 1940; and Gibson Committee, *Minutes of Evidence*, p. 187.
[89] There is a good account of the chronology of all these Bills in T. H. Kewley and J. Rydon, 'The Personnel of Commonwealth Government Corporations', *Public Administration*, III, no. 4 n.s. (December 1949), 133-4.
[90] Cabinet Minutes and Submissions, CRS A2697, vol. 6, Agenda no. 587 (1941).
[91] ABC Staff Association Minutes, 16 July 1941. See also Staff Association Information Bulletin no. 1, 15 May 1942, SP 724/1, Box 7, File no. 5/1/1, AA.
[92] *Aerial*, vol. 3, no. 1 (August 1944), in file marked 'Federal Council Newsletters', ABC Staff Association Archives.
[93] G. E. Caiden, *Career Service*, p. 277.
[94] T. Sheridan, 'Labour v. Labor: the Victorian Metal Trades Dispute of 1946-47', pp. 177, 181.
[95] R. Gollan, *Revolutionaries and Reformists*, pp. 130-1.
[96] B. Mitchell, *Teachers, Education and Politicis: A History of Organizations of Public School Teachers in New South Wales* (St Lucia, Qld, 1975), pp. 151-4.
[97] See record of meeting with Staff Association, 21 September 1942, Correspondence file on ABC Staff Regulations, ABC Staff Association Archives.
[98] Gibson Report, *Minutes of Evidence*, p. 189, and Cleary to Concannon, 6 January 1943, Correspondence file on ABC Staff Regulations, ABC Staff Association Archives.
[99] *Radio-Active* (September 1948), p. 14. See also Gibson Committee, *Minutes of Evidence*, p. 233.
[1] Parliamentary Standing Committee on Broadcasting, *Seventh Report*, p. 5.
[2] See draft memoranda from Moses to P. Daventry, and Moses to D. Bennett, 11 January 1945, SP 724/1, Box 7, File no. 5/1/2, AA.
[3] *Aerial*, vol. 3, no. 3 (October–November 1944), p. 2, SP 724/1, Box 7, File no. 5/1/2, AA.
[4] Bennett to Cleary, 18 December 1944, Correspondence file on ABC Staff Regulations, ABC Staff Association Archives.
[5] Parliamentary Standing Committee on Broadcasting, *Seventh Report*, pp. 5, 14; *Standard Weekly*, 29 June 1945.
[6] *Standard Weekly*, 29 June 1945.
[7] A copy of the draft regulations is contained in the *Seventh Report* of the Parliamentary Standing Committee on Broadcasting.
[8] Commission Minutes, 9-12 February 1943, and Statement by the Chairman, W. J. Cleary, to the Commission Meeting in Melbourne, 7-9 March 1945, Cleary Papers, MS 5539.
[9] Cleary's Statement to the Commission Meeting, 7-9 March 1945, *ibid*.

10. Statement by M. F. Dixon to the Commission Meeting in Melbourne, 8 March 1945, *ibid.*
11. *Ibid.*
12. Statement by T. W. Bearup to the Commission Meeting in Melbourne, 7-9 March 1945, *ibid.*
13. See Cleary's earlier comments about Moses' ambitions in Cleary to Brookes, 15 November 1938, Brookes Papers, Series 26. See also his remark about 'the existence of certain people in high places' who encouraged Moses, in Cleary to Medley, 19 February 1945, Cleary Papers, MS 5632, Resignation File.
14. See these newspapers for 26-27 February 1945, and see editorial in *SMH*, 9 March 1945.
15. *CPD*, vol. 181, 7 March 1945, p. 392, for Anthony's remarks. Other questions were asked in *ibid.*, pp. 110-11, 152. See also Cleary's own notes on p. 41 of Resignation File, Cleary Papers, MS 5632.
16. G. C. Bolton, *Dick Boyer*, pp. 122-3.
17. M. F. Dixon, *Inside the ABC*, p. 130.
18. Cleary to Medley, 19 February 1945, Cleary Papers, MS 5632.
19. Cleary to Cameron, 5 March 1945, Cleary Papers, MS 5539.
20. Cleary to Medley, 19 February 1945, Cleary Papers, MS 5632. See also bundle of notes headed 'Moses. Notes used at interview in Gardens on his return from England. Tuesday 8 May 1945' in Cleary's own handwriting, Cleary Papers, MS 5539.
21. From a document in the Brookes Papers, Series 26, file marked 'Talks', undated but obviously written during 1945 or later.
22. Quote taken from Cleary's own notes in Resignation File, Cleary Papers, MS 5539, p. 87. Dixon gave a slightly different version of the wording, namely, 'having found he could no longer rely on those from whom he had a right to expect loyalty, he thought it was time to get out' in 'ABC's Independence Day', *Review*, 3-9 June 1972, p. 935.
23. *Aerial*, vol. 4, no. 1 (April-May 1945), p. 1, in file marked 'Broadstaff', ABC Staff Association Archives.

7   The Return to Peace

1. Details of the victory celebrations may be found in *Daily Telegraph*, 10 May 1945, *ABC: Thirteenth Annual Report*, p. 11, and F. K. Crowley (ed.), *Modern Australia in Documents*, vol. 2: *1939-1970*, pp. 115, 129. A recording of Chifley's broadcast of 15 August is held in the Sound Archives of the National Library.
2. Figure given in *CPD*, vol. 188, 31 July 1946, p. 3319.
3. *ABC: Thirteenth Annual Report*, p. 3.
4. Boyer's biography has been written by G. C. Bolton, see *Dick Boyer: An Australian Humanist* (Canberra, 1967).
5. See, for example, comments by Medley reported in *ibid.* p. 123.
6. Cablegram from S. M. Bruce to the prime minister, 24 February 1945, and Telex from Fanning to Senator Don Cameron, 28 February 1945, CRS A461, Bundle 540, File no. Z422/1/6, AA; Cables from Boyer to Cleary, 27 February 1945 and from Cleary to Boyer, 28 February 1945, Cleary Papers, MS 5632, Resignation File.
7. See Cleary Papers, MS 5632, Resignation File, pp. 77, 89-91. See especially paper headed 'Diary of talks with WJC immediately before & after his [Boyer's] acceptance'.
8. Press statement issued by the prime minister, John Curtin on the appointment of Richard Boyer as chairman of the ABC, 12 April 1945—copy in SP 613/1, Box 1,

Notes (Chapter 7)

File no. 1/2/2, pt 1, AA. See remarks about who drafted the document written on the copy of the statement contained in the Cleary Papers, MS 5632.

[9] Cleary to Boyer, 5 May 1945, Box 1, File no. 1, Boyer Papers, MS 3181, National Library of Australia. See Boyer's ideas reported in *ABC Weekly*, vol. 7, no. 18 (5 May 1945), p. 5; 'Information Release — ABC Chairman Affirms National Broadcasting Policy', 28 June 1945, SP 613/1, Box 1, File no. 1/2/2, pt 1, AA; and Commission Minutes, 5-7 June 1946.

[10] Further details of these appointments are in *ABC Weekly*, vol. 6, no. 51 (23 December 1944), p. 3, and in Cabinet Minutes and Submissions, CRS A2700, vol. 13, Agenda no. 774, 1945, AA.

[11] *Aerial*, vol. 4, no. 2 (February 1946), p. 4, in Federal Council Newsletters File, ABC Staff Association Archives.

[12] *ABC: Fourteenth Annual Report*, p. 17; *ABC Weekly*, vol. 7, no. 43 (27 October 1945), p. 38; Bennett to Bearup, 20 March 1945 and Bearup to Bennett, 10 April 1945, SP 289/1, Box 3, File no. 15, AA.

[13] Details in memorandum from Chapple to the general manager, n.d. (*c*. mid-1945), and from McCauley to Moses, 30 August 1945, SP 613/1, Box 1, File no. 1/6/2, AA.

[14] *ABC: Fourteenth Annual Report*, pp. 17-18.

[15] These amendments are discussed further in T. Kewley and J. Rydon 'The Personnel of Commonwealth Government Corporations', pp. 135-6.

[16] There is a copy of the Staff Regulations in the ABC Archives.

[17] Absolute figure given in Secretary's Report to the Federal Conference, 1949, ABC Staff Association Archives.

[18] *Radio-Active* (March 1947), p. 3.

[19] Noted in *Daily Mirror*, 12 February 1947.

[20] A summary of the determination was printed in *Radio-Active* (March 1948), p. 13.

[21] *Radio-Active* (August 1948), p. 13, and Record of Proceedings of the Annual Conference, 15-17 November 1948, ABC Staff Association Archives.

[22] Details in *Radio-Active* (November 1948), pp. 3, 16.

[23] E. Blain, *Life with Aunty*, p. 157; ABC Staff Association Minutes, 3 February 1949.

[24] See discussion of the membership drop in Record of Proceedings of the Annual Conference, 15-17 November 1948, and in Secretary's Report to the 1949 Federal Conference, ABC Staff Association Archives.

[25] *Report of the Committee on Certain aspects of the Administration of the ABC, March 1948* (hereinafter cited as *Fitzgerald Report*), typescript copy, ABC Federal Reference Library, p. 40.

[26] Concern about these staff increases is expressed in memorandum from C. M. Toop to all states, 1 July 1946, SP 306/1, Item no. A 286, and from D. E. Felsman to the staff inspector, 18 July 1946, SP 306/1, Item no. A 283, AA.

[27] See paper headed 'Staff Economies resulting from the Amalgamation of the NSW Branch with Head Office', 26 June 1947, SP 306/1, Bundle 9, File no. A 260, AA.

[28] Figure from Staff and Establishment Files ABCA. Details of the administrative structure are given in the *Fitzgerald Report*, pp. 3-4, and in General Manager's Operational Instructions File, ABCA.

[29] Minutes of the Interstate Programme Controllers' Conference, 18 March 1947; Parliamentary Standing Committee on Broadcasting, *Tenth Report*, p. 5.

[30] Clewlow to the general manager, 13 September 1946, SP 613/1, Box 9, File no. 3/1/7, AA.

[31] See paper headed 'T. W. Bearup: Proposed Appointment to America: Minutes', File 2, Cleary Papers, MS 5632. Dixon notes that during Bearup's term as assistant general manager he had an office and a title but no work to do—see *Inside the ABC*, p. 146.

[32] A sketch of Finlay's career is in *ABC Weekly*, vol. 8, no. 35 (14 September 1946), p. 6, and in *Radio-Active* (December 1948), p. 4.
[33] Commission Minutes, 24-26 January 1946; Boyer's comments in Minutes of meeting of state managers and federal officers at Broadcast House, 21-22 November 1946, SP 613/1, Box 8, File no. 3/1/4, pt IV, AA; *ABC: Fourteenth Annual Report*, pp. 5-6.
[34] *Daily Sun*, 14 February 1947; Minutes of the Interstate Programme Controllers' Conference, 13 June 1947.
[35] *CPD*, vol. 190, 12 March 1947, pp. 524-5.
[36] G. C. Bolton, *Dick Boyer*, pp. 167-8.
[37] G. R. Curnow, 'The History of the Development of Wireless Telegraphy and Broadcasting...', p. 323.
[38] *Fitzgerald Report*, esp. pp. 8, 38-9, 50. See earlier comments on government obstruction of the ABC's building programme in *Gibson Report*, p. 17, and Parliamentary Standing Committee on Broadcasting, *First Report*, p. 17.
[39] Strictly speaking, this body was now called the Interstate Programme Controllers' Conference, but for the sake of clarity I shall continue to refer to it as the Federal Programme Committee, especially as it retained the same function. See Minutes of the Interstate Programme Controllers' Conference, 14-15 March and 29-30 August 1945, and memorandum from Barry to the director of Light Entertainment, 28 February 1945, Light Entertainment Department File, I (1937-47), R17, Box 70, ABCA.
[40] Minutes of the Interstate Programme Controllers' Conference, 29-30 August 1945.
[41] Commission Minutes, 17-19 October 1945.
[42] Minutes of the Interstate Programme Controllers' Conference, 23 November 1945; Commission Minutes, 1-3 May and 5-6 June 1946. Some technical problems caused the postponement of the original commencement date for the new arrangements of 1 July 1946.
[43] Minutes of the Interstate Programme Controllers' Conference, 23 November 1945 and 26-28 February 1946.
[44] *Ibid.*, 13 June 1947.
[45] Figures in *ABC: Fifth Annual Report*, p. 17, and *ABC: Sixteenth Annual Report*, p. 7.
[46] See Parliamentary Standing Committee on Broadcasting, *First Report*, p. 9. Figure from *ABC: Sixteenth Annual Report*, p. 10.
[47] *Fitzgerald Report*, p. 40.
[48] Details in *The Sydney Symphony Orchestra* (publicity pamphlet), ABC Federal Reference Library.
[49] R. Covell, *Australia's Music*, p. 123; press statement by the chairman of the ABC, 13 February 1948, Boyer Papers, Box 1, File no. 5.
[50] From *ABC: Sixteenth Annual Report*, pp. 24-5.
[51] More variety programme titles are listed in the ABC annual reports.
[52] Quoted in Minutes of the Interstate Programme Controllers' Conference, 12-13 June 1945.
[53] Figure in Douglass to W. T. Harris, 16 September 1947, Rural Broadcasts File, ABCA. See also *ABC Weekly*, vol. 7, no. 47 (24 November 1945), p. 8.
[54] Memorandum from Douglass to Barry, 13 February 1952, Rural Broadcasts File, ABCA.
[55] See J. Douglass, 'Address to Radio Farm Directors' Convention in Chicago, 1948' Rural Broadcasts File, ABCA; Commission Minutes, 17-19 October 1945; Barry to the general manager, 23 April 1947, SP 724/1, Box 43, File no. 17/1/5, AA; and *Fitzgerald Report*, p. 14.

Notes (Chapter 7) 211

[56] *Fitzgerald Report*, p. 27.
[57] Minutes of the Interstate Programme Controllers' Conference, 13 June 1947.
[58] M. F. Dixon, *Inside the ABC*, pp. 178-9.
[59] *Gibson Report*, p. 44.
[60] Memorandum from Wicks to the federal controller of educational broadcasts, 21 November 1940, MP 237/1, Box 21, File no. EDU/15, AA.
[61] Gibson Committee, *Minutes of Evidence*, p. 12. See also Federal Educational Broadcasts Advisory Committee Minutes, 15-16 May 1941, MP 237/1, Box 21, File no. EDU/15, AA, and *ABC: Sixth Annual Report*, pp. 32-33.
[62] *Proceedings of the Radio in Education Conference, 21-24 June 1946*, p. 6. Boyer also wrote an article, 'Radio in Education Conference', *Australian Quarterly*, XVIII, no. 1 (March 1946), 94-101.
[63] *Fitzgerald Report*, p. 24.
[64] N. Petersen notes that Dixon had a number of private meetings with Labor politicians from July 1940 onwards; see 'Policy Formation in the ABC News Service, 1942-1961', p. 79.
[65] Mentioned in *CPD*, vol. 188, 8 and 9 August 1946, p. 4097.
[66] Details in G. C. Bolton, *Dick Boyer,* pp. 162-3; *CPD*, vol. 188, 7 August 1946, p. 3792.
[67] M. F. Dixon, *Inside the ABC*, pp. 155-6.
[68] See comments on Henderson's statement in *CPD*, vol. 188, 7 August 1946, p. 3798.
[69] Parliamentary Standing Committee on Broadcasting, *Fourth Report* and *Fifth Report*.
[70] *CPD*, vol. 188, 7 August 1946, p. 3809.
[71] *Ibid.*, 8 and 9 August 1946, p. 4115.
[72] G. C. Bolton, *Dick Boyer*, p. 163.
[73] *CPD*, vol. 188, 8 and 9 August 1946, p. 4106.
[74] Boyer to Cleary, 13 December 1945, Cleary Papers, MS 5632, Resignation File; M. F. Dixon, *Inside the ABC*, p. 160.
[75] The decision not to proceed is recorded in Cabinet Minutes and Submissions, CRS A2694, vol. 15, pt 2, Agenda no. 1768, 5 May 1936.
[76] Parliamentary Standing Committee on Broadcasting, *Eighth Report*, p. 4.
[77] Cabinet Minutes and Submissions, CRS A2700, vol. 19, Agenda no. 958, 28 September 1945; L. F. Crisp, *Ben Chifley: A Biography* (Melbourne, 1963), p. 268.
[78] Boyer to Chifley, 19 February 1946, reproduced in P. Weller (ed.), *Caucus Minutes 1901-1949*, vol. 3, pp. 377-8.
[79] Figure in *Daily Mirror*, 18 June 1946. The *Daily Telegraph* gave a figure of £10 000.
[80] *SMH*, 11 July 1946.
[81] *Daily Telegraph*, 18 and 19 July 1946.
[82] Cartoon in *Daily Sun*, 29 April 1936. See other comment in, for example, *Sunday Sun and Guardian*, 3 May 1946.
[83] Readers' reactions recorded in *ABC Weekly*, vol. 8, no. 30 (10 August 1946), p. 9.
[84] Anderson Analysis of Broadcasting: Special Report on Listening to Federal Parliamentary Broadcasts in Sydney, Melbourne, Brisbane, Adelaide, Perth and Newcastle, 24-26 July 1946, MP 237/1, Box 45, File no. MGR/22, AA.
[85] Quoted in Parliamentary Standing Committee on Broadcasting, *Tenth Report*, p. 7.
[86] G. C. Bolton, *Dick Boyer*, p. 136; and see Commission Minutes, 16-18 October 1946 and 23-25 February 1949, and 'ABC Listener Research: Notes on methods of Sampling and Interviewing ...', 24 October 1945, MP 237/1, Box 45, File no. MGR/22, AA.

[87] Minutes of the Interstate Programme Controllers' Conference, 13 June 1947.
[88] Figure in memorandum from Pringle to the controller of programmes, 6 January 1948, Light Entertainment Department File, II (1948-59), R17, Box 70, ABCA.
[89] W. J. McKell to the prime minister, 6 April 1944, and the general manager to the director-general of the Postmaster-General's Department, 9 May 1944, MP 1170/3, File no. BS/5/1, pt 1, AA. See also Parliamentary Standing Committee on Broadcasting, *Summary of Evidence*, (1943-4), p. 173.
[90] Details of members' backgrounds in J. Rydon, *A Biographical Register of the Commonwealth Parliament, 1901-1972* (Canberra, 1975).
[91] Parliamentary Standing Committee on Broadcasting, *Ninth Report* (March 1946). Quotes from pp. 4 and 9.
[92] Mrs Ruth Tyson to Don Cameron, 8 August 1945, MP 544/2, File no. BA/7/5, pt 1, AA.
[93] National Talks Advisory Committee Minutes, 19-20 August 1946, SP 613/1, Box 6, File no. 2/4/1, II, AA.
[94] Minute Paper dated 16 August 1944, re Evidence before the Parliamentary Standing Committee on Broadcasting, MP 1170/3, File no. BS/5/1, pt 1, AA.
[95] G. C. Bolton, *Dick Boyer*, p. 159.
[96] L. F. Crisp, *Ben Chifley*, p. 267.
[97] Moses to Chifley, 12 December 1949, quoted in *ibid.*
[98] See, for example, *CPD*, vol. 183, 20 June 1945, p. 3328.
[99] Commission Minutes, 5-7 June 1946.
[1] *Ibid.*, 4-6 December 1946.
[2] See R. Gollan, *Revolutionaries and Reformists*, ch. 5.
[3] *Ibid.*, pp. 152, 178. See also G. C. Bolton, *Dick Boyer*, pp. 158-9.
[4] M. F. Dixon, *Inside the ABC*, p. 181.
[5] See Boyer's comments on Germany in Gibson Committee, *Minutes of Evidence*, p. 426.
[6] Details in *CPD*, vol. 186, 13 March 1946, p. 239.
[7] Calwell to Boyer, 29 November 1945, and Boyer to Cameron 20 November 1945, SP 613/1, Box 1, File no. 1/6/2, AA; Commission Minutes, 24 January 1945.
[8] *CPD*, vol. 192, 30 May 1947, pp. 3210ff.
[9] R. Gollan, *Revolutionaries and Reformists*, pp. 183-5; *SMH*, 16, 17, 19 and 20 November 1945; *Daily Telegraph*, 20 November 1945.
[10] C. Kiernan, *Calwell: A Personal and Political Biography* (Melbourne, 1978), p. 120.
[11] During the war he suspended the *Daily Telegraph* and four other newspapers which opposed his censorship regulations—see C. Kiernan, *Calwell*, pp. 98, 123-4. See also R. Gollan, *Revolutionaries and Reformists*, pp. 158-61.
[12] Calwell to Boyer, 20 December 1946, File marked 'Calwell complaint re Showdown script, 2 November 1946', R17, Box 70, ABCA. See also Commission Minutes, 22 January 1947.
[13] Details in *CPD*, vol. 192, 30 May 1947, p. 3213, and in G. C. Bolton, *Dick Boyer*, p. 165.
[14] Commission Minutes, 29-31 May 1947.
[15] M. F. Dixon, *Inside the ABC*, p. 176.
[16] Confidential Broadcasting Committee Paper no. 287, 'Notes of discussion with R. J. F. Boyer', Box 1, File no. 2, Boyer Papers.
[17] *CPD*, vol. 199, 27 October 1948, pp. 2132-7, and see provisions of Act no. 64 of 1948.
[18] *SMH*, 28 September and 29 October 1948.
[19] *CPD*, vol. 200, 24 November 1948, pp. 3456-7.

Notes (Chapter 7–Conclusion)

[20] *CPD*, vol. 199, 9 November 1948, pp. 2592-7.
[21] *Sun*, 9 August 1946 and 7 December 1946; *CPD*, vol. 188, 8 and 9 August 1946, p. 4100.
[22] *CPD*, vol. 198, 29 September 1948, pp. 987ff., and esp. pp. 998, 1016.
[23] *CPD*, vol. 199, 27 October 1948, p. 2138; vol. 200, 23 November 1948, p. 3324.
[24] *CPD*, vol. 200, 23 November 1948, p. 3320; *Caucus Minutes* vol. 3, 7 and 14 October 1948, pp. 462-4.
[25] *CPD*, vol. 200, 23 November 1948, pp. 3319-20.
[26] *Daily Telegraph*, 29 October 1948.
[27] Amendment discussed in L. F. Crisp, *Ben Chifley*, pp. 268-9.

Conclusion

[1] G. R. Curnow, 'The History of the Development of Wireless Telegraphy and Broadcasting . . .', p. 427.
[2] G. Serle, *From Deserts the Prophets Come*, p. 153.
[3] *Fitzgerald Report*, p. 7.
[4] W. F. Ifould, 'Moulding Public Opinion', in W. G. K. Duncan (ed.), *Educating a Democracy* (Sydney, 1938), p. 119.
[5] *ABC: Forty-Sixth Annual Report*, p. 14.
[6] *Ibid.*, pp. 15, 68.

Select Bibliography

I. Primary Sources

1. ABC ARCHIVES

Most of the ABC's records are in the process of being transferred to the Australian Archives. As this will involve a change in the numbering of files, ABC classifications have generally not been given below. All inquiries and applications for access should be directed, in the first instance, to the Australian Archives.

COMMISSION RECORDS:
Minutes of Meetings of the Australian Broadcasting Commission, 1932-48.
Miscellaneous personal correspondence files:
    Herbert Brookes File, 1932-8
    P. G. J. Foley File, 1942-4
    S. J. McGibbon File, 1940-2
    R. B. Orchard File, 1932
    E. C. Rigby File, 1940-2
    Chairman's Copies File

PROGRAMME COMMITTEE:
Minutes of Meetings of the Federal Programme Committee, 1936-48 (incomplete).
(After April 1940, these are referred to as the Minutes of the Interstate Programme Controllers' Conference)

MISCELLANEOUS FILES:
ABC Staff and Organization File, Victorian Branch, 1932-4.
File marked 'Advisory Committees', prepared for Commission Meeting, 14-15 March 1963.
Bernard Heinze Correspondence Files.
File marked 'Calwell complaint re Showdown script, 2 November 1946'.
General Manager Applications Files, 1932 and 1933.
General Manager's Correspondence Files, June 1932–July 1934.

Select Bibliography

General Manager's Correspondence Files with the Manager for Western Australia, July 1932–December 1933.
General Manager's Operational Instructions File.
Lawsons—Blue Hills Story File.
Objectionable Programme Matter: Correspondence with the Postaster-General, 1940-5.
Light Entertainment Department Files, I (1937-47), and II (1948-59), R17, Box 70.
Religious Broadcasts File.
Rural Broadcasts File.
'The Watchman' Files:
    Listeners' Letters pro 'The Watchman', 1938-40
    Listeners' Letters anti 'The Watchman', 1938-40
    Listeners' Letters complaints to the Postmaster-General
    Libel Case
    Overseas Visit
    Scripts of 'At Home and Abroad' and 'News Behind the News'.
Trade Union Talks Files, 1941-4, R17/19, Box 3.

PRESS CUTTINGS BOOKS, 1932-48:
These books contain cuttings from the following newspapers and journals:
Age
Australian Women's Weekly
Broadcaster
Broadcasting Business
Bulletin
Century
Commercial Broadcaster
Daily Mirror
Daily News
Daily Sun
Daily Telegraph
Herald
Home
Labor Daily
Radio Business
Radio Retailer
Smith's Weekly
Sports and Radio
Standard Weekly
Sun
Sunday Sun and Guardian
Sunday Telegraph

Sydney Morning Herald
Teleradio
Truth
Wireless Weekly

JOURNALS:
ABC Weekly, 1939-48.
Radio-Active, 1947-50, 1972.

MISCELLANEOUS ITEMS:
Document marked 'National Broadcasting in the Second World War—GM, 25/7/46'.
Transcript of Interview with Major Conder by John Cribbin, 1974.
Report by H. P. Williams to the Commission, 1932, in private notebook held by Miss Kelly.
Document marked 'Chairman's Advice to Mr Charlton, 1936'.
A. L. Holman's correspondence re Major Conder, 1935.

HELD IN THE ABC FEDERAL REFERENCE LIBRARY:
Australian Broadcasting Commission, *Annual Reports*, 1932-48.
Gibson Committee, Typescript of Evidence taken in camera.
Report of the Committee on Certain Aspects of the Administration of the ABC, March 1948 (Fitzgerald Report), typescript copy.
The Constant Voice: Radio Australia 30th Anniversary, 1939-1969, Melbourne, ABC, 1969.
The Sydney Symphony Orchestra, Sydney, ABC Publicity Pamphlet, n.d.

2. ABC STAFF ASSOCIATION ARCHIVES

Federal Executive Council Minute Book, 5 May 1938-19 August 1943.
Federal Council Minute Book, 11 October 1948-13 October 1949.
Loose sets of minutes: 2 and 3 January, 26 June, 24 July and 28 August 1947.
Record of Proceedings of the Annual Conference, 15-17 November 1948.
Relevant Papers and Minutes relating to the 1949 Annual Conference, including Secretary's Report.

3. AUSTRALIAN ARCHIVES

(a) New South Wales Branch:
ABC Files consulted were under the following headings:
SP 286/2, News Department, General Correspondence Files, 1936-50.
SP 286/6, News Department, News Commentaries and Commentators' Files, 1936-48.

Select Bibliography

SP 286/12, News Department, Shortwave and Department of Information Files, 1936-50.
SP 286/13, News Department, Wartime Organization and Censorship Files, 1939-45.
SP 286/17, News Department, Warren Denning Personal Files, 1939-48.
SP 289/1, Administrative Division, Legal, Formulation of Staff Regulations Files, 1938-51.
SP 300/1, Talks Department, Talks Scripts, General, 1937-50.
SP 306/1, Administrative Division, Staff Section, Administrative Files, 1936-51.
SP 341/1A, Programme Filing, General Correspondence Files, 1936-54.
SP 341/2, Unregistered Correspondence Files, 1936-49.
SP 613/1, Office of the Assistant General Manager, General Correspondence including Administration, Policy, and Artists' Contracts Files, 1933-63.
SP 617/1, Programme Division, Correspondence—Head Office, Drama Department, 1936-58.
SP 621/1, Administrative Division, Correspondence relating to Staff, Administration, Industrial and Establishment, 1936-61.
SP 655/1, Administrative Division, Staff Section, Correspondence relating to Staff Administration, 1937-63.
SP 724/1, Office of the Assistant General Manager, Correspondence including Administration, Policy, and Artists' Contracts Files, 1934-65 (incomplete).
SP 767/3, Publications Department, Correspondence relating to Publicity Control and Administration, 1938-46.
SP 985/1, Administrative Division, Correspondence relating to Staff Administration, Industrial and Establishment, 1936-62.
SP 1011/2, Press Cuttings and Written Publicity, General Television and Radio, 1938-68.

(b) Victorian Branch:
ABC FILES:
MP 237/1, General Correspondence Files, 1936-47.
MP 237/7, Listeners' Letters summaries, 1938-45.
MP 284/1, General Correspondence Files, 1936-47; Summaries of Listeners' Letters and telephone calls, and press publicity, 1938-40 and 1943.
MP 298/4, Talks Sessions Correspondence Files, 1940 and 1944-5.
POSTMASTER-GENERAL'S DEPARTMENT FILES:
MP 544/1, General Correspondence (unregistered), 1932-53.

MP 544/2, General Correspondence, 1931-60.
MP 1170/3, Broadcasting and General Correspondence Files, 1935-70.

DEPARTMENT OF INFORMATION FILES:
MP 272/1, Broadcasting Division, General Correspondence Files, 1940-6.
MP 272/3, Broadcasting Division, Secret Files (programme and transmission policy, including details of propaganda and political warfare policies), 1939-47.
MP 272/5, Broadcasting Division, William Macmahon Ball, Controller of Shortwave Services, Personal Files, 1939-48.

(c) ACT Branch:

DEPARTMENT OF INFORMATION FILES:
SP 109/3, General Correspondence, Central Administration, 1945-6.
SP 109/5, General Correspondence, Office of the Director-General, 1943-4.
SP 109/6, General Correspondence, Office of the Assistant Secretary, 1943-5.
SP 109/11, General Correspondence, Broadcasting Division, 1940-3.
SP 195/1, General Correspondence, 1939-45.
SP 195/2, General Correspondence, 1941-5.
SP 195/3, Secret Registry Files, 1940-3.
SP 195/9, Departmental History Files, 1939-45.
SP 195/6, General Correspondence Files, Office of the Director-General, 1940-3.

ATTORNEY-GENERAL'S DEPARTMENT FILES:
CRS A432, Correspondence Files, Annual Single number series, 1929-
CRS A467, Special Files, SF Single Number series, 1905-51.

PRIME MINISTER'S DEPARTMENT FILES:
CRS A461, Correspondence Files, Multiple Number Series, third system, 1934-50.
CRS A1608, Correspondence Files, SC Series, fourth system, 1939-45.

CABINET MINUTES AND SUBMISSIONS:
CRS A2694, Lyons and Page Ministries, 1932-9.
CRS A2697, Menzies and Fadden Ministries, 1939-41.
CRS A2700, Curtin, Forde, and Chifley Ministries, 1941-9.
CRS A2676, Advisory War Council Agenda Files, 1940-5.
CRS A2684, Advisory War Council Minute Files, 1940-5.

4. PUBLIC RECORDS

Commonwealth Bureau of Census and Statistics, *Labour Report*, no. 35 (1945 and 1946).
Commonwealth Parliamentary Debates, vol. 133 (17 February–17 March 1932) to vol. 200 (17 November–10 December 1948).
Report of the Joint Parliamentary Committee on Wireless Broadcasting (Gibson Report), and *Minutes of Evidence*, March 1942.
Report of the Royal Commission on Performing Rights, 1933.
Reports of the Parliamentary Standing Committee on Broadcasting, 1943-8:
  First Report, Miscellaneous Subjects.
  Second Report, Miscellaneous Subjects.
  Third Report, Funds for Programme and Technical Services of the National Broadcasting System; Powers of the ABC.
  Fourth Report, Broadcasting of News.
  Fifth Report, Broadcasting of News, *et al.*
  Seventh Report, The proposed ABC Staff Regulations.
  Eighth Report, The Broadcasting of Parliamentary Debates.
  Ninth Report, The Question of Broadcast Talks on VD and other Sex Matters.
  Tenth Report, National Programme Administration.
  Thirteenth Report, The Financing of the National Broadcasting System.
  Fourteenth Report, The Broadcasting of News.
Parliamentary Standing Committee on Broadcasting, *Minutes of Evidence*, 1942-3; *Summary of Evidence*, 1943-6; and *Record of Evidence*, 1946-9.
Official Year Book of the Commonwealth of Australia, 1932-48.

5. PERSONAL PAPERS

Sir Richard Boyer, Personal Papers, National Library of Australia, MS 3181.
Herbert Brookes, Personal Papers, National Library of Australia, MS 1924.
William James Cleary, Personal Papers, National Library of Australia, MS 5539 and MS 5632 (both restricted access).
Walter Tasman Conder, Personal Papers, National Library of Australia, uncatalogued.

II. Secondary Sources

1. BOOKS

Andrews, E. M., *Isolationism and Appeasement in Australia:*

Reactions to the European Crises, 1935-1939, Canberra, ANU Press, 1970.
Bainton, H., *Remembered on Waking: Edgar L. Bainton*, Sydney, Currawong Publications, 1960.
Ball, W. Macmahon, *Press, Radio and World Affairs: Australia's Outlook*, Melbourne, MUP, 1938.
Blain, E., *Life with Aunty: Forty Years with the ABC*, Sydney, Methuen, 1978.
Blainey, G., *The Tyranny of Distance: How Distance Shaped Australia's History*, Melbourne, Sun Books, 1966.
Bolton, G. C., *Dick Boyer: An Australian Humanist*, Canberra, ANU Press, 1967.
——, *A Fine Country to Starve In*, Nedlands, W.A., Uni. of Western Australia Press, 1972.
Briggs, A., *The Birth of Broadcasting* (vol. I of *History of Broadcasting in the United Kingdom*), London, OUP, 1961.
——, *The Golden Age of Wireless* (vol. II of *History of Broadcasting in the United Kingdom*), London, OUP, 1965.
——, *The War of Words* (vol. III of *History of Broadcasting in the United Kingdom*), London, OUP, 1970.
Burns, T., *The BBC: Public Institution and Private World*, London, Macmillan, 1977.
Caiden, G. E., *Career Service: An Introduction to the History of Personnel Administration in the Commonwealth Public Service of Australia 1901-1961*, Melbourne, MUP, 1965.
Clark, C. M. H., *A Short History of Australia*, Sydney, Mentor, 1969, revised ed.
Coleman, P., *Obscenity, Blasphemy, and Sedition: 100 Years of Censorship in Australia*, Sydney, Angus & Robertson, 1974.
Covell, R., *Australia's Music: Themes of a New Society*, Melbourne, Sun Books, 1967.
Crisp, L. F., *Ben Chifley: A Biography*, Melbourne, Longmans, 1963.
Crowley, F. K. (ed.), *Modern Australia in Documents*, vol. 1: *1901-1939;* vol. 2: *1939-1970*, Melbourne, Wren, 1973.
——, *A New History of Australia*, Melbourne, Heinemann, 1974.
Dixon, M. F., *Inside the ABC: a Piece of Australian History*, Melbourne, Hawthorn Press, 1975.
Duncan, W. G. K. (ed.), *Educating a Democracy*, Sydney, Angus & Robertson, 1936.
Etzioni, A., *Modern Organisations*, Englewood Cliffs, N.J., Prentice-Hall, 1964.
——, *A Comparative Analysis of Complex Organizations: on*

Select Bibliography

power, involvement, and their correlates, New York, Free Press, 1965.
Faulkner, C. C., and Corbett, J. D. (eds), *The Broadcast Year Book and Radio Listeners' Annual of Australia*, Sydney, Harbour Newspaper & Publishing Co., 1934, 1938-9, and 1946-7.
Game, P., *The Music Sellers*, Melbourne, Hawthorn Press, 1976.
Gollan, R., *Revolutionaries and Reformists: Communism and the Australian Labour Movement, 1920-1955*, Canberra, ANU Press, 1975.
Hasluck, P., *The Government and the People, 1939-1941*, Canberra, Australian War Memorial, 1952.
——, *The Government and the People, 1942-1945*, Canberra, Australian War Memorial, 1970.
Hobsbawm, E. J., *Labouring Men: Studies in the History of Labour*, London, Weidenfeld & Nicolson, 1968 [1964].
Kemp, C. D., *Big Businessmen: Four Biographical Essays*, Melbourne, Institute of Public Affairs, 1964.
Kiernan, C., *Calwell: A Personal and Political Biography*, Melbourne, Nelson, 1978.
La Nauze, J. A., *Walter Murdoch: A Biographical Memoir*, Melbourne, MUP, 1977.
Long, G., *The Six Years War: A Concise History of Australia in the 1939-45 War*, Canberra, Australian War Memorial, 1973.
MacKay, I. K., *Broadcasting in Australia*, Melbourne, MUP, 1957.
Mann, M., *Consciousness and Action among the Western Working Class*, Melbourne, Macmillan, 1973.
Marwick, A., *Britain in the Century of Total War: War, Peace and Social Change, 1900-1967*, London, Bodley Head, 1968.
McNair, W. A., *Radio Advertising in Australia*, Sydney, Angus & Robertson, 1937.
Mellor, D. P., *The Role of Science and Industry*, Canberra, Australian War Memorial, 1958.
Meo, L., *Japan's Radio War on Australia, 1941-1945*, Melbourne, MUP, 1968.
Mitchell, B., *Teachers, Education and Politics: A History of Organizations of Public School Teachers in New South Wales*, St Lucia, Qld, Uni. of Queensland Press, 1978.
Rees, L., *The Making of Australian Drama: a Historical and Critical Survey from the 1830s to the 1970s*, Sydney, Angus & Robertson, 1973.
Rivett, R., *Australian Citizen: Herbert Brookes 1867-1963*, Melbourne, MUP, 1965.
Ross, L., *John Curtin: A Biography*, Melbourne, Macmillan, 1977.

Rydon, J., *A Biographical Register of the Commonwealth Parliament 1901-1972*, Canberra, ANU Press, 1975.
Sawer, G., *Australian Federal Politics and Law, 1929-1949*, Melbourne, MUP, 1963.
Serle, G., *From Deserts the Prophets Come: the Creative Spirit in Australia 1788-1972*, Melbourne, Heinemann, 1973.
Siepman, C. A., *Radio, Television and Society*, New York, OUP, 1950.
Turner, I., *The Australian Dream: a Collection of Anticipations about Australia from Captain Cook to the Present Day*, Melbourne, Sun Books, 1968.
Walker, R. R., *The Magic Spark: the Story of the First Fifty Years of Radio in Australia*, Melbourne, Hawthorn Press, 1973.
Ward, R., *Australia*, Sydney, Ure Smith, 1969.
Weller, P. (ed.), *Caucus Minutes 1901-1949: Minutes of the Meetings of the Federal Parliamentary Labor Party*, vol. 2: *1917-1931;* vol. 3: *1931-1949*, Melbourne, MUP, 1975.

2. ARTICLES

Bell, R., 'Censorship and War: Australia's Curious Experience 1939-1945', *Media Information Australia*, no. 6 (November 1977), 2-3.
Boyer, R. J. F., 'Radio in Education Conference, Canberra', *Australian Quarterly*, XVIII, no. 1 (March 1946), 94-101.
———, 'The ABC—a Criticism', *Public Administration*, XII, no. 1 (March 1953), 56-59.
Burton, H. M., 'The Burlesque of Broadcasting', *Australian Rhodes Review*, no. 4 (1939), 77-88.
Cowper, N., 'The Control of Broadcasting', *Australian Quarterly*, no. 30 (June 1936), 52-64.
Curnow, G. R., 'The Origins of Australian Broadcasting, 1900-1923', in I. Bedford and G. R. Curnow (eds), *Initiative and Organization*, Melbourne, Sydney Studies in Politics no. 3, 1963.
Geeves, P., 'The Golden Jubilee of Australian Broadcasting', *Newsletter of the Royal Australian Historical Society* (April 1973), 3-5.
———, 'Australia's Radio Pioneers', *Electronics* (Australia), pt 1 (May 1974), 26-8 and 90; pt 2 (June 1974), 30-2; pt 3 (July 1974), 34-5 and 37; pt 4 (August 1974), 50-1 and 53.
Goot, M., 'Radio LANG', in H. Radi and P. Spearritt (eds), *Jack Lang*, Sydney, Hale & Iremonger, 1977, pp. 119-37.
Hilvert, J., 'More on Australia's Curious War Censorship', *Media Information Australia*, no. 7 (February 1978), 44.

Select Bibliography

Ifould, W. H., 'Moulding Public Opinion', in W. G. K. Duncan (ed.), *Educating a Democracy*, pp. 116-43.
Kewley, T. H., and Rydon, J., 'The Personnel of Commonwealth Government Corporations', *Public Administration*, VIII, n.s. no. 4 (December 1949), 132-7.
Moorhouse, F., 'The ABC's Search for Identity', *Current Affairs Bulletin*, XLVI, no. 10 (5 October 1970), 147-59.
Murdoch, W., 'The Tyranny of the Low-Brow', *Australian Quarterly*, IX, no. 1 (March 1937), 40-7.
Nettheim, G., 'Public Broadcasting and Government', *Australian Quarterly*, XXXV, no. 1 (March 1963), 36-42.
Porter, C., 'Broadcasting in Queensland', *Journal of the Royal Historical Society of Queensland*, VI, no. 4 (1961-2), 750-61.
Roberts, G. A., 'Business Interests and the Formation of the ABC', *Politics*, VII, no. 2 (November 1972), 149-54.
Robertson, J., '1930-39', in F. K. Crowley (ed.), *A New History of Australia*, pp. 415-57.
Rydon, J., 'The Australian Broadcasting Commission, 1932-1942: the Study of a Public Corporation', *Public Administration*, XI, n.s. (1952), 12-25; ditto '1942-1948', 190-205.
Sheridan, T., 'Labour v. Labor: The Victorian Metal Trades Dispute of 1946-47', in J. Iremonger, J. Merritt, and G. Osborne (eds), *Strikes: Studies in Twentieth Century Australian Social History*, Sydney, Angus & Robertson, 1973, pp. 176-224.
Stokes, C., 'The Politics of Radio', in R. Lucy (ed.), *The Pieces of Politics*, Melbourne, Macmillan, 1975, pp. 296-312.
Thompson, J. D. and McEwen, W. J., 'Organisational goals and environment: goal setting as an interaction process', in G. Salaman and K. Thompson (eds), *People and Organisations*, London, Longman, 1973, pp. 155-67.
Tildesley, B., 'The Cinema and Broadcasting in Australia: Reports Presented to the Pan-Pacific Conference of Women, 1934', *Australian Quarterly*, VI, no. 24 (December 1934), 129-36.
———, 'Broadcast Programmes', *Australian Quarterly*, VIII, no. 32 (September 1936), 62-9.
Watson, D., 'Anti-Communism in the Thirties', *Arena*, no. 37 (1975), pp. 40-51.
Wolfsohn, H., 'The Ideology Makers', in H. Mayer (ed.), *Australian Politics: a Reader*, Melbourne, Cheshire, 1966, 2nd ed., pp. 70-81.

3. THESES

Curnow, G. R., 'The History of the Development of Wireless Telegraphy and Broadcasting in Australia to 1942, with especial reference to the Australian Broadcasting Commission: A Political and Administrative Study', MA Hons thesis, University of Sydney, 1961.

Gash, L., 'The History of the Australian Broadcasting Commission's Children's Session, c. 1929-1945', BA Hons thesis, Monash University, 1975.

Hull, W. H. N., 'A Comparative Study of the Problems of Ministerial Responsibility in Australian and Canadian Broadcasting', PhD thesis, Duke University, 1959.

Mitchell, P., 'Development of the Australian Broadcasting Commission's News Service, 1932-1942', BA Hons thesis, University of Sydney, 1974.

Petersen, N., 'Policy Formation in the ABC News Service, 1942-1961', MA thesis, University of Sydney, 1977.

III. Interviews

The following people were interviewed, some on a number of occasions, between 1976 and 1978 inclusive:

Professor W. Macmahon Ball, 55 York St, Eltham, Victoria, 3095.

Mr T. W. Bearup, 'Boonah', 14 James Rd, Belair, South Australia, 5052.

Mr Ellis Blain, 12 Ferdinand St, Hunters Hill, New South Wales, 2110.

Mrs Sophie Kave (née Rockman), 21 Fellows St, Kew, Victoria, 3101.

Sir Charles Moses, then c/- Asian Broadcasting Union, 203 Castlereagh St, Sydney, 2000.

Mrs Pauline Watson (née Cleary), 2 Bingara St, West Pymble, New South Wales, 2073.

Mrs Wilga Wind (née Armstrong), 17 Summit Ct, Mooroolbark, Victoria, 3138.

IV. Miscellaneous

Argus, 1931-48.

Australian Broadcasting Company Yearbook, 1930, Sydney, Commonwealth Publications, 1931.

Conder, (Mrs) Judith, personal communication to the author, 1 March 1978.

Overseas Telecommunications Veterans' Association Newsletter, various issues, 1975-6.

Select Bibliography

Radio Pictorial of Australia, 1935-42.
'Proceedings of the Radio in Education Conference, 21-24 June 1946' (typescript).
Radio Trade Annual of Australia, 1933-9.
Sydney Morning Herald, 1931-48.
Who's Who in Australia, various years.

Index

Abbott, J. P., 157
ABC Weekly, 104-6, 131
Adkins, H. E., 70
advertisements, 14-15
Aerial, 135, 141, 145
Afford, Max, 71, 101
Age, 10, 88
Alexander, W. A., 59, 134
Amalgamated Wireless Australasia Ltd (AWA), 7, 22, 113, 116
amateurs, 6
Amour, Senator, 111, 123, 125, 139, 160
announcers, 28-9, 57-8, 129, 146-7
Anthony, H. L., 139
Argonauts Club, 40, 65, 96-7
Argus, 11
Ashley, W. P., 103, 114, 158
As Ye Sow, 71, 72
'At Home and Abroad', 84; *see also* 'The Watchman'
audiences: reactions of, 85-6, 88, 125, 149-50, 158; listener research, 42, 73-5, 130, 159; *see also* listeners' letters
'Austral, John Henry', 166
Australasian Performing Rights Association (APRA), 10, 36, 126, 164
'Australia Calling', 113
Australian Associated Press, 15, 38
Australian Broadcasting Commission Act, 12-16, 78, 80-1, 122-4, 135-6, 144, 146, 151, 156-7, 164-7
Australian Broadcasting Company, 8, 12, 16, 20, 22, 23, 24, 29, 34
Australian Broadcasting Control Board, 165-6
Australian Federation of Commercial Broadcasting Stations, 76, 159
Australian Institute of International Affairs, 82, 98
Australian Newspapers' Conference, 14, 38

Badger, Colin, 83, 98
Bainton, Edgar, 69
Ball, William Macmahon, 9, 73, 77, 82, 85, 90, 98, 110, 114, 115, 116, 117, 118, 128

Barclay, Edmund, 71-2, 101
Barry, Keith, 35, 53, 61, 65, 77, 78, 89, 95, 97, 128, 146, 147
Bearup, T. W., 22, 25, 51, 53, 64, 92, 93, 97, 103, 104, 110, 114, 126, 127, 133, 139, 148
Beasley, Jack, 8, 18, 25, 103, 114
Beazley, Kim, 149, 166
Beck, Haydn, 133
Bennett, D., 135
Benson, Rev. Irving, 112
Bentley, Dick, 99, 100, 110
Blain, Ellis, 4, 23, 27, 37, 57, 78, 129, 147
Blamey, General, 98, 100, 139
Bland, F. A., 162
Bloom, Harry, 70
Blue Hills, 73, 101
Bonney, E. G., 117, 149
Boyer, R. J. F., 122, 124, 142-3, 144, 145, 146, 150, 155, 156, 157, 158, 159, 162, 164, 173
British Broadcasting Corporation (BBC), 18, 37, 62, 75, 77, 96, 97, 100, 102, 105, 116, 128, 130, 148, 159, 163
Broadbent, Mollie, 97
Broadcast House, 21, 132, 141; *see also* Head Office
broadcasting industry, early history of, 6-8, 172
Bronner, Rudolph, 53, 77
Brookes, Herbert, 16-17, 25, 31-2, 36, 43, 48, 49, 50, 67, 102, 122
Brown, H. P., 9, 13, 32, 64, 102
Bruce, Stanley Melbourne, 17, 143
Bulletin, 88
Burdock, Heath ('Peter Possum'), 28, 40, 133
Burns, C., 109

Calwell, A. A., 114, 123, 125, 149, 158, 163-4
Cameron, Archie, 61, 80, 81, 88, 135
Cameron, Don, 111, 143, 158, 165
Cameron, R. G., 58, 140
'Canberra Calling', 103, 104
Caton, Anne, 84
Cecil, Lawrence, 71, 72, 97, 98

Index

'Celebrity Concerts': *see* concerts
censorship: political, 79-91, 106-9;
  internal ABC censorship, 83-4, 85, 89,
  91, 170; on moral grounds, 109-12,
  117, 159-61; 41-2; *see also* political
  interference
centralization, 53-4, 147-8; *see also*
  staffing polices
Chamberlain, N., 88-9
Charlton, Conrad, 28, 58
Charteris, Professor, 41
Chifley, Ben, 142, 149, 156, 157, 161,
  163, 164, 165
'Children Calling Home', 96
Children's Hour, 31, 39-40, 65, 155; *see
  also* Argonauts Club
Cleary, William James: background,
  45-7; views on broadcasting, 48-9, 50,
  56-9, 144, 169-70; and talks, 77, 78ff;
  and censorship, 81-2, 89, 91; and
  wartime ABC, 92, 95, 102, 103, 105,
  108, 109, 110, 111, 112, 114, 115; and
  staff, 131-2, 137; and Moses, 51-3, 54-
  6, 138-41; and listener research, 130;
  and Gibson Committee, 123-4, 137;
  and Parliamentary Standing
  Committee on Broadcasting, 125;
  resignation, 138-41, 143; also
  mentioned 51-76 *passim*, 122, 127,
  130, 150, 156, 173
Clewlow, F. D., 53, 61, 65, 71, 93, 97,
  100, 110, 145, 148, 154
Coles, Beryl, 97
Collings, Senator, 52, 56, 81
commercial radio, 75-6, 86, 123, 159,
  164, 172
communism, the ABC and, 161-2
Community Singing, 31, 34
composers' competitions, 35, 67, 152
concerts: 34-5; opposition from
  theatrical agencies, 68-9, 124;
  subscriptions to, 70, 151, 172; during
  wartime, 95-6; 34-5, 66-7, 151
Conder, Walter Tasman, 25-6, 27, 28,
  29, 32, 33, 34, 39, 41, 50-1, 54
Coombs, H. C., 162
Couchman, E. M. R., 9, 16, 17, 31-2, 43,
  48, 65, 122, 124
Country Hour: *see* rural broadcasts
Country Party, and the ABC, 11, 81,
  156, 165
Crawford, Dorothy, 97
cricket broadcasts, 11
'crooning', 100
Crosby, Bing, 100
Curtin, John, 67, 80, 81, 83, 94, 100, 103,
  117, 123, 124, 127, 139, 143, 144, 145,
  148, 166

Dad and Dave, 72, 94
Dakin, W. J., 41, 77
Davidson, Jim, 70, 96, 127, 131
Davis, Jean, 97
Dawes, Edgar, 143, 144, 155, 156
Deamer, S. H., 128
Denholm, Margaret, 97
Denning, Warren, 103, 123
Dixon, M. F., 3, 65, 88-9, 93, 102, 139,
  140, 156, 164
Douglas, Clive, 67
Douglas Social Credit, 109
Douglass, John, 153, 154
Doyle, Stuart, 16, 22
drama, 41-2, 71, 72, 101
Duckmanton, Talbot, 131
Dudley, Maurice de Lacy ('Billy
  Bunny'), 28, 40
Dumas, Lloyd, 15
Duncan, W. G. K., 77

educational broadcasts, 39, 43, 130, 152,
  155-6
election broadcasts, 83, 86
entertainment, 18, 19, 29, 34, 37, 49; *see
  also* light entertainment
Evatt, H. V., 103, 114, 115, 123
External Affairs, Department of, 89,
  115, 116, 163

Fadden, A. W., 165
features, 152-3
Fenton, J. E., 12-13, 80
finances, 21, 54, 62, 79-80, 124, 148-9,
  151, 165, 166, 172
Finch, Peter, 131
Finlay, A. N. ('Huck'), 65, 131, 148
Fisk, Ernest, 7
Fitzgerald, A. A., 149
Fitzgerald Report, 149, 164-5
Foley, P. G. J., 125, 144
Foll, H. S., 108, 111
Forces programme, 100, 120
Forde, F. M., 109
Foster, A. W., 84
Freer, Mrs, 78

Gibson, W. G., 123
Gibson Committee, 105, 107, 109, 110,
  113, 114, 115, 123-4, 126-37 *passim*
Goossens, Eugene, 151
Gordon, A., 134
Gullett, Sir Henry, 93, 102, 113

Haire, Dr Norman, 110-12
Hammond, Rev. R. B. S., 10
Hanlon, J. S., 145, 156
Harrison, E. J., 80, 90, 105, 113, 166

Hart, Fritz, 67
Harty, Sir Hamilton, 35
Hatherley, Frank ('Bobby Bluegum'), 28, 29, 40
Haylen, L., 157
Head Office, 21, 23, 54, 128, 147-8, 149; see also Broadcast House
Heinze, Professor Bernard, 24-5, 33, 35-6, 66, 67, 70-1
Henderson, K. T., 107, 112
Henderson, Rupert, 156
Herbert, Mary, 97
Higgins, Betty, 97
'highbrow' culture: see audiences
Hill, Alfred, 67
Hill, Ernestine, 125
Holman, A. L., 23, 128, 133, 147
Holmes, C. H., 114
Hope, A. D., 97
Horner, H. G., 22, 25, 86
Hosking, Charles, 23, 58
Hughes, William Morris, 13-14, 158

Information, Department of, 93-5, 102, 107, 113-16, 145, 163
Ingamells, Rex, 50
interstate network, 150, 153, 159

Jacklin, Paul, 99
Jacobs, Howard, 67, 70
James, W. G., 53, 66, 100
Japan: see propaganda
jazz, 35
Jensen, J. K. ('Jack'), 46, 47
Jones, Charles Lloyd, 16, 18, 20, 31, 32, 33, 39, 42, 43, 159
Jose, A., 134
journalists, 134
Joyce, Eileen, 67

Keavney, K., 133
Kent, Ivy, 144
Kirke, Basil, 23, 29, 55, 58, 61
Kisch, Egon, 84
Kitto, J. W., 64, 122

Labor Party, and the ABC, 11-12, 14, 81, 103, 108, 109, 123, 124, 125, 126, 145, 156, 158
Lang, J. T., 11-12, 47, 164
Lawson, Lionel, 133
Lawsons, The, 73, 100-1, 153-4
Lewis, E. J., 23, 27, 58
Liberal Party, and the ABC, 156, 165; see also United Australia Party
light entertainment, 99-100, 120, 149-51
Lindsay, Norman, 49, 83
listeners' letters, 42, 155
listeners' licences, 6, 7, 22, 42, 54, 79, 92, 120, 126, 149

'Listening Groups', 98-9, 127
'Listening Post', 113
Lucke, Judy, 40, 65
Lyons, J. A., 8, 12, 13, 18, 66, 82-3, 86, 157

MacArthur, General, 118, 119
MacKay, R. W. G., 108
Makeham, Mark, 133
Makin, N. J. O., 158
Mann, Edward Alexander: see 'The Watchman'
Marr, Sir Charles, 123
Mason, Arthur, 32, 102
Masuda, Sgt J., 116, 119
McCall, R. C., 102, 148, 161
McCance, Norman, 28
McGibbon, S. J., 122, 123
McLachlan, Alexander, 14, 68, 80, 81
McLeay, G., 135, 157
McLeod, John, 133
Medley, J. D. B., 125, 140, 143, 144, 156
Menzies, R. G., 77, 92, 104, 108, 123, 124, 126, 139, 162
Meredith, Gwen, 100-1
'Merry Go Round': see Dick Bentley
Millar, Gladys, 97
Molesworth, B. H., 53, 61, 77, 103, 107, 127, 128, 133
Moses, Charles Joseph Alfred: and staff, 55-6, 57-60, 62, 68, 131, 133; and political interference, 83, 87, 88; and wartime ABC, 92, 100, 102, 105, 107, 111; and Cleary's resignation, 138-41; also mentioned 27, 28, 52, 54, 124, 127, 128, 129, 143, 144, 147, 148, 149, 151, 154, 156, 161, 169
Munich Settlement, 88-9
Murdoch, Keith, 102
Murdoch, Nina, 40, 65; see also Argonauts Club
Murdoch, Walter, 41, 58, 75, 77, 130
music, 33-6, 66-71, 120-1, 124, 126, 127, 130, 151-2, 153, 171, 172
'Music through Movement', 70

Nash, Senator 111
National network, 150, 153, 159
National Talks Advisory Committee, 77, 89, 98, 103, 127, 160
'Nation's Forum of the Air', 110
'News Behind the News', 84; see also 'The Watchman'
news broadcasts, 37-9, 65-6, 101-4, 120, 156-7, 167, 172; see also M. F. Dixon
News Department, 139, 149

Offenburg, Kurt, 85, 116
'Official Listeners', 159
Open Mike, The, 135

Index

Orchard, R. B., 16, 17, 43, 122
orchestras, 34-5, 69-70, 151-2
Osborne, Ida ('Elizabeth'), 97
'Out of the Bag': *see* Dick Bentley

Page, Earle, 11, 13, 18, 165
Parkhill, Archdale, 44, 48, 80, 81
parliamentary debates, broadcasts of, 157-9
Parliamentary Standing Committee on Broadcasting, 124, 125, 131, 132, 137, 138, 145-6, 156, 157, 159-60, 164, 165-6
Parry, G., 99
Paterson, A. B., ('Banjo'), 16
Pearce, Sir George Foster, 48
Philips, Thea, 95
plays: *see* drama
'Pleasant Sunday Afternoon', 112
political interference, 78-84, 106, 107-8, 109, 124, 129, 159-60, 161, 162, 166-7, 170; *see also* censorship
Political Warfare Committee, 115, 117; *see also* propaganda
Portus, G. V., 77, 78
postmaster-general: powers in relation to broadcasting, 16, 64, 78, 79, 108; influence in Cabinet on ABC issues, 43-4, 80
Pratt, James, 96
press: *see* news broadcasts
Price, A. Grenfell, 123
Pringle, Harry, 100
productions: *see* drama
Programme Committee, 62, 65, 128, 149, 150, 151, 159, 169
Programme Development Fund, 147-8
programme policy, 29-30, 61, 127, 150-1ff, 155, 159, 169; *see also* entries under individual programme categories (e.g. music)
propaganda: domestic, 92-5; overseas, 93, 113-19
Proud, J. C., 98, 99

racing broadcasts, 10-11, 37
Radio-Active, 146
Radio Australia, 113-16, 119, 163-4; *see also* propaganda (overseas)
Radio Vigilance League, 110
Rankin, Senator Annabelle, 165
recordings, 36, 62
recruitment: *see* staffing policies
Rees, Leslie, 71, 72
Reith, John, 18, 168, 170; *see also* British Broadcasting Corporation
religious broadcasts, 112
Rigby, E. C., 122, 124
Riordan, W. J. F., 123
Robertson, Sir Macpherson, 26

Robinson, J. W., 23, 27
Rodgers, Judith Halse, 97
Rorke, H. A., 108
rural broadcasts, 100, 152, 153-4
Ruth, Rev. T., 112

Santamaria, B. A., 162
Sargent, Dr Malcolm, 67
Sawer, Geoffrey, 115, 163, 164
school broadcasts: *see* educational broadcasts
School Broadcasts Advisory Committee, 155
Scott, Ernest, 9
Scott, F. G., 134
Scullin, J. H., 8, 12, 18, 123
sealed-set system, 7
Senior Officers' Association, 60-1, 134, 135, 138, 145, 169
sex broadcasts, 110-12, 159-61
Shead, Isobel Ann, 65
Sheehan, Nancy, 135
Sheehan, P. J., 59
Sholl, E. K., 131
shortwave broadcasts: *see* Radio Australia
Smith's Weekly, 48, 104-5
Spanish Civil War, 88
sport, 37, 65, 120, 154-5, 172
Staff Association: formation of, 59; and Staff Rules, 60; and Staff Regulations, 129, 131, 133, 134-8, 145, 146, 147, 169; *see also* staffing policies
staffing policies: conditions of work, 24, 26-8, 56-7, 59-61, 128-9, 146-7, 169-70; and political activity, 161; staff numbers, 53, 54, 130-1, 147; Staff Rules, 59-60, 61, 133-4, 137; during wartime, 131-8; Staff Regulations, 145-6, 166-7, 169
Standing Committee on Broadcasting: *see* Parliamentary Standing Committee on Broadcasting
state advisory committees, 130; *see also* Western Australian Advisory Committee
state managers, 22-4
Stevens, Captain A. C. C. ('Uncle Steve'), 28
Stewart, Douglas, 101

Tait, E. J., 68
talks, 31, 40-1, 107, 121, 127; *see also* B. H. Molesworth, National Talks Advisory Committee
Tate, Frank, 9
Taylor, Bryson, 40, 133
technical services, 21, 54, 64, 116-17, 165, 166

Thomas, Wilfrid, 99, 100, 128, 153
Thorby, H. V. C., 79-80, 89, 109
Trade Diversion Policy, 86-8
trade unions, talks by, 95; *see also* Staff Association and staffing policies
Turner, Alexander, 101

unionism: *see* Staff Association and staffing policies
United Australia Party, 8, 81, 104, 109

variety programmes, 152, 159; *see also* light entertainment
'Voices from Overseas', 97

Wallace, R. S., 16, 17, 43
Ward, Mary, 97
wartime programmes, 92-121

'Watchman, The', 77, 84-91, 107, 109
Watts, H. M., 74
Wells, H. G., 78, 82
Western Australian Advisory Committee, 58, 130, 144
White, Colonel T. W., 87
Wicks, C. C., 106
Williams, H. P., 24-5, 36, 39
Williamson, J. C. Ltd, 10, 21, 25, 28, 34, 68-9
Wilmot, Chester, 97-8, 142
'Wives Calling Husbands', 96
women: women's sessions, 42; women in the ABC, 97, 132
Wood, G. L., 39, 51, 52, 77
Woodruff, H. A., 112

Yorke, Stephen, 70

PN 1991 .3 .A8 1980

DATE DUE